Wittgenstein and Political

WITTGENSTEIN AND POLITICAL THEORY

The View from Somewhere

CHRISTOPHER C. ROBINSON

Edinburgh University Press

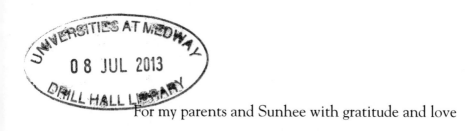

For my parents and Sunhee with gratitude and love

First published in 2009 by
Edinburgh University Press Ltd
22 George Square, Edinburgh
www.euppublishing.com

This paperback edition 2011

Typeset in 11/13.5 pt Goudy by
Servis Filmsetting Ltd, Stockport, Cheshire, and
printed and bound in Great Britain by
CPI Antony Rowe, Chippenham and Eastbourne

A CIP record for this book is available from the British Library

ISBN 978 0 7486 4298 4 (paperback)

Contents

Acknowledgments

In many ways, this is a book about the resilience and flexibility of trust, and, ironically, I think I managed to strain every relationship I have in writing it. And, so, this set of acknowledgments is also a set of apologies.

First, I want to thank my teachers. In my senior year in high school, I really had no clear plan for college. This all changed when I stepped into my AP class in the History of Political Thought. Vincent Buscareno taught it. Dr. Buscareno was a dynamic teacher, with a strong moral compass that he instilled in his students. I was mesmerized both by him and by the material. My debt to him is enormous; I continue to mourn his passing and honor his memory. In college, I was very fortunate to arrive on campus at the same time as Kathy Ferguson. I had never felt so challenged and intellectually alive than when I was in her classroom. Her many writings, and her friendship, continue to mold my thinking and embellish my love for political theory. In graduate school, I studied and wrote my dissertation with John G. Gunnell. To this day, I am in awe of him as scholar and teacher. Studying political theory and the philosophy of language with Jack Gunnell was a privilege. His many kindnesses and the toughness of his criticisms of my work give way to a feeling of gratitude impossible to articulate.

My colleagues and friends at Clarkson University have been wonderfully supportive. Dan Bradburd, Jerry Gravander, and Dick Pratt, in their respective administrative roles have made Clarkson a warm and friendly place to teach and research. Colleagues from across the campus have contributed in countless ways to the completion of this work. Thanks to: Fran Bailey, Jen Ball, Owen Brady, Ellen Caldwell, Stephen Casper, David Craig, Kimberly DeFazio, Laura Ettinger, Lew Hinchman,

Lou Ann Lange, Sarah Melville, John Serio, Linda Snyder, Annegret Staiger, Sheila Weiss, Rick Welsh, Tom Langen, Michael Twiss, Tino Tamon, Al Rossner, Andrea Ferro, Steve Yurgartis, Al Bender, Amanda Pickering, and Deanna Errico. Joe Duemer, a poet, shares my interest in Wittgenstein, and I have been the beneficiary of countless conversations with him. Bill Vitek has been a remarkable friend and patient reader over the years. We have engaged in what is now a ten-year conversation that is a constant reminder of how fortunate I am to have such a friend.

Other friends I need to thank are: Hugo, Miles, Maria, Andrew, Elizabeth, Caroline, Ian, Hyoejin Yoon, Michael Shapiro, Sam Chambers, Michael Bérubé, David Freeman, Matthew Moore, Jeff Johnson, Ed Warzala, Pat Ferraioli, Sue Behouniak, all the great theorists I've met through the Association for Political Theory (APT), John Nelson, Jane Bennett, Ellen Rocco, and my friends over at North Country Public Radio.

I need to thank my brothers, Dave and Sean Robinson, for their friendship and love. I thank them also for bringing Fawn and Michelle into our family. My nieces Breanna, Cali, and Julia, and my nephew, David, have been so kind despite our long-distance relationship. I have dedicated this book to my parents. My daughters, Sarah Robinson (who sacrificed more than anyone) and Minji Hill, and my dear Nicholas Brino, have been inspirations.

I share a loving life with Sunhee Sohn-Robinson, and she has certainly received the short end of the stick in this deal. I tell my students that the most important lesson I can offer them is when you choose a life companion, be sure he or she makes you laugh, is smarter than you, and wields a prescription pad. This is one area where I practice what I preach.

Introduction: Wittgenstein and the Scene of Contemporary Political Theory

Political theorists have been at a loss on what to do with Wittgenstein. The form his work most often takes is that of the remark. It is a style that defies coherence, both because Wittgenstein sought to write what and as he saw, and this was fragmented; and because he did not "want to spare other people the trouble of thinking." His work therefore suggested many directions, but pursued only a few. For some, the way to work with Wittgenstein is indirectly through surrogate "Wittgensteinians" like Peter Winch or Thomas Kuhn, who focus on aspects of the work, create a coherent account of that aspect, and then apply it to an area of interest – the study of primitive culture or how a body of knowledge changes over time from within. Those who wish a more direct route display a tendency, following Hanna Pitkin, to consider the "significance" of Wittgenstein's philosophy for the enterprise of theorizing. Making the connection between Wittgenstein and political thought is a difficult one precisely because Wittgenstein did not talk about politics in any specific way, and his remarks regarding theory were anything but positive. One area where Wittgenstein and political theory could be said to overlap, noted Pitkin and others who followed her, is in the activity of reading. Political theorists read difficult texts, ponder the historical changes reflected in concepts such as politics, democracy, justice, and so on, while Wittgenstein describes words and contexts in language-games as tools that derive meaning from their place and use in sentences and social practices. Throughout the 1970s and 1980s, Wittgenstein was conceived mainly as offering a non-Derridean method for close readings of the canon that bridged the continental–analytic divide.

More recently, social and political theorists have been investigating Wittgenstein's writings for conceptual strategies to deploy against the erasure of national and cultural differences by "globalization" (the neutral academic and journalistic term of art that has supplanted "imperialism" with all its evil economic and cultural connotations) discourse, technologies, and policies. It was Wittgenstein who thought to use the line "I'll teach you differences," from *King Lear* as the motto for his *Philosophical Investigations*, and who castigated the ethnocentrism of James George Frazer's claim in *The Golden Bough* that various "primitive" magical and religious views and practices are unscientific, insane, and, most importantly, false. Those who partake in these perspectives and rituals, notes Frazer, have not benefited from the progress of Western science in demystifying reality. These are backward savages in Frazer's view. What is revealed in Frazer's account, argued Wittgenstein (1993), however, is not a state of abject primitivism in need of educational reform and table manners, but rather Frazer's cultural myopia and "how impossible it was for him to conceive of a life different from that of the England of his time." Our task as philosophers, anthropologists, scientists, Wittgenstein said, is to *describe* practices different than our own, expanding our own imaginative and perceptual capacity only to recognize: "this is what human life is like" (119–55). Description is a celebration of even those differences incommensurable with the sources of our identity (whomever we may be); it does not entail inquiry that reveals practices to be logically, structurally, or cognitively the same and reconcilable through generalization/homogenization (the goal of "infantile theory"). Because description occurs from close up, accounts for only that which can be seen, responds to perceptual limits with movement, and is done with care, identity is revealed to be the source of difference.

For Pitkin and others in the postbehavioral era of Political Science and Political Theory, the problem of connecting Wittgenstein to political theory was directional. The task was conceived as one where something in his philosophical writings (family resemblances, forms of life, critical remarks pertaining to solipsism and private language) could be extrapolated and used to illuminate and latch onto a key term of theorizing (for example, interpretation, pluralism, communitarianism, multiculturalism, antifoundationalism). Isolated remarks from Wittgenstein's works were employed merely to substantiate a claim or offer a catchy turn of phrase.

But the direction has changed. From a range of schools (critical legal studies, rhetoric, democratic theory, liberal reconstructionism, identity theory, deconstructionism), political, social, and legal theorists are rethinking the dualisms – theory/practice, aesthetics/politics, mind/body,

2

and agent/structure – at the core of the contemporary discourse and their identity. That is, these theorists have moved away from an ontological duo-verse and toward an ecological recognition that the surface world before us is all we have. The resulting monism dissolves the conception of the world as composed of binary oppositions. More comprehensive readings of Wittgenstein are presented as monistic alternatives to dualism, an ethical way of coping with a universe (taken literally) that offers no certainty, no fixed Archimedean perceptual vantage point, no transcendence, and dooms us to a life of friction. On this Wittgensteinian plane, we can acknowledge the experiences and pains that gave rise to metaphysical flights by past philosophers and poets. We observe that these pains do not go away once the "craving for generality" is resisted.

This tension between metaphysical impulses and the pull of gravity suffuses the efforts of all theorists working with Wittgenstein today. Indeed, it suffuses the work of Wittgenstein. Despite professions of amazement at the novel character of his work, there remains the strong tendency among theorists to use Wittgenstein in service to some theoretical goal or orientation, as my engagement with the works of Chantal Mouffe, Robin Holt, Simon Glendinning, and Nigel Pleasants will show. These ambitious works illustrate the place of Wittgenstein, for better and for worse, in the discourse of contemporary political theory because each can be taken as representative of a larger set of liberal, phenomenological, and postmodern claims about theory's relation to politics in the contemporary era. Mouffe argues, as will I, for a Wittgenstein who reveals something new and important about the challenges of theorizing in the contemporary age, but struggles mightily against the unrelenting conventionalism and contingency of his philosophical adventures. Holt and Glendinning follow the Pitkin path of seeing Wittgenstein contributing clarifications to discourses within political theory: human rights (Holt) and political ethics (Glendinning). Finally, Pleasants raises profound questions about whether Wittgenstein has anything to say about theorizing beyond criticisms of the epistemological excesses of those writing in the enterprise. If I were to mark my place amid these positions on Wittgenstein and political theory, it would look something akin to a perturbed reconciliation between Mouffe and Pleasants. Wittgenstein's *Philosophical Investigations* makes transparent the work of theorizing today, and attending to this work is a matter of accepting that politics and political life are viewed best without recourse to regulative ideals like "the political," or surrogate images wrested from the Great Tradition of Western Political Thought.

3

In her *The Democratic Paradox* (2000), Chantal Mouffe is blunt in her appraisal of Wittgenstein's philosophy: It offers a *"new way of theorizing* about the political," she writes, "one that breaks with the universalizing and homogenizing mode that has informed most of liberal theory since Hobbes" (60–1). Hanna Pitkin was the first to announce that Wittgenstein offered a "new way of theorizing" politics, but her work did not deliver on this promise. Instead, Pitkin's magisterial *Wittgenstein and Justice* (1972) inaugurated the tradition of instrumentalizing Wittgensteinian philosophy to substantiate already existing methods available to theorists. Given this backdrop, we need to consider similar promises with skepticism. Is Mouffe arguing that Wittgenstein leads us to new ways of thinking about theorizing and engaging in it, or is she setting us up for a metatheoretical argument where Wittgenstein is used to illuminate a darkened corner of Carl Schmitt's concept of "the political"(a concept central to her enterprise)? For Mouffe, Wittgenstein promises a way to traverse or dissolve this logical and experiential boundary between theorizing politics in an academic context and a life of political engagement. This promise appears built into his philosophical project of pushing philosophers from the frictionless, logical purity of metaphysics and returning them to the streets of the city. "Back to rough ground!"

The rough ground for Mouffe, as I hinted earlier, is Schmitt's concept of "the political." It appears in its current hegemonic form as a plurality of incommensurable differences (ethnic, national, gender-based, economic, ideological, and so on) that float upon a nourishing sea of democracy. Democracy perpetuates such differences without any claim to knowing a higher or deeper source of unity or closure. The paradox Mouffe addresses pertains to the modern form of democracy – liberal democracy – composed of two distinct historical traditions and sets of values. Symptoms of this uncomfortable alliance include individual liberty vying with democratic popular sovereignty; attempts to safeguard freedom with laws running afoul of attempts to enhance freedom by expressing dissent; and the inclusive grammar of human rights being undermined by the exclusivity of a democratic polity whose parameters are formed by us (citizens) excluding them (non-citizens). These are secondary in relation to the central liberal democratic paradox: the irreconcilability of the desire of liberals to universalize the rights of humans with the direction of modern democracy that Mouffe describes, citing Claude Lefort, as moving toward the political expression of "the dissolution of the markers of certainty" transforming all other areas of human knowledge and existence (Mouffe 2000: 18).

4

For Mouffe, the contemporary form of liberal democracy is characterized by an asymmetry favoring neo-Liberal centrism. In political life, this inequity can be observed in the pragmatic and meta-ideological policies of Tony Blair, Gerhardt Schröder, and Bill Clinton that function to absorb the platforms and passions of left democratic parties. In social theory these advocates of free market centrism are described by Anthony Giddens, for one, as "beyond left and right." Left unchecked, neo-Liberalism seeks to end left/right adversity, but succeeds only in destroying democratic values and institutions while creating an ideological vacuum filled by increasing violent right-wing parties.

Enter Wittgenstein. "[W]e find in the late Wittgenstein," contends Mouffe, "many insights which can be used to envisage how allegiance to democratic values is created not through rational argumentation but through an ensemble of language-games which construct democratic forms of individuality"(Mouffe 2000: 11). Mouffe develops this defense of democracy she finds in Wittgenstein by conceiving it as an "agonic" departure from the liberal rationalist's choice between Rawlsian metaphysics and Habermasian epistemology. While Rawls seeks justification and an escape from politics in the speculative prehistory of the "original position," Habermas tries to burrow beneath the vicissitudes of political discourse to the grammatical universality and safety of an ideal speech situation. Mouffe's criticisms of the apolitical qualities of Rawls and Habermas are as compelling as they are cogent, but I want to concentrate on her inventive use of Wittgenstein to imagine a "new way of theorizing the political."

There is an immediate conceptual paradox that is perhaps insurmountable. Mouffe does not employ Wittgenstein as a combatant for democracy, nor does he offer a philosophical lens through which we can see how the plurality of perspectives and voices constitutive of the democratic political cohere in the constructed identities of democratic individuals. These suggestive ideas are posited, but not argued or substantiated. Rather, Wittgenstein offers Mouffe a skeptical (read: nonrationalist, nonuniversalizing) way to view "the political" – one that enables us to question whether liberal democracy is the best, most just political order. This is the problem: As we use Wittgenstein to denaturalize teleological and universal claims about liberal democracy, "the political" is presented as ontologically prior, autonomous, essential, and universal. Is Mouffe offering another rationalist-universalist political theory then?

From a Wittgensteinian perspective, politics is one form of life among many. We can expand this topographical map of reality temporally by noting that forms of life can be actual and potential. That is, what we see before us in this mosaic does not include forms of life that faded out of existence, and we can certainly argue that all the possibilities for human organization have not been exhausted. Any of the constellations of conventions undergirding forms of life can be altered; and this would, in effect, reorganize our reality. This is the dynamic quality of Wittgenstein's Weltanschauung and why the descriptivism he proposes as the way to engage in philosophy is such a tricky business. The tendency is either to step too far back to achieve uniformity of perspective or to engage in a search for stable foundations possibly hidden by the polymorphic surface. For Wittgenstein, conventions are as close to bedrock as we get and we need to accept this. Mouffe does not. She allows for experimentation in the forms the political might take, but the political itself is conceived as a natural one behind the many artifacts.

To be more consistent, what Wittgenstein leads us to is a more fundamental question, one that can be answered historically and anthropologically: Is politics the best, most just way to organize ourselves? What are the possible alternatives? In this sense, Wittgenstein unleashes the political imagination by presenting a malleable, nontotalizable and multifaceted reality where creativity and responsibility rest solely with humans in their linguistically constituted worlds. Democracy would be defended in these conventional contexts, but only if we succeed in resisting the liberal rationalist temptation to universalize ordinary human practices. Mouffe fails on this crucial point perhaps by missing a deeper paradox embedded in the oxymoronic idea of a "democratic order."

The value of Mouffe's work for political theory does not end at this aporia, but rather begins with the connections she draws between Wittgenstein and the universalizing ambitions of human rights discourse and the dynamic constitution of democratic citizens. I explore these features of Mouffe's work in Chapter 3 of this volume. Recent studies by Robin Holt, Simon Glendinning, and others explore aspects of this connective terrain as well.

Holt's *Wittgenstein, Politics and Human Rights* (1997) is a provocative study that nevertheless remains within the procedural parameters of instrumentalism and the substantive parameters of communitarianism. Wittgenstein is trimmed and retrofitted to be shoehorned into these categories. In Holt's view, Wittgenstein helps us to conceive of human rights as a product of ongoing conventions, customs, and a dominant culture, rather than as an extension of the liberal contractarian idea that human rights issue from the autonomy of the individual subject, the abstract claim that we are all the same under the skin, and the corresponding interest in preserving the smooth functioning of the marketplace. Wittgenstein, contends Holt, is more than a therapist to the communitarian position, however; Wittgenstein leads us to a new way of thinking about human rights. Here again is the promise regarding the transformational effect Wittgenstein has on political theory and it should set off an alarm. Holt calls the newly shaped discourse "ordinary human rights."

The idea articulated here is to eliminate the ontological duo-verse that serves to create a transcendent realm to house the universalized language of rights. This follows Wittgenstein's (1958b) reflection that: "What we do is to bring words back from their metaphysical to their everyday use" (sec. 116). We (philosophers following Wittgenstein) engage in this activity not simply to eliminate the putatively privileged stance of philosophers – what Wittgenstein describes in terms of "houses of cards" – but also to enhance the philosopher's perceptual appreciation of this world. From a distance, we miss much, and, as Holt reminds us, not all we overlook is beautiful. The rhetorical effect of the terms of universal rights – freedom, dignity, equality – is not simply to extend these rights to every human, but it is also to miscast suffering in abstract terms. In returning the language of human rights back to the "rough ground" of ordinary political discourse, we efface the most insidious effect of human rights when they are conceived as guaranteed: these concepts mask differences between cultures; regiment what forms of dissent can be regarded as legitimate; hypostatize existing power relations between and within nations, classes, genders, and cultures; and blind us to the denials of these rights that occur on a daily basis and in a wide variety of circumstances. Human rights discourse, notes Holt, can and does engender "an illusion of calm" (19).

Ordinary human rights, by contrast, combat the temporal suspensions, ontological dualisms, and reifications of the lexicon of universals. They create instead a dynamic "confessional space" within language that does not privilege an abstract subject or an abstract notion of the just order; rather, ordinary human rights serve as an antidote to conceptual rigidity (dogmatism). At this point, a concrete example would help clarify this purported effect achieved by trading universal rights for the ordinary variety, but Holt does not offer one. This weakens the effect of the argument. I imagine that what might serve to help is something like what Nussbaum (2000) calls the "the capabilities approach," which she employs to embellish the perceptual acuity of those engaged in the traditional discourse of human rights as articulating universal standards for justice. In the capabilities approach, we are to see and respect cultural variation, and observe closely the detrimental effects of gender inequality, racism, and poverty, while seeking an equality that each culture might define differently. What we recognize is, and here a concrete example clarifies, a woman in the Indian countryside has fewer resources – nutrition, health care, education – available and more obstacles to overcome in terms of religious and patriarchic tradition, to achieve "equality" than a woman from a culture that spawned this ideal. This "capabilities approach" has the needed effect of cultivating real-life examples to politicize what might otherwise stand as a sterile abstraction, and it is steeped in Nussbaum's own deep and generous reading of Wittgenstein through an Aristotelian lens.

Holt's notion of the "confessional space" engendered by ordinary human rights is one such sterile abstraction. In the space of the confessional, self-creation is achieved by overcoming the liberal opposition between the subject and the world. This is accomplished as the eye is turned toward the encompassing medium of language where we are reconceived as linguistic beings residing in a linguistically constructed environment. These constructs are provisional and fragile. The confessional is described as both a space in this fluid order and as a "technique for living" with this impermanence and motion. "Confession for Wittgenstein was not an attempt to re-gain lost equilibria, reveal truths or attain prescribed goals by filling out an ideal," observes Holt, "but a continual attempt to make oneself one's own object, to face and re-face oneself"(18). How this conception of ordinary human rights as a process of self-creation will prevent cruelties and mass death while enfranchising the world's dispossessed populations and extending to them the rights delineated in the International Charter on Civil and Political Rights is not made clear. We can certainly note the deficiencies of the Charter and the way it is implemented, but the need for an effective international commitment to end genocide, torture, and inequities in the distribution of resources that lead to malnutrition, starvation, and the technological gap remains.

The strength of Holt's work lies not in his ordinary language prescription, but in his critical appraisal of the language and pretense of universals as a form of dogmatism. Wittgenstein conceived of such idealized language as a seductive and entrapping ice world. By contrast, the language of rights must be fluid and sensitive to change over time and across cultures. Rights have been extended over time to slave populations and prisoners of war; they can be expanded to include non-human species or to sentient machines in the future. Flexibility and sensitivity to change demand that rights emerge from political struggle rather than being imposed from above.

Why we require Wittgenstein to help us advance this politicized notion of rights is a question that Holt does not take up directly (and this is true also of the way Wittgenstein is used by Rawls, Dworkin, Sandel, and others in their inquiries on rights). Nietzsche, for instance, could provide us with an even more provocative occasion for re-evaluating liberal human rights discourse and the perceived necessity for couching these rights in terms of teleological or deontological foundations. Stanley Fish (1999), as another example, reassesses the insularity and purported incorruptibility of "neutral principles" in American jurisprudence and the principled tolerance supporting "boutique multiculturalism" without resort in any explicit way to Wittgenstein. What does Wittgenstein offer that we cannot gain from other philosophical or rhetorical traditions?

Holt responds indirectly by assessing Wittgenstein's remarks on ethics from the *Tractatus* to his late writings. This is a common scholarly tactic for those interested in exploring the political implications of Wittgenstein's work, and Holt does this well. As noted earlier, politics was not included in Wittgenstein's philosophical journey. Ethics, if we can follow Aristotle's path for a moment, abuts politics and offers some tantalizing hints about what Wittgenstein might have said in conversation with the political theorists of his day. From this classical suggestion, Holt then adds contemporary remarks on ethical and political existence by Oakeshott, Rorty, Derrida, Deleuze, and others. All these thinkers seem to indicate indebtedness to Wittgenstein by arguing that our political ideals emerge from everyday political practices, which then function to disguise these humble origins. This is perhaps an important reminder of what lies before us. The legitimacy and authority of universal human rights is eroded by the experiences of the twentieth century: the Holocaust, Hiroshima, Nagasaki, the killing fields of Cambodia, genocides in East Timor, the Amazon basin, and the list goes on. If human rights are to have any consequence for improving our lot as a species, it will emerge by our reinvesting ourselves in ordinary political practices of civility. Using tools from Wittgenstein, Holt cuts through thick veils of illusion to get to this simple, yet vital point.

Holt leaves us with a project of investigating political practices that efface distance and effect a humanization of others. Simon Glendinning (2002) undertakes a preliminary investigation of human interactive practices in his essay, *On Being With Others*. Glendinning provides an interesting response to the traditional philosophical problem of other minds. The question, "How can I be sure the other has a mind like my own?" smacks of abstraction. Certainly students encountering the question for the first time think this. But the inhumanity that can occasion a negative or skeptical response is anything but abstract. We know this blindness to lurk at the core of the rhetoric of war employed to prepare soldiers to kill, the political rhetoric of scapegoating, and various expressions of racism and sexism. The problem of other minds is more an ethical than epistemological question, as Wittgenstein knew.

Glendinning's study opens with a reflection on Heidegger's critique of humanism as an expression of antinaturalism predicated on an incorporeal notion of "the self-conscious subject" that invites and is itself vulnerable to the skeptic's questioning of other minds. What Glendinning seeks is a "reframing" of skepticism along Heideggerian lines, in order to then extend the resulting naturalism in a way that eliminates any separation between human and non-human beings. While this may entail the extending of rights down the phylogenetic chain, I think the most significant effect of this conception is the erasure of the Enlightenment division between humans and nature. This would eschew attempts to fashion a "new humanism" that would serve to reaffirm the old image of reality as a hierarchy with humans at the apex, argues Glendinning, while engendering a new vocabulary for the description of human behavior. The behavior that Glendinning is most interested in re-describing is reading and writing, and this places his work in the shadow of Hanna Pitkin.

The difficulty with Glendinning's overall project is the kind of most un-Wittgensteinian generalizations he must undertake to synthesize the distinctive philosophical enterprises and images of language offered by Heidegger, Derrida, J. L. Austin, and Wittgenstein. Heidegger ontologizes language, conceiving it to be "the house of being." An apt analogy for Derrida's conception of language would be the layers of an onion, but for one problem: when you finish peeling away an onion you have nothing; Derrida's peeling of language arrives at something: pre-Babelian "arche-writing" or the Ur-language. Austin describes language in terms of three levels of performative contexts: the locutionary, the illocutionary, and the perlocutionary. Within those contexts a finite range of performative and constative utterances is possible and context altering or affirming (Shapiro 1981). There are no such ontologically secure parameters for language in Wittgenstein. To understand the spirit of the walk though

language-games Wittgenstein describes in the pages of his *Philosophical Investigations*, you must imagine yourself on the most precarious of grounds. Each step brings you in contact with a writhing surface that could give way at any moment. Think of the vertigo-inducing pull of the surf that leaves you teetering even as your feet sink into the sand. You trust you can go on, and so you do. Language is really nothing at base but conventions with possibilities for change, miscommunications, and meanings that far exceed what Austin envisioned. Wittgenstein's language is best thought of as an irreducibly large set of tools or conveniences that help us to disclose features of the world, communicate to others, command attention and respect, articulate pleasing sounds, and so on. It is old, new, and unpredictable. Combining these distinctive philosophical conceptions of language and the relations humans have to language, as Glendinning would like to do, cannot be accomplished without eliding differences and ignoring nuances.

Glendinning's use of Wittgenstein for how we interact (or "read one another") and construct our identities is nevertheless effective and sure-footed. The starting point for this exercise is Wittgenstein's (1958b) claim: "If one sees the behaviour of a living thing, one sees its soul" (sec. 357). This is an expression of what is often called Wittgenstein's "rule of externalization." Our Cartesian heritage leads us to conceive of our "minds" – an occult substance or property located somewhere under our hats and behind our glasses – as the ultimate source of knowledge, certitude, and meaning. To break this bad habit, Wittgenstein asks us to externalize our private soliloquies and mental pictures so that we can hear them as in conversation or so they appear as objects like paintings or photographs. Using this rule over time will break down the inner/outer, mind/body conception of our self. This is a more accurate description of how we are able to "read" one another. There is no essentially private component to our act of saying something and meaning it. What has been conceived in the Cartesian tradition as an "inner" event is available to others through "criteria," another Wittgensteinian technical term. After reviewing the secondary literature on how Wittgenstein used criteria and noting a general agreement among these sources, Glendinning offers an alternative account that highlights his unique contribution to the problem of other minds.

Wittgenstein's use of criteria, notes Glendinning, departs from the ordinary use of the word (and this raises an important question about the ordinariness of ordinary language philosophy that cannot be answered

11

here). When we, in the everyday sense, establish the criteria one must fulfill to obtain a university degree, "we" are the recognized authority to do this. "[W]e establish the identity of the thing," the degree; criteria tell us what this degree is, what it means, what it represents (pp. 133–6). Conversely, there is no determinate, authoritative "we" setting criteria in Wittgenstein's sense of the term; criteria are not used to fix identity. "What is the criterion for the sameness of two images?" asks Wittgenstein (1958b), "What is the criterion for the redness of an image?" (sec. 366). These queries are not answered with certitude by appealing to a mental or metaphysical source of redness or sameness; rather, these queries are calls to examine particular instances when identity and color are brought into question. The criterion we may employ is specific; it is neither determinate nor determining. Particularity – the hard work of describing specific behaviors or events – eschews exactitude, notes Glendinning, and this is the point of these examples of criteria-in-use.

When it comes to the problem of other minds, Wittgensteinian criteria do not supply a response to the skeptic's question "Can we really know the mind of another?" Criteria do not "reveal the inner state of another." Conceived in the form of this skeptical inquiry, the problem of other minds is caught in the "humanist restriction" of subject/object, mind/body, and human/animal antinomies.

I can recognize, acknowledge, or "read" a criterion for pain such as wincing because, as Glendinning argues, it is an "iterable trait," or behavioral regularity that I have seen before, perhaps in the mirror. When I read the wince in the face of another, it is not presented as a conduit that leads me to conclude, "she is in pain." Rather, as Wittgenstein observed, the wince can exist independently of the moment; why it functions as a pain criterion has to do with my response. My response or reading of the wince is as a member of a community of language (for I can imagine different responses to a wince from different communities). Reading criteria is an activity of response, what Cavell (1976) described as "acknowledging" or a compassionate response that unites me with another living being and a community of language users. There is a temporal element here that needs emphasis: I did not read the wince and then respond. The response, observes Glendinning, *is* the reading. Were there a temporal gap, this might lead us to conclude that the community and the other are somehow external in relation to me. Response to pain is a sentient response to a sentient being/soul; our compassionate response, for this reason, is not to the area of affliction (a pain in the hand, to use

Wittgenstein's example), but to "the sufferer: one looks into his face" (Wittgenstein 1958b: sec. 286).

The skeptic leads us astray by divining a division between "us" and "others" that distorts the unity of our "being there" together betokened by Wittgensteinian criteria. We fall into the skeptic's trap, continues Glendinning, when we "conceive of the presence of criteria as something which will *ground* my response to the other" (149). We acknowledge the minds of others automatically, re-iterably, in a continuum of interactions; criteria involve partaking in this unity, they do not individuate or provide occasion to call the mind of the other into question. When we grasp this, the epistemological rendering of the problem of other minds is supplanted by a less exact and inclusive ethical description. The implication of this transition from epistemological problematic to ethical description returns us to Mouffe's suggestion regarding Wittgenstein and the formation of the democratic citizen. This is an area still to be worked out.

What unites the discussions of Mouffe, Holt, and Glendinning is an acceptance that Wittgenstein offers theorists a way to deal with social and political questions and problems philosophically. Although I have specific disagreements with their respective treatments of Wittgenstein, I am in agreement with the thesis that Wittgenstein gives us a new way of theorizing political life. One who questions this sort of rendering of Wittgenstein most contentiously and effectively is Nigel Pleasants in his study *Wittgenstein and the Idea of a Critical Social Theory* (1999).

Pleasants' argument is quite clear and strong. He states, "I regard the idea of a Wittgensteinian *theory* (of anything) as irreparably oxymoronic" (1). To substantiate this claim, he culls the works of Wittgenstein for remarks against theory, lists most of them, and then argues that "Wittgenstein's critique of philosophy can be a valuable resource for revealing the incoherence and impotence of critical social theory," as that enterprise is represented in the works of Winch, Giddens, Bhaskar, and Habermas (2). In Wittgenstein's remarks opposing philosophical theory, one finds a powerful foe of the ontological essentialism or "metaphysical extravagance" used to bolster the authority of these proponents of critical social theory in relation to society.

There are two arguments regarding the marginal place of Wittgenstein in the discourse of social and political theory presented by Pleasants. First, most theorists confront Wittgenstein's philosophy as a "proto-social theory" because of the influential writings of Peter Winch. This requires a reassessment of Winch's fundamental claim that Wittgenstein's remarks on rules and rule-following behavior lead to a "rule generated ontological picture of social life." Eventually, this reinvestigation should lead us to "liberate" Wittgenstein from Winch. Second, even theorists who read Wittgenstein tended to approach his work as though the remarks added up to a coherent picture of reality. Pleasants indicates agreement with the claim made first by Cavell that there are two levels to a theorist's reading of Wittgenstein. The first level is a street-level view of Wittgenstein as he travels through language learning, language-games, forms of life, perception, private language, solipsism, other minds, perspicacious presentation, and so on. The fragmentary, episodic form of Wittgenstein's writing is what is emphasized from this immanent perspective. The second level is that of the "observing theorist" who stands above the text and employs various theoretical devices not found in Wittgenstein – tacit rules, tacit knowledge, assertions about the nature of social life and language in general – to explain how the philosophy coheres into an ontological claim. The critical social theorists explored by Pleasants exhibit Winchean influences that lead to the observing theorist's infelicitous reading of Wittgenstein.

Winch is therefore included in this category of Critical Social Theory (CST), which makes the category itself seem overly broad. Pleasants describes CST as "the new consensus" in social theory and it includes the following characteristics: First, although theorists of this stripe oppose positivism and empiricism, they nevertheless believe that social reality can be represented accurately (in opposition to postmodernist antirepresentationalism). Indeed, they hold "it is vital to have a correct 'ontological picture'" of social actors and their social structure (176). A correct picture of social actors shows them to be "knowledgeable, reflexive, active agents" who artfully construct their social worlds. Second, CST theorists conceive of their task as providing a theory of society that will be of use to social scientists; moreover, by opposing the view of social actors as mere reflections of their social order, CST theorists believe they have fulfilled a crucial critical function for society. Third, these theorists conceive of their relation to political society and the agents who construct it as a "double hermeneutic." That is, they conceive of themselves as traversing two logically distinct realms or rationalities: the critical rationality of social scientific and scientific inquiry, and the commonsense or ordinary rationality of social life. On this point, CST theorists depart from the hermeneutic or descriptive orientation to the social world represented by Winch's Wittgenstein, which they consider a hopelessly conservative position, for critical-explanatory analysis predicated upon the epistemic authority of their social scientific, second order perspective. This perspective marks a methodological end to the old positivist dispute that separated hermeneutics from empiricism. What is available to CST theorists, thanks to the postempiricist philosophy of science, is a consilience between the poles of the traditional *Methodenstreit* that retains the explanatory status of scientific theory while acknowledging the unsurpassability of hermeneutics, even in natural scientific inquiry. The only remaining distinction between natural and social sciences, according to CST, "is their respective subject matters . . . and this is an *ontological*, not an *epistemological*, difference" (174–8). This is a restatement of the double hermeneutic, which now is to be regarded as an explanation for the epistemologically privileged stance of CST theorists and the scientific authority of their social critiques.

Pleasants responds to these components of CST by simultaneously defending Wittgenstein against the charge that his descriptivism is inherently conservative. This defense goes beyond just *saying* Wittgenstein's work is itself a non-conservative critical orientation within philosophy; Pleasants *shows* us how to use the philosophy to reveal the baselessness of CST's various claims to epistemological and ontological privilege. This presumed privilege does not translate into a strong social voice. Indeed, argues Pleasants, "it can hardly be said of the theories of structuration, communicative action, or discourse ethics, that they have anything much to say about *changing the social world*" (47). As Mouffe observed, the only social effect CST appears to have (and here we can speak only of Giddens and Habermas) is as a voice of intellectual justification (propaganda) for the free market centrism of "Third Way" leaders in Britain, Germany, and the US.

CST is an esoteric philosophical enterprise with political and social pretenses. The irony of its emphasis on accurate representation and explanation of individual agency is that practitioners deflect critical attention and reflection from real-world problems. The CST theorists' only reality is their abstract theoretical construct. Wittgensteinian therapy reveals the confusion and incoherence of this ontologization of social reality. "[W]hy should the postulation of hidden cognitive powers . . . and an external transcendental order of rules, in itself, count as a critical perspective on, or intervention in, social life?" asks Pleasants (78). The unreflectiveness of CST theorists that this question begs bespeaks the hermeticism of their respective ontologies.

15

Wittgenstein is employed by Pleasants to illuminate the category error at the base of CST. Theorists in this school confuse second order (metatheoretical) assertions for first order (political) criticisms and potency. One pervasive example of this confusion in CST is the imposition of "tacit knowledge" – a theoretical construct – as an explanation for the rule-following behavior of agents acting in the social world. Tacit knowledge is part of a general conception of rule following and an abstract definition of the social actor as the knowledgeable constructor of meaningful social structures. It is not a description of how humans interact socially. Indeed, according to CST, social actors do not access their tacit knowledge ordinarily; rather, it requires the hermeneutical skills of the social theorist to translate the agent's ordinary "knowledge how to" (tacit knowledge) into the "knowledge that" (explanatory knowledge) of CST. Thus, tacit knowledge has two metatheoretical functions: it works like the concept of mind in behaviorism as an esoteric explanation for why a person is predisposed to act in such a way; and it serves to bolster the theorist's claim to epistemic authority by demanding special skills to make the tacit explicit. The consequences of such authoritative insights for social criticism are, notes Pleasants, negligible. At best, the view of social agents as knowledgeable social constructors can be employed to confront similarly second order theoretical constructs. This is not inherently bad, Pleasants continues; it just ought not to be confused for actual social engagement. The amelioration of such conceptual or boundary confusion is an effect of Wittgenstein's philosophical therapy.

I want to extend this Wittgensteinian critique further in an ethical direction to reveal the critical dimension of what I take to be a new kind of theorizing encouraged in Wittgenstein's work. This is also an opportunity to tie together the various strands of argument issuing from the works I have considered here. Traditionally, political and social theorists have argued for the necessity of critical distance to produce a theory of political society. This distance can be expressed spatially as the span between the mountaintop and the city, or temporally as the distinctive pace of philosophical reflection in comparison with the technologically accelerated pace of modern existence. Most often, these metaphors are further abstracted as the creative manifestations of vocation, unique perceptual acuity, privileged mental aptitude, or the defense of theory's critical potency from the corruption of politics. In the end, however, it is only perceptual distance, notes Wittgenstein, and this distance is dehumanizing. In abstracting the person into subject or agent, in abstracting

16

the world into theoretical idealizations, theorists are (benignly, usually) contributing to the effacement of what Levinas (1987) called "the ethic of visual proximity" (61–74). The further we stand from people, the less we care what happens to them. Wittgenstein expresses this distance as at the heart of "the darkness of our time."

Pleasants does a serviceable job of examining the conceptual confusions in Critical Social Theory, but he does not take the additional step, acknowledged by Wittgenstein, to get to the real-world pains experienced by theorists that lead them to seek escape from politics by climbing ladders that lead to ontologies of politics. In this, theorists are like physicians who wish for a longer stethoscope to avoid the odors of their dying patients. The social world of the twentieth and early twenty-first century is an increasingly smelly place and so the urge to escape into metaphysics grows ever stronger. This is why Wittgenstein felt his own work so important: Illuminating our darkness is possible only from positions of immanence, achieved by physical motion, that enable us to see ideality and reality as inextricably intertwined. When we supplant dualism with monism, we countenance the pains and joys of human life with compassion and imagination, and without resort to flight in the guise of critical thought. Enhancing perception on this crowded plane by combating the captivity of ontological and epistemological dogmatism and by encouraging notice and description of differences is the ethical mission of the immanent theorist.

Through training, our tendency as theorists is to view metatheory as offering a superior perceptual vantage point *over* the world. Even critics of metatheoretical inflations of the theorist's knowledge, like Pleasants, tend to conceive of the orders of knowledge/discourse as arranged in a hierarchy. Wittgenstein (1958b), however, was interested in flattening all such pyramidal conceptions. Any strategic, perceptual advantage of second order philosophy (like the transcendence it appears to offer), he stated, is illusory. There is only first order philosophy in this sense (sec. 121). What is called metaphilosophy – talking about what philosophers do when they philosophize – exists on the same plane as philosophizing. They are distinctive language-games. To traverse their boundaries requires acknowledgement of their distinctiveness, acceptance that there are no alternative scenic or subterranean routes, and a willingness to endure the friction-filled walk across them. Following Wittgenstein, theorists need first to reconceive nonhierarchically the relations between metatheory, political theory, and politics. Then we need to consider the visual and ethical consequences of this horizontal rearrangement.

17

This is what I hope to accomplish in the following chapters. I aim to reconceive theorizing politics using Wittgenstein's work on language and seeing, to both foreground the obstacles to seeing politics clearly that are unique to our times and that render older, epic examples of theory otiose; and to show the rough ground of language to offer paths that surmount these obstacles. This project is achieved through engagement with various schools, arguments, and thinkers composing contemporary political theory. The starting point is the recognition that Wittgenstein is not a mere tool for theorizing. Instead, his philosophical works in all their anti-Cartesian glory provide us with an intimate view of how a theorist goes about the hard work of seeing clearly and describing with a felicity that illuminates what Cavell (1988) has called "the uncanniness of the ordinary." Uncanniness is a feature of our contemporary political life underappreciated by those who wish to escape its unpredictability with equations, textual analogues, and the promise of epistemological heights.

The peripatetic character of the philosophizing in Wittgenstein's *Philosophical Investigations* guides the organization of the book. As with the remarks of that compose this most unusual and important philosophical work, there are perceptual modulations in my study of what it takes to theorize politics today. At times, I will walk in close to notice darkened corners and smaller obstacles to attain the clear seeing that should be the goal of political theory in any age. At other times, I will try to step back a little to gain a wider perspective. This is not to be taken as resignation to the strong impulse to transcend the limits to vision posed by the street-level perspective endemic to life in the city of language; rather, it is a mundane move shaped by the accidental experience of turning a corner and finding an unexpected open field, instead of another row of apartment buildings and a car-lined street.

Chapter 1 offers a focus on immanent theorizing as a form of therapy that breaks the hold of epic political theory. The opening remarks of the *Philosophical Investigations* are read best as an invitation to follow the philosopher through the language-games that he himself is discovering now that he has broken with his older conception of language as composed of a single, logical act of picturing by attaching word to object. Travel, then, is conceived as liberation from a mistake of considering a neighborhood of the city of language the entirety of language. The picture that held theorists captive, I contend, is one where they stand above the city enjoying the panoramic view offered by the fixed perspective of the mountaintop, a height conceived in the lexicon of both metaphysical and epistemological privilege.

In the second chapter, I examine some of the obstacles and problems unique to contemporary theorizing that warrant a break from the epic past. This is the beginning of a strand of argument about the fragmented character of political life today that is carried through my study. Even if epic theory were achievable, I will argue, it is expressed through a vocabulary of order unbefitting the sporadic character of political life today necessitated by and resistant to the predominant form of collective order: bureaucracy.

The third chapter is an examination of citizenship that follows from the effect of travel through language-games on how we come to define ourselves. The forms of entrapment or impediments to motion examined here are philosophical and religious dogmatism, as I work through the conversation between Socrates and Euthyphro, and Azar Nafisi's memoir of her life in Tehran during the reign of the Ayatollah Khomeini. Along the way, I flesh out the notion of citizenship conceived along Wittgensteinian lines by encountering critically and appreciatively the work of Chantal Mouffe and Aletta Norval. The resulting dynamic account of political life leads me into Chapter 4, which takes up the radical quality of Wittgenstein's conventionalism (an argument about language's lack of natural or metaphysical groundedness) in opposition to those who read his work as a call to conservatism and a renunciation of philosophy's critical role in relation to the other claims to knowledge audible in society generally or in the other faculties of the university.

Chapters 5 and 6 examine Wittgenstein's remarks on perception, including his accounts of aspect-blindness, continuous seeing, seeing aspects, and the relation between the experience of seeing in the world and the experience of meaning in language. These remarks form a walking trail that lead to a deeper historical affinity with the ocular and illuminative metaphors at the root of theorizing. As I noted at the beginning, political theorists have long investigated the connection between Wittgenstein and theorizing, and it is in his studies of seeing – in particular seeing as noticing change – that I locate this connection.

Chapter 7 is regarded best as a Wittgensteinian reading of a play by Samuel Beckett, *Catastrophe*. This chapter entails a perceptual shift in relation to the rest of my study. Where I have emphasized the horizontal travel through language by immanent theorists, in this chapter I illustrate this movement by stepping from politics and political theory into (literary) culture (Dean 2000); however, I also examine the space for vertical movement within language. Wittgenstein suggests this thickness in his distinction between surface and depth grammars, and his thoughts on the relation of trust, conceived as irreducible, to language-games. The distance between surface and depth in language is miniscule: to get to the "bedrock" of trust in language you do not have to dig too deep. This is also the distance separating those of us who enjoy the privileges that attend membership in a political community and the abjection of what Giorgio Agamben describes as "bare life." Through torture, exile, imprisonment, and other forms of inhumanity illuminated in the techniques of concentration camps, humans are deprived of what makes them human. When this political life is bared completely, we see that what are effaced are the relations of trust undergirding language. When this thin membrane is eroded, victims fall through language into death. In Beckett's *Catastrophe*, trust is exposed and threatened. But there may be a redemptive moment in the end, and this possibility mirrors what I perceive as the optimism that suffuses Wittgenstein's philosophy. It is a constructive moment, and the proper place to end this study of the condition of theorizing political life today.

Chapter 1

Theorizing as a Lived Experience: A Wittgensteinian Investigation

For me a theory is without value. A theory gives me nothing.
Wittgenstein to Friedrich Waismann (Waismann 1979: 117)

I. Introduction

Themes of entrapment and escape are pervasive in Wittgenstein's philosophy. Indeed, the philosopher or theorist's apparent preference for being chained to a given picture of reality is the target of Wittgenstein's therapeutic skepticism and his corresponding call for a return from metaphysical language to ordinary language use. This call should be understood as more than a break from one picture and a step into another. For Wittgenstein, ordinary language lacks any pretense to epistemological or perceptual privilege and affords a great range of horizontal motion that, if recognized, will challenge any future forms of entrapment. The pictures or zones of regularity in ordinary language run into one another and invite horizontal travel. Entrapment, then, is really a matter of intellectual laziness. Returning to ordinary philosophy involves a transformation of at least one large and influential philosophical tradition. That is, Wittgenstein's call entails a reversal of Plato's cave parable: the return to the cave from the sunlit outer world is to be considered now as an escape from enslavement to static philosophical abstraction.

Ordinary language, by contrast, is dynamic and defies both simplification and claims to mastery by language-users. There is room for self-criticism that arises when travel across language reveals the errors and limitations that arise when you mistake the part (a language-game) for the whole. "A *picture* held us captive," wrote Wittgenstein in response to the

21

reductive picture he propounded in his earlier work, the *Tractatus Logico-Philosophicus*. This reduction, called the picture theory of language, first shrank language down to the proposition, and then claimed the discovery of the underlying logical form in which all propositions partake. For this early work, those human experiences and expressions that escaped the rigid formalism of the picture theory of language were simply excised from Philosophy. Philosophy was rendered anemic as a result of this account of language; while we were to understand that what was truly interesting about life existed beyond the province of philosophical analysis. Philosophy could come to a quiet end at this point, and those who once called themselves philosophers needed to find new jobs in poetry or gardening.

Wittgenstein returned to philosophy in the work that would culminate in his posthumously published *Philosophical Investigations*. There were two entwined components of this return. First, he saw the theory of language that animated his *Tractatus* and gave him the sense that he had brought philosophy to an end as the result of a category error. He took one dimension of language, the proposition, and thought it the whole of what could be called language. In this conception of language, surface differences between words would give way to a deeper sameness in meaning: meaning was a product of the linear relation between words and the object they represent. Conversely, ordinary language in the *Philosophical Investigations* is composed of a complex and dynamic array of language-games that float loosely on a river of equally complex, living conventions. There is no bedrock of sameness. Meaning is a residue of the way words are arranged in sentences or utterances. Sometimes even infelicitous uses of words manage to convey the desired information or effect; but miscommunication is a common feature of language-use. Rules in language serve as "signposts" for language-use, but they have no regulative or deterministic effect.[1] At base, there is only a trust that this world of language and the relations it permits coheres in some way. In this, language has no ontological stability, and the real job of the philosopher/theorist is to travel from language-game to language-game, while resisting the desire to say something general about the nature of language (for it has no nature), and avoiding the misplaced synecdoche of the young Wittgenstein.

The second component of Wittgenstein's (1958b) criticism of his earlier philosophical work is understood best as an inevitable consequence of the return to ordinary language. As he observed, this return involved friction (sec. 107). Intimacy with ordinary language entails, in other words, intimacy with oneself – the embodied philosopher or theorist – and intimacy with others. All those corporeal, emotional, and spiritual concerns of the person so neatly exiled from the concerns of Philosophy in the *Tractatus* make a return in the *Philosophical Investigations*. They return not in the form of occult, inner processes, but rather as expressions and practices in and across language-games. We live these experiences that are then reached and describable by the philosopher through travel (walking) and a compassion for others that emanates from our coexistence in the stream of language.

In sum, the critical point of the *Philosophical Investigations* is to escape the picture of Philosophy and Language offered in the *Tractatus*. The effect of this escape is the liberation of the embodied philosopher and the opening of philosophical or theoretical vision by uniting seeing with bodily motion. Emancipation is the spirit of his later work. "What is your aim in philosophy?" Wittgenstein (1958b) asked of himself, "To shew the fly out of the fly-bottle" (sec. 309).

There is a picture holding contemporary political theory captive, I will argue, and it is the epic self-image of the theorist borrowed from religious and mythological narratives, and from Plato who is extolled for prefiguring and originating the tradition of epic political theory. This self-image is in emulation of "the combination of power, knowledge, and prevision," described by Wolin (1985), as "most perfectly realized in Yahweh. He performs the supreme political act: he does not merely create the world; he constitutes it, that is, he orders it, differentiates levels of power and being, assigns jurisdictions and issues rules for their regulation" (228).[2] There is nothing nefarious about this self-image; indeed, it tells us something important about the visual rootedness and goal of theory. It is an enterprise devoted to seeing. But the epic theorist mistakes clear and coherent sight from a fixed point of view regarded as divine and timeless for the kind of perspicacious seeing available to mere mortals capable of overcoming some perceptual limits by walking. Young (1990) captures the impulse to generalize in the epic tradition while resisting the temptation to "construct a theory of justice." "A theory of justice" in the epic tradition, she writes,

> typically derives fundamental principles of justice that apply to all or most societies, whatever their concrete configuration and social relations, from a few general premises about the nature of human beings, the nature of societies, and the nature of reason. True to the meaning of *theoria*, it wants to see justice. It assumes a point of view outside the social context where issues of justice arise, in order to gain a comprehensive view. The theory of justice is intended to be self-standing, since

23

it exhibits its own foundations. As a discourse it aims to be whole, and to show justice in its unity. It is detemporalized, in that nothing comes before it and future events will not affect its truth or relevance to social life. (3–4)

The epic project of creating a theory of justice exemplified in the work of Berlin, Rawls, Nozick, Walzer, Sandel, and others fails on two counts, Young continues. First, it is constructed to function as an absolute normative standard that can be employed to evaluate the justness of activities and institutions in the concrete realm of human political and social activity. But any epic concept of justice is too abstract for this kind of comparison. Second, the construct is never as cleanly extrapolated from the particular context as epic theorists would like to believe. The concept of justice is not so much a product of theoretical seeing as it is a matter of hearing and attending to calls for justice and protests against injustice from within political practices or the language-game labeled by Lyotard as "the game of the just" (Young 1990: 4). "The traditional effort to transcend the finitude toward universal theory," Young (1990) concludes, "yields only finite constructs which escape the appearance of contingency usually by recasting the given as necessary" (5). Renouncing the veneer of universality supporting the epic self-image of theorizing does not lead to the demise of the enterprise; rather, the turn back toward concrete political life is also a return to the mundane activity of seeing that animates theorizing.

The immediate effect of introducing Wittgenstein's philosophy into the discourse of political theory would be twofold. First, the epic self-image would be de-divinized, even while encountering the very human impulse to transcend creatively the mundane. Second, the stark, vertical division between the epic theorist and political life, that bespeaks privileged vision on the part of the theorist, would be flattened. From this eye-level view, we can begin to see the relation between political theory and other activities (politics, Political Science, and so on.) as distinct language-games that can and may abut and overlap, permitting travel between them. And this is the way we theorists live in and among these games. The perceptual and critical results of such a reconceptualization for the enterprise of theorizing politics are the interrelated subjects of this book.

So far, I have intimated a close relation between Wittgenstein's philosophical activity in the *Philosophical Investigations* and the activity of theorizing. Let me now clarify this relation. I will argue that Wittgenstein's travel through language-games, his inquiries into solipsism and personhood, the experience of seeing changes, and his thoughts on the relation between the conventions undergirding language and the activities

24

constituting the surface, yield intimate views of what it is to engage in theorizing. This is a claim that I will have to substantiate. Among Wittgenstein scholars, my thesis is contentious. Against those who consider him an antitheoretical thinker, those who take Wittgenstein's own injunctions against theory (and I included some of this at the beginning of this chapter) too literally or inclusively, I argue that whatever cohesiveness the ultimately and necessarily incomplete *Philosophical Investigations* possesses is a product of deep concern with the condition of theorizing (expressed more accurately for Wittgenstein as "philosophical seeing") in the latter half of the twentieth century.

As an example of this dispute, insightful commentators on Wittgenstein's work like Genova (1995) and Diamond (1991) see his celebration of pluralism (that vast mosaic of language-games) composing linguistic reality as inescapably antitheoretical. "For Wittgenstein," writes Genova (1995), "the connection between language and world is so tight that we cannot isolate the two variables in order to have a theory" (211). Genova's reading of Wittgenstein as antitheoretical is the product of two kinds of entrapment. First, she conceives of theory as synonymous with transcendence. This is very much part of the self-image that informs epic theory. Theory is achieved from a height that affords synoptic perspective. Second, and I will argue this further, Wittgenstein's remarks critical of theory are seen more accurately as criticisms of metatheory. If what might count as theory is a claim about the conventional and provisional nature of linguistic reality, then Wittgenstein has a theory and is a theorist. His antitheoretical remarks target a distinct range of claims about how theory can be used to justify, legitimate, and bolster a philosophical argument. Thus what we should find unique about Wittgenstein's theorizing, and why it is so often mistaken for something else, is the immanent (or anti-epic, antitranscendent) and dynamic perspectives from which it is articulated. Descriptions of that "tight connection" between language and world noted by Genova, emanate from internal points of view achieved by walking and careful seeing (Wittgenstein 1958b: secs. 203, 455–7). Wittgenstein's theorizing is not the product of a bedridden abstraction, but that of an alert, embodied walker.

From a less contentious angle, I want to show that Wittgenstein takes the activity of theorizing, along with its optic and illuminative correlates, too seriously for summary dismissal. The *Philosophical Investigations* is replete with observations on liberating perception, on traps that limit seeing that are to be evaded and obstacles that impede vision to be

25

surmounted, by treading along the "rough ground" of language. In this, walking is employed by Wittgenstein as both a renunciation of transcendence and a celebration of what it is to be human. I treat this human condition of theorizing described by Wittgenstein as three interrelated aspects: First, embodiment opposes the sovereignty of the traditional epic stance, both ethically and politically; second, the vision that comes from embodiment or the lived-life of the theorist is provisional and descriptive in relation to the conventional nature and organization of linguistic reality; and, third, it is peripatetic and unapologetically immanent (even if it comprehends the creative impulse behind transcendence). Theorizing, following Wittgenstein, is divorced from the traditional epistemological concerns with justification and explanation. Again, this is the stuff of metatheory, and such *ex post facto* (mis)uses of theory imply a version of truth as accuracy or coherence that is itself an obstacle to theorizing understood as an ongoing description of the components and topography of reality from various positions within.

What follows in this chapter is an example of immanent theorizing in action, and the action that I focus on is its critical regard for epic theory. I will explore some of the implications of the descriptions of forms of epic theory offered by social and political theorists. The common belief running through these images of theorizing is there must be a fixed spatio-temporal distance between the theorist and politics that provides the theorist with a privileged, panoptical perspective. This vantage, tacitly or explicitly, depending on the theorist in question, replicates the sacral relation between the Creator and her or his creation. Supporting this God's-eye point of view, "the view from nowhere" as it is termed by Nagel (1986), is a network of theological and epistemological claims that appear immutable and inscrutable, but are actually quite vulnerable, as Wittgenstein shows, to his skeptical regard for metaphysics as a self-deluded attempt to step out of ordinary language. Epic theory and the foundational claims enlisted to protect it from ideological corruption and the violence of ordinary human existence are, claimed Wittgenstein, part of a larger "generalizing impulse," endemic to the culture, that is both an understandable response to, and a contributing element of, "the darkness of this time." Stereotyping, scapegoating, nationalism, sexism, violent heteronormativity, and racism are manifestations of this same proclivity to resist face-to-face intimacy, escape the unpredictability of politics, and judge/view others and events from a safe distance. For Wittgenstein, then, epic models of theory are to be criticized on ethical grounds. It

26

results, he observed, in the disembodiment of the theorist, and abstract, soulless notions of others. As creative an enterprise as this is, the vacuum engendered by eschewing corporeality is filled quickly with the distrust that breeds barbarism.

This mainly ethical argument serves to reposition the theorist in the city, which Wittgenstein (1958b) achieved metaphorically (sec. 18). He then extols the virtues and rewards of immanent theorizing by traveling the streets of this city of language. This travel closes the distance between perceiver and the objects of perception, and it reveals and revels in the all too often unnoticed creativity of ordinary seeing. Perception is not the passive exercise described by empiricists. Once we grasp the inescapable intimacy of theory, language, and world, there is no stronger argument against the impulse to generalize available or needed. The fragile bedrock of trust supporting the floating platform of language-games is all we have, and that, Wittgenstein contends, is sufficient for human happiness.

II. THE EPIC SELF-IMAGE

An immediate impression formed in confronting contemporary descriptions of the activity of theorizing is how pregnant they are with religious, largely Judeo-Christian, imagery. It is often difficult to distinguish theory from theology (Taylor 1991). As their common prefixes indicate, there is etymological justification for this conflation of religion and political vision. "*Theoreos* means someone who takes part in a mission to a festival," observed Hans-Georg Gadamer (1975). "Such a person has no other qualification or function to be there. Thus the *theoreos* is a spectator in the literal sense of the word, who shares in the solemn act through his presence at it and in this way acquires his sacred quality: for example, of inviolability" (111). Although there is no direct or necessary connection between this *theoreos* and contemporary conceptions of the theorist and theoretical activity, recent descriptions of the theorist do appropriate the sacred quality of the theory to event relation, and respond to the vulnerabilities, the lack of "qualification and function," experienced by the ancient spectator, with claims about the necessity of distance for theoretical vision.

I do not want to initiate this investigation into how political theory is defined today with an impression that there is widespread agreement among practitioners. There is not. Contemporary theorists exhibit a wide range of fears and dissatisfactions in the definitions and justifications they offer to describe and ground what it is they do. Security is a critical and ongoing theme, and it pertains to the autonomy political theory can claim in relation to other academic activities, especially Political Science and Philosophy.[3] In defining themselves, then, theorists are usually responding to a perceived threat within or against the university.[4] But there are also expressed concerns for the theorists' larger intellectual role in political society, and for political society's capacity to receive and appreciate theoretical truth. Responding to these arenas of actual or potential conflict, theorists ignore or resist explicitly the passivity implied in the depiction of *theoreos* as dilettantish spectator and identify instead with the activist role of the philosopher advanced most memorably by Marx in his *Eleventh Thesis on Feuerbach*. To move beyond mere interpretation of the world by changing it, or at least to eliminate threats to theorizing, was understood to necessitate an embellishment of theory with claims to privileged knowledge and a perceptual vantage inaccessible to ordinary citizens. The combined effect of the fear of impingement by other faculties in the university, and the desire to play an authoritative and incorruptible role in political society, leads to a transcendent self-image that emphasizes the theorist's "sacred quality" of "inviolability" noted by Gadamer.

The irony is that this self-image contradicts many of its desired effects. Theory's claim to autonomy, for instance, is undermined ultimately by all its borrowing from epistemology, metaphysics, (the philosophy of) science, historiography, and theology. The distance prerequisite to claims to superior political knowledge negates any potential for political activism.[5] Moreover, for theoretically adduced knowledge about politics to remain inviolable, it must be perceived as separate from the taint of ideology and mutable political opinion.

Overcoming these contradictions, "like shewing the fly out of the fly-bottle," requires a new conception of the activity of theorizing politics and a new self-identity for the political theorist. I will pick this point up momentarily. For now, we need only to observe that traditions and habits rendered rigid and sacred by fear are exceptionally challenging forms of entrapment, as Wittgenstein knew. The rigidity of disciplinary boundaries in this case remain invisible and unacknowledged until you attempt to oppose it. When you do make a case for interdisciplinarity, for example, you find that you are trapped by the vocabulary of the discipline from which you emerged. This is an especially damning problem for political theorists trained in the epic tradition. It is a tradition that inspires love on the part of practitioners. Reading and learning from the products of the epic tradition – *The Republic*, *The Prince*, *Leviathan*, and so on – is a bond shared by theorists. Yet, the view of politics offered by the heroic theorist is a trap. An entire constellation of concepts emerges around the agreement that politics is a form of order, and these concepts are accepted so readily they may serve to keep us from seeing how politics, the political life, is actually lived today. For theorists following Wittgenstein's path to immanent theorizing, what is valued above all else is mobility. Part of the lived-life of the theorist walking the neighborhoods of language is concerned with the destruction of those conceptual "idols" that serve to end inquiry. This may lead to new readings of old works of theory. But the critical task of the theorist's way of life is a matter of constant vigilance to resist the metaphysical impulse, "and that means not creating a new one [idol] – for instance as in 'absence of an idol'" (Wittgenstein 1993: 171).

Part of my contention is that political theory is incapable of resisting the metaphysical impulse – the need to imagine itself floating safely above politics – so long as theorists believe that epic distance is a necessary precondition for, and an effect of, theorizing. The allure of the epic stance is very strong, and the alternative posed by Wittgenstein of voyeuristic theorizing from a street-level, is unheroic, exposed, and initially at least, unattractive. Transcendence, too, has its dangers and corruption. Think of Arendt's dismissal of Heidegger's Nazism as a "change of residence" renounced, at least symbolically, in his return to the heights of philosophy, or the kind of metaphysical inanity that calls to mind Aristophanes' unflattering but funny portrait of Socrates in The Clouds. For Wittgenstein, immanence is not the mirror of transcendence. Immanence is a perspective that precludes transcendence by presenting a view of reality devoid of ontological dualisms like heaven and earth, sacred and profane, noumenal and phenomenal, mind and body. There is but one plane of human existence and this is the landscape the theorist shares with everyone else. This monism is the source of the irony in his quip, "Never stay up on the barren heights of cleverness, but come down into the green valleys of silliness" (Wittgenstein 1980b: 76).

There are strands of dissatisfaction with the epic self-image expressed within political theory today. Wittgenstein's brand of immanence shares features of various forms of Aristotelian, Nietzschean, and Deleuzean political theory, for example. But the pull of the general is a hard habit to resist for the three reasons I outlined earlier: the desire to emulate the divine, a need to embellish theory's claim to autonomy in relation to its constitutive outside, and a distaste for actual politics. Each desire is nourished by knowledge claims emanating from rationalist and empiricist

29

(or some post-Kantian hybrid) epistemology. However, the unintended effect of the desire to establish a critical perspective outside and above the spheres of ideological influence is the production of various knowledge claims that serve to rationalize and justify power relations existing within society, particularly ethnocentrism and the priority of order over freedom. These predispositions were raised to eye-level in an exchange on the relation between theory and politics prompted by what Isaac (1995) called "The Strange Silence of Political Theory" in the wake of the 1989 events in Eastern Europe and the former Soviet Union. Isaac described this silence as "a shocking indictment of academic political theory" (637).

Much of the analysis of the relation of political theory to political events provided by Isaac is a gloss on the historical work of other theorists who focus on the academicization of the discourse as an explanation for its negligible political voice. But the strength of the Isaac piece lies in its polemical character. What Isaac manages to evoke is the often hidden dimension of political theory's estrangement from politics – its epic self-identity. Academicization may illuminate the logical and institutional division between theory and politics – you cannot be in two places at once – but epic distance is justified both in terms of the superior perceptual vantage it offers and in terms denigrating to politics as a locus of corruption and where the vicissitudes of public opinion leave little time or patience to consider theoretical takes on even the most momentous of events.

The professional responses to Isaac illuminated the central contradiction in the epic identity disclosed earlier: the juxtaposition of the theorist's purported need for spatial and temporal distance from politics and the incapacitation this distance induces in theorists who wish to comment on issues in the political world. Wolin (1997) captures this contradiction in his defense of epic political theory of the present. "Theory," he observes, "is in a bind: it wants to be local and restricted" in its desire to respond effectively to political events, "but the structures of power – political, economic, and cultural – are national and global. To theorize the inside one must theorize the outside" (para. 10). Following this odd argumentative path for achieving immanent theory through transcendence, Wolin responds to Isaac's question, "What is wrong with political theory today?" with a question of his own that simply underscores the structural problem of epic theory: "Why is political theory so difficult today?"

Wolin's answer to his own question is a remarkably evocative defense of epic distance along temporal lines. It recalls Augustine's apology for Christianity in The City of God: The separation of sacred time from human time absolved Christianity of any blame for the fall of Rome. Wolin's similarly bifurcated notion of time is somewhat more complicated than Augustine's, but it shares his rhetorical goal of absolution, though for political theory in this instance. Wolin notes first that there is no uniform "political time." Rather, the political pace of a society with democratic aspirations is different than the normal political time of societies at peace. Generally, and transnationally, however, political time is far faster than the temporal rhythms of the larger culture. This contrast is cast into clear terms when we compare normal political time with the historical and preservationist tenor of political theory's cultural voice. For Wolin, then, this temporal contrast plus the conflation of power and politics in contemporary political society yield a political reality that makes it all but impossible for a theorist to discern what should count as a political event until it can be viewed retrospectively. Connolly (1995) offers another argument in support of temporal distance that conforms to the Nietzschean celebration of untimeliness. "It is important to be untimely sometimes to explore as profoundly as you can the messy corners of the world in which you live" (655). In response to such arguments, what Wittgenstein reveals for political theorists today is the trade-off that epic distance demands that is unnecessary. The temporal division between theory and the democratic messiness of Central Europe in 1989 is a barrier to perception. It is not as though we theorists do not view events as they happen; nor does contemporaneous seeing somehow prevent further thought and vision in the future. Conceived in terms of language-games, timeliness and untimeless, and all the benefits to vision achieved through their reconciliation, are conjoined in the lived-life of political theorists. With vertical metaphors, theorists are conceived as something like political tourists. It is down to the Piraeus to observe the Dionysian ritual and then back up again to do some theorizing. This is not how we live.

Brown (1997) responded to Wolin's remarks with a more traditionally spatial argument for political theory's epic stance in relation to politics. In responding to political events of the moment, she argues, political theorists are in danger of relinquishing their uniquely synoptic perspective. Invoking lessons from Merleau-Ponty and Foucault, Brown contends that distance and indirection are time-honored tactics theorists must employ if they are to avoid "becoming just another hubristic pundit." Although Brown warns against privileging theory over political action, it is difficult to see how to avoid this, given her sweeping suspiciousness of political opinions arising from sources others than political theory. In

31

this, Brown happens upon an area of concurrence shared by Isaac, Wolin, and Connolly: They all agree that the place for the theorist is above politics in the same conceptual sense that *episteme* is above *doxa*, and heaven is above hell. In truth, if pressed, I would admit to liking political theory more than I like politics, but I still find in Wittgenstein an accurate description of my daily wanderings between the two activities.

Significantly, no respondent to the Isaac polemic presented anything more than a cursory analysis of the political problems of Central Europe undergoing democratization. Even in these general remarks, politics was taken either as the "*putative topic*" and dismissed, or intellectual surrogates, most often the writings of Havel, Michnik, and Žižek, supplanted it. Isaac's challenge was taken unanimously as a cue to defend one's beliefs about the correct way to engage in political theory as opposed to taking it as an opportunity to look anew at the relation of theory to practice. Given the attenuated parameters of the responses then, we are left with the intriguing question posed by Kiss (1995): "So, how would the field of political theory look different if we followed Isaac's advice?" (668). The difference would be negligible. The epic self-image exposed by Isaac remains unchallenged, like a true divinity.

The theological dimension of epic theorizing – the creation of order out of chaos, something from nothing – has been conditioned by the philosophical discourse of the twentieth century. Criticisms and cultural analysis offered by Nietzsche, Heidegger, Wittgenstein, Foucault, Derrida, Rorty, Cavell, and postmodernists have advanced by eliminating ideas of an overarching rationality, a language of nature, and an Archimedean standpoint as regulative ideals in philosophy and literature. But these older beliefs continue to resonate in some political theory circles. From the rationalist tradition of Habermas, for example, we hear McCarthy (1990) arguing that "we need . . . to develop concepts of reason, truth, and justice that, while no longer pretending to a God's-eye point of view, retain something of their transcendent, regulative, critical force" (367).

The centrality and promotion of theory's epic self-image must be understood in the historical and institutional context of its relation with other subfields of academic Political Science, as well as with the other disciplines constitutive of social science in American and European universities.[6] The epic image was appropriated from the history of political thought and employed to both justify political theory's existence as a tradition, from Plato to Marx, and to provide if not an instruction book on how to theorize, then a sense of duty to defend the (sub)discipline.

Just as epistemology served to explain and justify the place of philosophy in relation to religion and science, so the epic tradition, with its own embedded epistemological contentions, provided political theory with a raison d'être.

III. WITTGENSTEIN AND THE ETHICS OF EPIC DISTANCE

The antitheoretical remarks of Wittgenstein are undeniably blunt and acerbic. Theory, in his view, is what Plato's world of forms was for Aristotle: a pointless complication that draws attention away from the way we live and entails disrespect for this world of humans and things. Throughout Wittgenstein's writings, his antitheoreticism is advanced as a chasm between living an ethical or religious life, and speaking philosophically about ethics and religion. Living a political life was an area of the city of language he did not explore, but his concern about the linguistic entanglements and degraded perceptions that would arise should we confuse meta- or third order reflections of politics for politics, can be inferred from his critical remarks about philosophically idealized accounts of ethics and religion. Where the philosophical perspective on activities involves judgments and justifications of the activities, as in the example of Frazer's description of tribal magic as "false," an injustice has been perpetrated in the form of a deluded attempt to rise to a height external to language to remark on linguistic phenomena or any other species of human activity. For Wittgenstein, "our only task" as practitioners and describers of language-games "is to be just. That is we must only point out and resolve the injustices of philosophy," the claims to epic or privileged stances in political theory, dogmatism in religion, or the ethnocentrism of anthropology, "and not posit new parties – and creeds" (Wittgenstein 1993: 181). Nor do we need any fictive vantages onto the world; language provides ample, actual points of view.

Thus far, I have examined the epic self-image in political theory as composed of various spatial and temporal claims to distance from political life, and the role the so-called tradition of great works in political thought have played (unnecessarily) as surrogates for politics. There is a third, phenomenological manifestation of the epic avoidance of politics achieved by burrowing beneath the surface of forms of political life to locate their foundation in "the political." This is a notoriously difficult term to define, but, generally, "the political" refers to the rules and conventions underlying political practices as essential to those practices (Hauptmann 2004: 34–60). Moreover, these essential rules form rigid boundaries separating "us" from "them," friends from enemies, as in Schmitt's influential work, and are delineated within political relations described as agonic. Eschewing liberal bourgeois notions of politics as compromise exposes this agonic or polemical quality of the political. For Schmitt (1996), the political is the most human of all associations; and it is the ground of life-and-death struggles over the beliefs that divide us. This arena where we are willing to kill and to be killed is what distinguishes politics from other aspects of life and make it human and meaningful. Other versions of "the political" lack the gore and antiliberal vehemence of Schmitt's, but they share the contention that the political is grounded in human nature, expressed as a deep and regulative agreement that gives shape to politics in all its surface manifestations, and is a somehow necessary beginning of a linear and con-tinuous tradition culminating in the politics we see today.[7]

Immanent theory, following Wittgenstein, takes on claims that "the political" is that underlying aspect of political life that tethers it to timeless and immutable human nature. Illuminating features of Wittgenstein's own claims about theory and language achieve this. For Wittgenstein, politics is a language-game composed of various activities that play upon the communicative, constructive, critical, and disclosive aspects of language. Beneath and on the surface of these activities are rules and conventions that serve as "signposts" for participants. The only bedrock undergirding political play is trust (which I explore more fully in the final chapter). These "signposts" do not determine activity. Rather they function to give the game parameters – the game of chess is different from the game of checkers even though they are played on the same board – and show the relation of the game being played to both games played in the past and games that are similar. In this, we can think of the relation of rules and conventions to the activities on the surface on the language-game as illustrated by the relation footnotes have to the text above them on the page. Asking if the text created the footnotes or if footnotes create the text is not terribly illuminating. What is important is the interplay between innovation and tradition made visible by the contrast of text and note.

"The political" is an overly deterministic reading of the conventions of political life. If the subject of the political theorist is political life, then "the political" as a hypostatization of politics is the product of metapoliti-cal theory. This activity of responding reflectively to what are themselves products of reflection is the source of Wittgenstein's antitheoretical ire. As I noted earlier, Wittgenstein erred in either categorizing metatheory as theory, or in conflating the two levels of philosophical reflection. Let me show this by examining Wittgenstein's critical response to claims about the foundations of mathematics. Note how similar these foundational claims from the philosophy of mathematics are to the relation of "the political" to politics.

For Wittgenstein, the idea of a philosophically adduced foundation of mathematics is, at base, a brand of philosophizing that accomplishes nothing for either philosophy or mathematics. The person engaged in mathematical calculation, who understands and can apply the rules of this particular manipulation of symbols, gains nothing from an exploration and justification of the rules being applied (provided such a proof is possible). "*You cannot gain a fundamental understanding of mathematics by waiting for a theory,*" asserted a young Wittgenstein (Waismann 1979: 129). This injunction pertains to any language-games the philosopher or theorist walks into. "[T]here can be no question of a *justification* for a game: if one can play it, one understands it" (Monk 1990: 307). Wittgenstein's contention here against justification is reminiscent of the answer Mark Twain gave when he was asked if he believed in infant baptism. "Believe in it? – I've seen it done!" (van Inwagen 1992: 138).

We see this argument about the irreducibility of activity again in Wittgenstein's treatment of the relation of religious belief to theological justification and anthropological explanation. "Frazier's account of the magical and religious views of mankind [sic] is unsatisfactory: it makes these views look like errors," he wrote. "Was Augustine in error, then, when he called upon God on every page of the *Confessions*? But – one might say – if he was not in error, surely the Buddhist holy man was – or anyone else – whose religion gives expression to completely new views. But *none* of them was in error, except when he set forth a theory" (Wittgenstein 1993: 119). Some descriptions of practices and experiences are better than others in terms of clarity and attention to detail, you can say, but neither the experience nor the description of the experience can be considered mistaken. Error arises when you seek deeper justification for the practice or experience, or for criticism (disenchantment) of the practice or experience (Wittgenstein 1958b: secs. 200, 291–2, 373).

What one gains from these examples of the philosophical justification or explanation of mathematical and religious practices is that metamathematics and metatheory are unnecessary, ornamental, and obfuscating because they erase the idiosyncratic characteristics of the activity being studied. The error Wittgenstein speaks of is an error in direction: The metadiscourse he calls "theory," serves to bolster the authority of the perceiver rather than add anything to the description of the perceived. That is, metatheory is performed in order to aggrandize some putative critical role of philosophy and theory in relation to other activities, rather than disclose features of distinctiveness within the activity and its relations of similarity with other activities. Magic described from a meta-anthropological perspective as pre-science, writes Dienstag (1998) perceptively, not only "washes out everything that is distinctive about it," but it also "washes out everything that is unscientific about *ourselves* as well" (593).

Once again, the role of metatheory within the activity of political theory is, in the form of the epic stance, to present an image of theorist who is above and exterior to politics, but who can act authoritatively and influentially in politics. This authority is achieved, in actuality, not in political life, but in a tamed image of politics derived from the writing of other political theorists that is then called "the political." These projects are provocative, creative, learned, and interesting, to be sure, but they are not what they claim to be. They are not theoretical engagements with political life and institutions; indeed, their goal is to distance theory from politics. For the purposes of this chapter, grasping this distinction between metatheory and theory creates room to begin to describe the work of Wittgenstein not as merely "significant for" or "influential on" political theory, but as an example of theorizing itself. On this point, my reading of Wittgenstein converges with that of Feyerabend.

"Today I would say that Wittgenstein severely reduced the independence of theoretical speculation," wrote Feyerabend (1995) in this vein (93–4). There is a language-game, a zone of language, distinguishing political theory from other activities. But, as Feyerabend suggests, by Wittgenstein's account, the time a theorist spends in this language-game should be limited.[8] Travel into other games – politics for example – is travel into areas where theorizing can occur. The rigidity of conceptions of "the political" or "Theory" distorts the ease of travel between political theory and politics. "The confusions which occupy us," Wittgenstein (1958b) writes, "arise when language is like an engine idling, not when it is doing work" (sec. 132).

For Feyerabend, Wittgenstein's attack on metatheory is compelled by an ethical argument that the complexity of the world ought not be sacrificed by the conceptual simplification that epic distance invites. Any attempt to circumscribe reality with metatheoretical rigidity involves spillage; the boundaries of concepts like "the political" cannot hold adequately the rich diversity of phenomena and processes it seeks to categorize and explain. Moreover, the activity of generalization itself must be performed at such a distance that the modulating capability of ordinary vision described by Wittgenstein (1958b: 213–14) in terms of "seeing aspects" or "continuous seeing" is at best devalued and at worst rendered useless. Generalization from a fixed stance leads to a condition described by Wittgenstein (1958b) as "aspect-blindness."[9] See Chapters 5 and 6 for a consideration of Wittgenstein's remarks on perception.

From this ethical and perceptual argument emerges a logical contention that attacks the purported external stance of the epic theorist. Externality here, it bears repeating, is not a matter of observing the distinctiveness of political theory; rather it is a claim that the proper place of the theorist is untimely and apart from the range of activities composing human life and language. This externality, I have shown, is manifested in the discourse of contemporary political theory through claims to privileged vision, untimeliness, regulative ideals, and a most un-ordinary lexicon of apparently timeless "perennial questions" or "essentially contested concepts" that lend epic theory an air of universality.[10] No theory of games is possible, wrote Wittgenstein in this regard, because such a theory would itself be a game. The allure of transcendence, the very idea of an ideal language, is thwarted, in Wittgenstein's view, by the inescapability of ordinary language. Even the most refined mathematical or symbolic language is but an extrapolation of the language we use daily.

Wittgenstein's description of the world of the peripatetic philosopher/ theorist is composed of a range of internal stances suffused with the language of religion. In abandoning the pretense of a God's-eye perspective, theorists enter into a passionate, antinomian life of faith – faith that language coheres somehow, while acknowledging that this larger unity is beyond the human perceptual field. By accepting the limits to vision, theorists first "destroy . . . houses of cards," then "battle against the bewitchment of our intelligence by means of language," address "disquietudes," demystify "superstition . . . produced by grammatical illusions," and finally come "to use language full-blown." The Wittgensteinian encounter with one's perceptual and linguistic limits is tantamount to releasing one's impulse and capacity to move and create (Eldridge 1997).

The theorist as walker is emancipated from wisdom's coldness. Wisdom in Wittgenstein's view is the lexical equivalent of epic theory: "Wisdom merely *conceals* life from you. (Wisdom is like cold grey ash, covering up the glowing embers.)" (1980b: 56). But the task of the theorist engaged in the return to ordinary language is not to blend quietly into sublime surroundings. Breaking from the entrapments of the epic self-image and tradition serves to enhance the power of theoretical perception through intimacy with the particulars of political life and motion. Theory remains a distinctive activity in ordinary language because of its conscious effort to see clearly and describe carefully. "[W]e shall constantly be giving prominence to distinctions which our ordinary forms of language make us overlook." Nevertheless, Wittgenstein (1958b) warned, it is not "our task to reform language" (sec. 132). This urge to reform is perhaps heightened by the clear view immanent theory has to the conventions of political activity.

Ordinary language also entails a return to what it means to be human rather than God. Yet, it does not provide a formula for an ordinary, unreflective life. Philosophers and theorists have long described the turn back to the cave, or entry into the city as painful and dangerous. Wittgenstein concurs. "The *edifice of your pride* has to be dismantled. And that is terribly hard work" (1980b: 26). "It's only by thinking even more crazily than philosophers do that you can solve their problems" (1980b: 75). The *Philosophical Investigations* is an examination of what it is to be human in this age, and it discerns a long list of tools, or what Foucault termed "technologies of the self," that language provides for this discovery or recovery. That we have to be reminded of what it is to be human is necessitated not only by the aspirations of theorists to be God-like, but also the conditions of inhumanity that punctuated Wittgenstein's lifetime.

IV. CONCLUSION: THOUGHTS ON THEORY/ PRACTICE AND OTHER DICHOTOMIES

Immanent theory involves the slaying of epic theory (and this can be thought of as an act of child-killing rather than parricide, since epic theory is an idealized extrapolation of the ordinary desire to transcend immanence). To answer the question of what political theory becomes when returned to the friction of ordinary language requires extensive rethinking of the enterprise, its relation to Political Science, Politics, and other related language-games, and the self-image of practitioners. But Wittgenstein conceived of the demise of metaphysical and epic pretensions in philosophy and theory in terms of peace. "Unrest in philosophy," he contended, "comes from philosophers looking at, seeing, philosophy all wrong, i.e. cut up into (infinite) vertical strips, as it were, rather than (finite) horizontal strips. This reordering of understanding creates the greatest difficulty" (1993: 195). How else are we to account for all the ink spilled over the relation of theory to practice, or such philosophical problems regarding our relation to external reality, or how the particular partakes in qualities of the universal? Are these problems that arise in the way we live? We pay an enormous price in terms of time and "unrest" in viewing a complex world from afar. The source of this expensive struggle lies in the space of incommensurability between how we see ourselves as theorists and the way we go about theorizing.

Following Wittgenstein's diagnosis and prescription for the malaise of philosophy, political theory is miscast as a product of transcendence achieved by training, vocation, and/or the need to see politics from on high. The epic self-image is a source of pain not only because it runs afoul of the way we really go about seeing politics by traveling from one game to another, but also because it becomes a fetter on travel and a source of self-doubt. There is a palpable therapeutic effect in seeing that theorizing is cast more accurately as a primitive activity involving seeing and walking. Freeing theorizing from conceptual entrapment encourages that range of activities that will result in the new self-image of the immanent theorist.

Primitivity or primordiality in Wittgenstein's (1958b) writings refers to the horizontal or first order character of seeing and walking (sec. 121). There is the perspective of primitive people that Wittgenstein (1958b) enters empathetically as a playful point of contrast with more modern forms of life that conceive themselves as "advanced" (sec. 194). But there also is the somewhat deeper sense, explored in his late writings, of the primitive as the bedrock of conventions that underlie the panoply of language-games. On this level, labeled by Wittgenstein (1958b) as "depth grammar," what theorists see is an underlying commonality that dissolves all dichotomies regarded heretofore as ontological in nature (sec. 664). This common base informs all language-games, renders their boundaries permeable, and invites travel on the part of those whose activity is primarily visual. This is the trust that Aristotle singled out as the source of political associations, but Wittgenstein perceives more widely as what makes language even imaginable. To be sure, trust is not the essence of language in Wittgenstein's view; rather it is itself an effect of the teaching and learning of language in the closeness of tribes, families, and communities. What we can say about trust is that it does not ontologize language by giving it a definitive shape or something-ness; but trust can be seen in the continuity of language-games over time, as from generation to generation.

The freedom to travel into politics is not danger free. Political theorists nourished on examples of politics as a form of order that defines freedom in terms of stability and safety find themselves ill-equipped for the throes of change and the forces of coercion at work in political language-games. Without transcendence as a means for rising above the vicissitudes and dangers of political life, escape could be conceived in terms of the theorist's ability to detach herself or himself from politics by traveling back into the language-game of political theory. Walzer criticizes this element of what I have been calling immanent political theory.

For Walzer (1983), Wittgenstein presents a model of philosophical detachment in stark contrast to the long list of "connected critics" and "organic intellectuals" he admires and studies. For this reason, he regards Wittgenstein's ordinary language philosophy as a misstep for political theory today (75–99). This is an important criticism. Walzer opens his short treatment of Wittgenstein with a well-known statement included in a posthumous collection of Wittgenstein's (1967) remarks, *Zettel*: "The philosopher is not a citizen of any community of ideas," he wrote. "That is what makes him a philosopher" (sec. 455). In my account, this remark belongs to Wittgenstein's various warnings against becoming entrapped in dogmatic pictures of reality. But for Walzer, as for other critics of Wittgenstein like Marcuse and Gellner, this remark is emblematic of a political quietism or conservatism that pervades his writings. For Walzer, Wittgenstein's celebration of the philosopher as political outsider implies a contentment that amounts to abandonment of the moral mission of the intellectual. When he writes, "philosophy leaves everything as it is" (1958b: sec. 124), this is because, for Walzer (1983; 1987), Wittgenstein has distilled any notion of social responsibility out of the philosophical enterprise. Let me respond to this serious charge by illuminating the consequences of the immanent theorist's eye-level view of the conventions of politics.

"When you are philosophizing," taught Wittgenstein (in another statement where "philosophizing" can be replaced with "theorizing"), "you have to descend into primeval chaos and feel at home there" (1980b: 65). If the theory/practice dichotomy reveals anything, it is that theorists are not at home in chaos. Indeed, as noted, the epic tradition is wholly unequipped to grapple with the level of change Wittgenstein associates with even the normal state of conventions. For Walzer, the connected critic descends to or evokes this same depth in order to protest. For Wittgenstein, descending to and illuminating conventions is a matter of assembling reminders of what is so often forgotten in political life: its malleability. From this perspective, it is difficult to see Wittgenstein as somehow detached from the grounds of human existence. For Walzer, the mark of the connected critic and organic intellectual is her or his alignment with a particular group or party wherein she or he lends intellectual credence to the group's politics. It is a move replete with perilous temptations, Walzer (1988) notes, and any engaged intellectual who manages to stand by her or his principles will always be disappointed by the form the group or movement's politics takes on. For Wittgenstein, this alignment of the theorist or intellectual with a movement bears the traces of the theory/practice dichotomy. This calls for a twofold response. First, political action and institutions are in no need of theoretical justification. It is a matter of false intellectual chauvinism to think otherwise.[11] Second, theorizing as an activity does not require a group or political movement to justify its worth. Such a contention implies a denigration of theorizing. Moreover, such justification, when sought, comes with a heavy price of entrapment in a particular, dogmatic, and goal-oriented view of reality.

What is left once the theory/practice dichotomy is escaped is a view Wittgenstein would regard as a product of justice. It is horizontal and modifiable by walking in one direction and then another, up closer and then back further. In the language-game of theorizing, justice is a matter of casting out entrapments and traversing grounds around obstacles. It is to find the good and the beautiful in the ordinary; it is to countenance injustice on the plane in which it occurs and to remind others of its conventionality. Finally, it is to resist the impulse to turn inward or upward when faced with whatever ugliness and horrors exist in political life today. The immanent theorist's response must be to look and describe.

NOTES

1. "Not only is a rule not (metaphysically or conventionally) fixed, according to Wittgenstein, it is not even intrinsically better than (what within our form of representation counts as) deviant practice. Use cannot justify a rule, let alone some essence of language" (Zerilli 2003: 136).
2. For other descriptions of epic theorists and theorizing, see Wolin (1970); Oakeshott (1975); Gunnell (1979); Arendt (1990).
3. As an example, consider the argument for autonomy articulated by Kateb (1977). This call for a Political Theory liberated from the hostile confines of behavioral

Political Science was anchored in earlier academic calls for the creation of new departments of political theory, beginning at UC Berkeley. See Hauptmann (2005).

4. "Thus to inquire 'What is political theory?' Is to ask about its constitutive outside as well as its techniques of dissimulating this constitution" (Brown 2004: 103). What I offer here is a small yet representative list of such inquiries: Ashcraft (1983); Ricci (1984); Gunnell (1986; 1993); Ball (1995); Vincent (2004).

5. As a counter-example to be fleshed out later, Wittgenstein leaves us seeing theory and politics as distinct language-games shaped by permeable boundaries. Political action on the part of a theorist is a matter of walking from one area to another.

6. This literature is quite large, and so, once again, I am supplying only a representative cross-section: Gould and Thursby (1969); Graham and Carey (1972); Chandler (1977); Freeman and Robertson (1980); Nelson (1983); Farr and Seidelman (1993); Farr, Dryzek, and Leonard (1995); Vincent (1997); Gunnell (1998); Frank and Tambornino (2000).

7. "I shall take the *political*," says Wolin (1996), "to be an expression of the idea that a free society composed of diversities can nonetheless enjoy moments of commonality when, through public deliberations, collective power is used to promote or protect the well being of the collectivity. *Politics* refers to the legitimized public contestation, primarily by organized and unequal social powers, over access to the resources available to the public authorities of the collectivity. Politics is continuous, ceaseless, and endless. In contrast, the political is episodic, rare" (3).

8. Such travel is nutritional, Wittgenstein says (1958b: secs. 255, 593; 1967: sec. 382).

9. Aspect-blindness, for Wittgenstein, is a condition he posited to show the relation between perception and understanding. The blindness refers to the inability to "get a joke," for example. To see the humor in a joke is a matter of being in or moving to the correct perspective. "What is it like for people not to have the same sense of humor? They do not react properly to each other. It's as though there were a custom amongst certain people for one person to throw another a ball which he is supposed to catch and throw back; but some people, instead of throwing it back, put it in their pocket" (1980b: 83).

10. "Proponents of the essential contestability thesis," notes Ball (1997), "are correct in claiming that conceptual contestation is so persistent and recurrent a feature of political discourse that it amounts almost to a defining feature of that domain. But to claim that a particular concept is essentially contested is to take a timeless and a historical view of the character and function of political concepts. Not all concepts have been, or could be, contested at all times. Conceptual contestation remains a permanent possibility, even though it is, in practice, actualized only intermittently. The now-ubiquitous disputes about the meaning of 'democracy', for instance, are of relatively recent vintage, whilst the once-heated arguments about 'republic' have cooled considerably since the late eighteenth century – indeed they now rage only amongst historians of political thought, and not amongst political actors or agents" (35–6). For an investigation of forms of essentialism and timelessness in feminist political theory carried out by a theorist influenced by Wittgenstein, see Heyes (2000).

11. This is an observation that can be found in Castoriadis and Arendt as well, and articulated in a way that illuminates the creative side of Wittgenstein on theorizing. "Both Castoriadis and Arendt question the idea that politics, as a register of human doing,

requires participants to supply, or be able to supply, a complete theory of their activity," notes Zerilli (2005). "Neither thinker associates this lack of knowledge with the failure to think critically, with nonreflexive activities, or with the mindless compulsion of habit. Like Wittgenstein, they affirm that our rule-governed practices are underdetermined, that is, that they are neither justified all the way down nor in need of such justification to count as part of a creative and critical relation to the world" (38).

CHAPTER 2

Wittgenstein's Philosophy after the Disaster

The sickness of a time is cured by an alteration in the mode of life of human beings, and it was possible for the sickness of philosophical problems to get cured only through a changed mode of thought and life, not through a medicine invented by an individual.

(Wittgenstein 1967: 132)

I. INTRODUCTION

Where is the disaster in Wittgenstein's writing? Where are the protracted reflections on what humans are capable of doing to one another found in contemporaries and near-contemporaries like Adorno, Sartre, Merleau-Ponty, Bataille, Benjamin, Russell, Arendt, and even Heidegger? Where are the meditations on scenes of horror from the wars, pogroms, purges, the Holocaust, Hiroshima and Nagasaki? Did Wittgenstein think these scenes too sacred to be appropriated and profaned by philosophy? Is the level of inhumanity unique to the twentieth century that edge separating speech from silence he posited in his *Tractatus*?

In my reading of Wittgenstein, he is categorized best with writers like Karl Kraus, George Orwell, Samuel Beckett, Primo Levi, and George Steiner who observed and argued that language was the first victim and best measure of the damage done by exposure to, and use in, totalitarianism, total war, and abject horror. Wittgenstein opposed those philosophers who believed language has an essence (religious, ontological, cognitive, and so on) impervious to damage in human time. But he also went further than those like Orwell and Arendt, who measured the harm done to language in term of decreased and profaned vocabulary, mangled grammar, hateful graffiti, and flights of political escapism in the form of euphemism and overly academic prose. Because of the integral relation he posited between language and life, Wittgenstein could see the erosion of trust or the constriction of mobility as a result of authoritarianism and inhumanity. Threats to trust and mobility as features of language and theorizing in Wittgenstein's philosophy and life will be the focus of this chapter. The damaged landscape investigated and used by Wittgenstein involved self-diagnosis of his own thinking; there is no transcending "the sickness of a time," and, so, critical self-reflection and self-improvement had to be part of the project.

I want to examine the view of language as composed of a plurality of language-games that emerged in Wittgenstein's thought after 1930, and search for evidence of a philosophical response to the damage to thought, the fragmentation of everyday life, and the challenges to the belief in progress at the heart of Enlightenment philosophy that occurred as a result of the shattering, dehumanizing political and military events of Europe through the twentieth century. There is a relationship between the philosophy and the life that Wittgenstein asserted as an antidote to dehumanizing philosophical abstraction. But this relationship is not marked by the construction of identity primarily, but rather in terms of the necessity of mobility for seeing. That is, Wittgenstein's philosophical conception of language and his assessment of the damage done to and reflected in language are entwined, but distinguishable (permitting movement). I seek to illuminate this feature of his thought here. I begin with the assumption that Wittgenstein was a product of his time, and that the darkness of the time found its way into his philosophy and was made manifest in his concern with perception. After the *Anschluss*, Wittgenstein could not return to Vienna to be with his family. "Presented with the choice of being a German Jew or a British university lecturer," notes Monk (1990), Wittgenstein "was forced, with some reluctance, to choose the latter" (395). Philosophy would not be a source of solace for him, or an escape. It was the creative activity in which he engaged, out of a sense of duty to his own abilities as Monk contended, to find his way through the world. Philosophy was his way of seeing; and his view of language permitted the free movement denied by anti-Semitism and nationalism in the Europe of his day. Yet he thought often of leaving philosophy to train in medicine or some other activity he regarded as more useful.

Despite the fragmentary character of his remarks, Wittgenstein manages to create a world; or at least the feeling of being in a world is produced for the reader. Whenever I read his remarks, I am impressed by the sense that I am traversing a threshold and stepping into an atmosphere whose pace and weight are different than my own. The *Philosophical Investigations* are written as an invitation to walk with the philosopher on the page and see as she or he sees. Wittgenstein's command, "Back to rough ground!" is rendered possible by the book's atmosphere. The view from this lexically produced vantage is largely across the pockmarked and obstacle-strewn surface of the world occluded by the physiological limits of human eyesight; but there are imaginatively synoptic moments in the book that give the world some provisional shape.

Accordingly, there are two distinct sets of tropes deployed by Wittgenstein to describe our relation to language. First, language is like a toolbox and the language-games or forms of expression are tools that aid us in shaping our world and achieving communicative successes. Second, we are not exactly tools of language; rather, language is a landscape or city that permeates and pervades what we think of as our inner and outer aspects, and permits us to compose our personhood by travel through and membership in various constellations of language-games. The language-game we play shapes the contours of what we see, but perception can be altered through movement to other language-games or by bringing past experiences in other language-games to bear on the one we are in now. In permeating our being (and here I am wrestling with the vocabulary to distinguish Wittgenstein's horizontal or open view of language from Heidegger's enclosing conception of language as "the house of Being"), language effaces Cartesian duality with its occult thinking substance posited as the seat of personal identity, and the divided universe of Kant that promises blissful transcendence as the answer to hostile immanence. In Wittgenstein there is only immanence (even for philosophers and theorists, as noted in the last chapter); overcoming limitations in vision are achieved through horizontal travel and the help of others. The form language takes is humanly unstable; we cannot know the whole of language or even that it coheres into a whole. Our concept of language as something unified is therefore an expression of faith and our limited experience amid a finite number of language-games.

We tread across language, as illuminated by the metaphor of the city of language (1958b: sec. 18); and language permeates our being, showing the inner and outer to be distinct, but entwined. When language is conceived in these fluid terms, flowing like respiration into and out of the body, the traditional philosophical problems of access to the mind or our relation to external reality simply dissolve. If Descartes's duality can be conceived

46

as a strategy for privileging and protecting the *cogitans* from the uncertainty of the senses and the harshness of the *extensa*, then Wittgenstein's conception of the human being is utterly vulnerable to a more thorough trauma than dualism permits. But this more vulnerable conception of human being-in-the-world speaks accurately of the forms of inhumanity unique to the twentieth century (and here, think of the images of "the walking dead" "the drowned," the *Muselmänner* depicted in Primo Levi's memoirs), as well as the central place of uncertainty in the language-games constitutive of the sciences (Prigogine and Stengers 1984).

The human form our language takes is susceptible to damage. We express pain, for example, through language, and yet it is more than a conduit for emotion. At base, language is nothing more than grunts and scratchings codified over time (Rorty 1982; 1991). But, still, codification is related intimately to the growing trust cultivated through language use. Moreover, the way we talk about language reveals subtle shifts in the way we live. Accounts of language cast in sacred/profane binaries as a gift from God or the plurality of languages as a divine punishment, for example, have all but been supplanted by the monistic, de-divinized, scientific vocabularies of Chomskyan linguistics, evolutionary biology, neurology, and cognitive psychology.

The elimination of ontological dualisms somehow foregrounds the two dimensions of the way we use language: world-disclosure and world-making, critical and utopian, what is and what could and should be (Kompridis 1994). What I want to say here is that language feels pain and seeks to mend itself, but Wittgenstein is not Heidegger and, for him, language has no inner, mystical unity. Language, for Wittgenstein, does not speak; and we need to resist the continuing temptation to conceive the language we use today as a linear descendant of the language of the pre-Babelian world. God cannot be heard to speak in language if only we attend to it closely enough; but if God were to speak to us, he or she would have to use human language for us to understand what is being said. The oldest things in what we call our language, Wittgenstein acknowledges, are not divine or natural in origin; they are the conventions or rules that undergird and guide practices within language-games. They do not speak either. They are living "sign-posts" we can use and produce in our journey through language.

II. GROWING INTO LANGUAGE

The orientation of the philosopher/theorist to the world entailed, for Wittgenstein, acceptance of both disorder and the oscillations and fragility of an apparent order. There is, for Wittgenstein, a performative dimension to description. He therefore challenged the linearity of word-to-things relations posited by Positivists and the equation of describing with passive representationalism or mirroring found in Empiricism. A "perspicuous representation" is not a static achievement of the theorist (or anyone else) that can be likened to a snapshot of reality. Theorizing is not a passive enterprise separated from the stage upon which reality acts by a thick pane of safety glass. The quality of perspicuousness takes the form of struggle to attain a clear view of how we actually use language; the greater the struggle, measurable in terms of pain that gives way to increased mobility, the better the theory (or clearer the view).

In following Wittgenstein, philosophers and theorists need to resist the temptation to impose order on disorder, and this resistance is against essentialism primarily or other strategies of simplification like reductionism. In contrast to Wittgenstein, essentialism is a fractal-like argument that regards disorder as ephemeral and superficial; order, however, can be discovered if we dig deep enough. If this order gives way to deeper disorder, then we continue on the path downward and, eventually, we are assured, the unifying essence or truth of the thing will be uncovered (*altheia*). The history of philosophy reveals that this path can move in either direction on the vertical plane. The transcendental impulse informing Cartesian epistemology, phenomenology, Freudian psychoanalysis, Heideggerian onto-theology, and the logical investigation of the *Tractatus*, is toward the subterranean truth or order. If we train our eyes upward, transcendence beyond the realm of appearances to embrace the larger, extraterrestrial universal sphere of reality posited by Plato or Kant is possible. The emphasis on politics as order in political theory can be traced back to these dual philosophical sources. Describing disorder, the fragmentation of what is before us, Wittgenstein (1958b) knew, is a corrective against the essentialism and metaphysical impulses that dehumanize philosophy and disembody the philosopher (secs. 97, 98, 116, 345). It is, I argue, a more accurate path for describing politics today, and this is the most compelling reason I can give for why theorists need to consider Wittgenstein.

There is consonance between the perspectivism of Wittgenstein and Nietzsche's (1974) path to philosophical vision in *Worldly Wisdom*: "Don't stay in the field! / Nor climb out of sight. / The best view of the world / is from a medium height" (43). This medium perspective is the dramatic consequence of the demise of the pretense of a God's-eye point of view in Wittgenstein's world and an acceptance of uncertainty as central to what it means to be human.[1] It is reasserted in the image of the theorist as a wanderer or peregrine within and between the constitutive forms of human life, as I argued earlier, and a corrective to the fixed stance associated with political theorist in the epic tradition (1967: sec. 455). In addition to placing inhumane pressures on the philosopher to discover or uncover truth, the source of certitude, the essentialist conception of language and world presents an account of learning that is likened to a uniform path we all travel, and where, as in the picture of education Plato presents in his line and cave parables, some go farther than others. Wittgenstein's description of learning begins with a far richer and variegated account of the world. How we go about the lifelong process of education is by playing in and then moving from one language-game to another. We can imagine prescribed orders of travel in compulsory education, the move from learning numbers to simple functions to equations in mathematics, for example. But most of our learning occurs in contexts that are playful and fluid, and so the way to describe us thickly is by describing the games we play and have traveled.[2] Generally, then, we can speak of our learning in terms of the number of perceptual vantages we have encountered or achieved in a lifetime. This is overly simplistic, however. How we see does not only conform to what the vantage offers physically – as looking through a keyhole gives a keyhole shape to what we see – but is a product of experiences we have garnered through travel up to that point, as well.

The broader implications of Wittgenstein's work at least suggested an answer to the question: For whom did he write? In a real sense, he wrote for himself, a philosopher in need of therapy. "The philosopher," wrote Wittgenstein (1978), "is the man who must cure himself of many sicknesses of the understanding before he can arrive at the notion of sound human understanding. In the midst of life we are in death, so in sanity we are surrounded by madness" (302). His other audience was composed of similarly afflicted philosophers and theorists who, for any number of reasons, turned away from the ordinary business of life, and sought metaphysical relief from uncertainty and from a life lived interdependently with other humans in vacillating conditions of trust.

Solipsism was but an extreme manifestation of this dissatisfaction with the ordinary and ephemeral, yet Wittgenstein's therapeutic plan was fairly uniform for a range of philosophical maladies from solipsism to metaphysical escapism. Therapy was conceived as a matter of returning philosophers to the pre-linguistic primordial and then guiding them through mazes of contingent, opaque but permeable and overlapping language-games to give a sense of language's capaciousness and insurpassability. It is akin to the speech therapies a patient rendered aphasic as a result of a stroke might undergo. For the stroke patient, new neural pathways around the damaged area of the brain are encouraged and formed. For the philosophical patient, a new appreciation for and trust in ordinary language's vast resources for meaning and creativity or lexical travel are encouraged and (hopefully) formed. In the end, the therapy is successful if the philosopher can renounce his or her solitary confinement in a fictive, hidden world above or below ordinary language, and go about living a human life amid disorder, friends, and even enemies. Put differently: The therapy is successful if the philosopher can stop doing metaphysics or stop justifying philosophy's existence, which is the function of epistemology, and remember what it is to be human (Wittgenstein 1958b: sec. 133).

What is being reformed in therapy, therefore, is not language *per se*, but the philosopher's particular uses of an extrapolated portion of language. Examples of extrapolation include the celebrations of "ideal language" like mathematics, symbolic logic, or Esperanto. These forms of expression are described as having escaped the prejudices, emotions, and infelicities of ordinary language. Wittgenstein shows there is no escape from ordinary language, however. The strategy of extrapolation to fashion an ideal language is itself an expression of self-imposed entrapment in a particular language-game (as in the example of the philosopher facing away from the door and who cannot find his way out). This entrapment results in "bewitchment" – a falsely static view of the world likened to language on "holiday," exemplified by the depiction of language in Wittgenstein's early work.

The *Philosophical Investigations* is a sustained argument (with ameliorating effects) against the "craving for generality," condemned first in the *Blue and Brown Books*, and against what Cavell has described as skepticism's "anxiety about our human capacities as knowers" by placing philosophers back on a plane that permits and cultivates interaction with others (Wittgenstein 1958a: 18; Cavell 1988: 4).[3] This "craving" should now be understood as the consequence of trying to see the world from the vantage afforded by a single language-game of one's own making, and it gives rise to two related problems. First, private languages, like ideal languages, are not what they purport to be. That is, they are not external to ordinary language, but rather the intuitions that give rise to the idea of a private language (Wittgenstein 1958b: secs. 243, 256) are, as Kripke (1982) noted, governed by rules the larger community observes (87–9). Moreover, those intuitions of sensations and thoughts that the person experiencing them believes knowable only to her or him are what Wittgenstein (1993) called "techniques of use," which are indeed taught, and what Cavell regarded as inner experiences in need of and susceptible to outer criteria (448).[4] Second, generality is itself a manifestation of the mistaken belief, described earlier in terms of epic theory, that we can see the world in its coherent entirety by imagining what it would look like rather than doing the legwork necessary to travel through its constitutive localities. Such travel would reveal the impossibility of such a totalized view of language.

The text opens with the traveling theorist/reader as a child surrounded by adults who pass on this very human endeavor of symbol manipulation or language use. Simultaneously, Wittgenstein (1958b) offers a criticism of "the philosophical concept of meaning" posited by St. Augustine in his personal recollection of how he first acquired language (sec. 2). In criticizing Augustine for being overly general after reducing meaning to a correspondence between words and things, Wittgenstein confessed his own guilt by association.[5] He had made a similar generalization resulting in a reductive account of language in his *Tractatus*, although the idea of language as a "picture of reality" explored there was supplemented by the unexplored, decodable complexity of what Wittgenstein (1922) called "colloquial language" (4.002).[6]

The language learner is never alone as she or he moves from significant others in the familial context of Augustine's recollection, through a group of workers, to the general public occupying Wittgenstein's city. In this we understand why Wittgenstein chose Augustine's autobiographical take on language learning as opposed to something from a member of the Vienna Circle or British Empiricism. What Augustine offers in addition to his circumscribed view of what can count as language is the insight that learning a language involves entering into a community. There is reciprocity between language and language user. "The children are brought up to perform *these* actions, to use *these* words as they do so, and to react in *this* way to the words of others" (1958b: sec. 6). What Wittgenstein shows using Augustine's example is the close tie between language acquisition and our notion of what language *is*.[7] Acquiring language is an experiential matter of being acquired by language (1958b: sec. 19). But this idea of being acquired by language avoids an ontologization of language like that posited by Heidegger. Travel through these language-games, and exposure to the laundry list of language uses contained in and encouraged by the

variety of games, results in the maturation of the learner whose competence grows even as the endless plurality of, and creativity encouraged
by, language is revealed. This instability of language is reflected in the
identity of the learner that appears endlessly provisional. "New types of
language, new language-games, as we say, come into existence, and others
become obsolete and get forgotten" (1958b: sec. 23).

Wittgenstein's reflections on language lead him to see beyond the assur-
ances of certitude promised by the correspondence of words to objects and
the contention emanating from Aristotle that language is but a tool for
the conveyance of information related deeply to our capacity to live and
act politically.[8] Correspondence and communication provide the security
of knowing that our language is anchored in reality, and that it can be
mastered and reshaped for projects that require greater precision, and, if
need be, transcended. The illusions this reductive view of language as a
possession can sustain for philosophers and theorists include the belief we
control our entries into, and exits from, language; that concepts (political, religious, ethics, and so on) are fixed cognitively and take the same
form today that they did in the past and so theorizing, for one, need not
change or move; that idealizing language through extrapolation of parts is
possible and the basis of mathematics and symbolic logic; that examples
of events and phenomena culled from history will correspond to and illuminate features of contemporary life; and that our identity as philosophers
and theorists can be revealed by appealing to the way thinkers of the
past described what they were doing even if they did not call themselves
philosophers or theorists. Because language is a uniform and stable tool
we employ (in much the same manner as Plato and Aristotle), there is no
reason for us to live or theorize differently. For political theorists exhibit-
ing a kind of intellectual necrophilia, a steady diet of examples of political
phenomena from a set of historical texts revered as the "Great Tradition"
is sufficient. We can act upon history and circumscribed historical examples because of the temporal distance we are afforded by presence and the
spatial distance between our tools and us that permits possession of language. There is apparently nothing unique or transformative about contemporary conditions and trauma – at least for an epic theorist conceiving
of herself or himself as hovering above and impervious to (existentially
and linguistically) political life and language.

We can and do defer the experience of instability that living in language should evince. We do so because we use language to communicate
with the expectation of success and because we are often successful in our

attempts to convey information. The larger, dynamic field of language breaks into our illusions of stability at times when we are misunderstood, when we try to express something difficult and "the words will just not come" (Wittgenstein 1958b: 187), and when we recognize (or are forced to confront) that we have been blinded by coercive power relations that shape the discursive formations we have inherited. I suppose my first memorable experience of this relation between linguistic and existential instability occurred when my father invited a co-worker to dinner. I was probably about five at the time. During the meal, conversation turned to religion. My father's co-worker revealed at that point that he was an atheist. Raised as I was in a Catholic household in a Catholic neighborhood and in a Catholic school, the category of not believing in God did not exist for me. That a person *could* go about not believing in God was simply inconceivable. Belief was therefore not so much a matter of faith as it was an inevitable effect of cultural compulsion and blunted imagination. But now, suddenly, nonbelief was conceivable (though not at the time acceptable). This possibility was experienced as a doubling of the universe and the formation of questions for which there were no words the day before.

For Wittgenstein, that we could sustain the illusion of cultural, intellectual, and moral progress in the face of mounting countervailing evidence – genocide, atomic weapons, world wars – amazed him and revealed something deep and important about how what we see can be manipulated.[9] How do we perpetuate these images that fly in the face of empirical reality? Maintaining belief or disbelief is more than a matter of craving generality and something akin to the comfort selective blindness affords. Belief and disbelief can issue from focus on the particular. We can, for example, from up close, claim that a given event or atrocity is an aberration. We fail, because our focus is so localized, to see this one spasm of ethnic cleansing, for example, as part of a larger pattern. If we do manage to see the pattern, we can also create distance between it and us. That is something that happens over there. Because it happens over there, it serves to illustrate the progress toward morality here.

What we see in theorizing from a Wittgensteinian perspective is a two-part process: First is the awakening that occurs when we see patterns develop between particulars. This is a resistance to the soporific effect of Newtonian or reductive science and perhaps a tacit acceptance of something akin to Goethean science. But, second, we see a middle ground being forged between politology and political theory,[10] between the entrapment in the particular that Wittgenstein evades with travel, and the synoptic vision from an illusory epic stance that Wittgenstein regarded as inhuman and as entrapping as the parochialism it was designed to evade. It is the space between entrapment and transcendence that Wittgenstein traveled himself and in which he placed the now-healthy theorist/philosopher.

Within language-games are activities governed by rules that constitute the activities themselves. Playing chess, evaluating the play of others, even assessing creativity in strategy, is in accord with a set of criteria that give the game parameters and distinguish it from other such games, as Geertz (1973) and Winch (1977) observe. As a chess player, when I am in the game, I feel the rising and pleasurable stress of playing to win. What I do not feel is uncertainty about the rules of piece movement. In this instance, then, I do not experience the existential trigger to philosophizing or theorizing expressed as "I don't know my way about" (1958b: sec. 123). This sort of contrast between knowing your way about and not knowing is in one sense pervasive. It is, for example, a common experience for students graduating college. They have spent sixteen or seventeen of their twenty-two years in the context of compulsory education and they have proven their grasp of the criteria of success in the academic arena. But now they must step out of the game and enter into a larger arena where the rules are less clear, where language-games are more varied, and their response is usually a mixture of fear and exhilaration. At this point, however, they engage in self-motivated critical self-reflection that begins with big questions, variations on the quest for the meaning of life, and an acknowledgment that they are moving into regions beyond the campus where they do not know their way about.

The idea of growing into language is an appealing one even as it opposes the goal of eventual mastery over or possession of language. At best, we achieve varying levels of competence in language-use. We would like to think we get better at it as we grow older. Wittgenstein shows that within language-games we do grow in expertise and experience, perhaps. There are all kinds of yardsticks we can turn to for intellectual progress. But in a second sense, growing into language is a matter of growing into life and this entails acceptance of our mortality. That is, we confront the contrast between our limited time in and with language, and the relative immortality of language itself.

The life of the theorist, then, can be understood best as one that tries to live in the maelstrom of unknowns formed along the edges of language-games. In particular, if the political theorist can be said to have a home, the residence is the particularly liquid one along the edge of a political life that is disorderly, dissenting, and sporadic. The trick is to resist forces of security that give the illusion of knowing one's way about.

III. The Irreducibility of Trust

The feeling of fragmentation and the experience of existential free fall cannot be sustained, and it is supplanted by adjustment to a new feeling of coherence. What is the source of this coherence? What holds the pattern of social practices Wittgenstein called "language-games" together? Wittgenstein is most explicit about the role of rules. These rules, themselves relatively crystallized patterns of patterns of successful practice, give guidance to players and shape to the game itself. Checker and chess are both games, played on the same board, but the pieces and the rules distinguish them from one another. Discussions of rules pervade this book, but, for now, I want to focus some attention on an intangible that Wittgenstein (1969) tries to make visible in his remarks on language-games, and that is the role of trust. "I really want to say that a language-game is only possible if one trusts something (I did not say 'can trust something')" (sec. 509). We see in this remark, and particularly in the distinction between "if" and "can" in a trusting relation, the vulnerability of the language-game to experiences that erode the capacity for trust.

Notice also that Wittgenstein does not pay attention to the role coercion might play in perpetuating a language-game. Play within a language-game demands varying degrees of freedom and equality. In Wittgenstein's conception of language-games, there can be no slavery. A person responding to a command like "Bring me a slab!" is responding to an articulated rule. This rule, in turn, is not deterministic or foundational in Wittgenstein's view. It is a "sign-post." The responder can hear and obey, not hear or hear mistakenly, or willfully ignore, the command. In the end, the bounds of the language-game are permeable and conventional. The person can always turn and leave; or retreat into an inner realm of thinking that is in a continuum with but freer than the language-game's public side. At least, this is how it is in Wittgenstein's linguistic landscape. There are no guards on the game's perimeter checking identification cards or armed posses charged with the responsibility of hunting down fugitives and returning them to their owners.

The lack of engagement with the question of coercion's role of holding language-games together has been an area of contention for political theorists and philosophers reading Wittgenstein. Lyotard's (1984; 1988) examinations of the dissensus and competition within and between heterogeneous language-games are examples of attempts to address a perceived lack of political vision in Wittgenstein's philosophy. But Wittgenstein's emphasis on freedom implicit or embedded in our understanding of rules, our capacity to travel, and our trust that the language-games we populate produce and lend life meaning, reveal Lyotard's project – even in his emphasis on conflict – to be an answer to the question of whether language holds together by necessity or by ontology. By contrast, Wittgenstein holds that there is no such *thing* as language. There are only the constitutive features of conventionally recognizable linguistic phenomena that are so integral to human being as to preclude an outside perspective that offers synoptic vision. It is not that Wittgenstein does not confront the elements of coercion, enslavement, and hierarchies of inequality and power in language-games; rather, we should understand that these traumatic relations that efface trust are presumed. The role of Wittgenstein's particular examples of language-games are *"objects of comparison"* that shed light on freedoms rendered ordinarily invisible by "the route traveled by enquiry" patterned by habit or command that exempts these very patterns from the disturbance of doubt (1958b: sec. 130; 1969: sec. 88).

When Wittgenstein talks about the bedrock of language being forms of life, he is making a case for the irreducibility of trust. This insight illuminates the relation posited by Aristotle between language and politics, but places the relation in a contemporary setting where our capacity for trust has been effaced by inhumanity and threats of extinction by nuclear conflagration. Consistent with the dual perspective offered by Wittgenstein and his invisible interlocutor in the *Philosophical Investigations*, trust plays two roles. First, the theorist in the street trusts that the linguistic landscape before her or him actually does form a coherent whole. Skeptical questions in the work raise the possibility that we impose coherence on language that is not there.[11] But we have to live as if it forms a system or world. The *as if* is created by trust manifest in the coherent, narrative quality of our descriptions of what we see even as this act of seeing produces fragmentary and changing percepts and aspects. Second, trust in language-games serves as an antidote to overly deterministic readings of the role of rules in these games. While trust is irreducible, it can be effaced completely. This is the profound insight Wittgenstein shares with Samuel Beckett whose scaled-down, minimalist language indicates a path to some postapocalyptic, postlinguistic muteness. I draw a more comprehensive comparison between Wittgenstein and Beckett in the final chapter.

Countering the images of the traveling philosopher/theorist as a homeless sort whose relation to a language-game is tentative and whose deepest desire is to speak above or beneath the strictures of language-games, are relationships described with extraordinary intimacy. The sites of encounters with others in Wittgenstein's work involve no suspicion, distrust, anxiety, or fear; rather, he conceives the atmosphere of these encounters in terms of mutual comprehensibility, communication, and space engendered by shared language. This language is not only a tool for talking. The linguistic criteria we share for expressing personal pain, feelings of elation, aesthetic or religious experiences of the ineffable, are invisible, comforting tethers to one another. Language permeates both parties, and in what could be thought of as an anti-Cartesian insight, it renders both transparent to one another.

This is another instance and effect of the two Wittgensteins. As noted earlier, in the pages of the *Philosophical Investigations* there are modulations in the perceptual vantage of the walking theorist. There is the street-level walker and there is the vantage of one who reflects upon what the walker sees. Here the doubling of Wittgenstein is a difference not so much in perception but in outlook. There is the pessimistic Wittgenstein (1980b) who sees the taming of civilization at the hands of science in terms reminiscent of Weber's vision of the "iron cage" of bureaucratic formalism as the culmination of modernity's forces of rationalization. And then there is the Wittgenstein who measures the quality of life in terms of friendships, and acceptance of the limits of and surprising vistas afforded by habitation in language.[12] This is the Wittgenstein that opposes his own public reputation typified by Blanchot's (1986) description of him as a philosopher who "gives one the feeling . . . that he is alone and isolated . . ." (139). The counter-image of theorizing in the streets is one where the walker is not merely surrounded by people, but dependent upon them as well. The activities of seeing, thinking, speaking, writing, and reading described by Wittgenstein occur not in the various symbols of isolation – the mountaintop, hermitage, or wilderness beyond the city walls – that populate most works of philosophy, but rather with and through others.

These moments of friendliness and occasions for less transient relationships that occur in the *Philosophical Investigations* do indeed run up against the larger culture of mistrust cultivated in the concentration camps, designed to use and subvert traditional scenes of political life,[13] and the threats Wittgenstein must have felt as a Jew and as a gay man. When I contemplate the fate of his contemporary and one-time student Alan Turing, I think I glimpse the fear and suspicion that must have been an integral part of Wittgenstein's daily life.[14] And, so, the street-level views presented in Wittgenstein's writings in some way express an ideal or optimistic view that extends how life is into how life should be. Contemporary theorists might recognize it as, *pace* Marcuse, the utopian dimension of philosophy that presents itself as perspicuous description.

What Wittgenstein opposes philosophically is the metaphysical exclusiveness and abstract rationalism of the Cartesian subject who has privileged access to its own mind and cannot know the minds of others. This exclusivity rests upon two foundations of privacy: the privacy of sensation and private language. And these foundations of privacy, in turn, rest upon a separation of mind and body common to post-Cartesian philosophy, but not at all common in the context of how we think of ourselves ordinarily. The subtlety of Wittgenstein's argument leads the reader against the idea that there is an ontological barrier between others, and us, but this opposition is not achieved by eliminating privacy; rather, it is achieved *through* a language (not *the* language) conceived as flowing through and uniting us (at least within language-games). In this vein, Davidson (2001) opens his investigation of what we can say, generally, about the nature of language by posing a question: "How many speakers of a language must there be if anyone can be said to speak or understand a language?" (107–22). The argument Davidson presents could be mistaken as another account against the very idea of a private language, but really what he wants to achieve here is comprehension of the practical implications of the idea that we are competent users of a language. "[W]e all talk so freely about language, or languages," writes Davidson (2001), "that we tend to forget that there are no such things in the world; there are only people and their various written and acoustical products" (108). Our commonplace conceptions of language as a thing, like a hammer, which we can pick up, possess, and use, do not withstand scrutiny. We cannot, therefore, answer the questions of "what" and "where" language is.

The logical consequence of this insight is that language does not depend upon speakers for its existence and so "there must be an infinity of 'languages' no one has ever spoken or will speak."[15] But Davidson does not pursue this "theoretical" or logical direction; rather, he makes a "practical" or Wittgensteinian turn toward language as the medium for truth, speaking to others, and understanding the utterances of others.

How is this achieved? Answering this question is a descriptive enterprise, Davidson shows (thus illuminating this feature of perspicuous representations in Wittgenstein), conducted with and through language. "The main point of the concept of a language, then, and its attendant concepts like those of predicate, sentence, and reference, is to enable us to give a coherent description of the behavior of speakers" (Davidson 2001: 109). We cannot ascertain with certainty which of the infinite number of languages the speaker is speaking, but we can "form the expectation," as interpreters, that the speaker is speaking one language. Part of this expectation pertains to the speaker's intentions.[16] Davidson takes us into a physical/ mental dualism that he holds as the antidote to the radical skepticism Kripke (1982) finds in Wittgenstein. Kripke's position eliminates duality by positing that knowing a language is to know and follow the rules of the language (1958b: secs. 198–9). Knowing a rule is not a matter, therefore, in Kripke's view, of occult possession, but of public display. It is a unifying feature among language users.

In response, Davidson takes us back to the scene of learning our first language. Kripke, Davidson asserts, overstates the relation between language learning and rule following found in Wittgenstein's writings. To the contrary, Davidson argues, "rules can be a help in learning a language, but their aid is available only in the acquisition of a second language." We *acquire* a second language based on our first language; but we *learn* our first language. The role of rules distinguishes these two activities and achievements. Moreover, communication between people across different languages does not require that they follow the same rules, only that they intend to communicate. Following Davidson's example, then, if there were only two people in the world, one a speaker of English and the other Sherpa, then they would be able to understand one another because they share a world. Communication and speaking do not require agreement over rules. Moreover, "it is probably the case that no two people actually do speak the same language." This idea of a language only one person speaks is a sustainable, un-Wittgensteinian, account of what might be called a "private language."[17]

But can there be a private *first* language? Davidson pursues the public character of language by evading the questions of rules, customs and conventions as tools for assessing felicity in usage. The tack he takes is to examine interactions between humans as possible because of the eliminability of self/other, inner/outer dualities. He notes, memorably, "that a creature cannot have thoughts unless it is an interpreter of the speech of another" (Davidson 1984: 157). All that we consider inner and private can be externalized through the path of language. This is a most Wittgensteinian conclusion that raises profound questions about the prevalence of mistrust among humans and, by implication, the importance and fragility of trust.

The secondary philosophical literature on this "problem of other minds" in Wittgenstein is dense, animated by internecine disputes on, as an example, the nature of direct and indirect sensation, and interesting. I do not want to recapitulate this literature or to add to it here; rather, I want to approach Wittgenstein's remarks on approaching others from the vantage of a political theorist. What is exposed in Davidson's reading of Wittgenstein's remarks is a public unity that is missed when we start with individual agents and then try to see how communities or political societies are formed. The community is in place at Wittgenstein's starting point. It can be seen in the family intimacy of Augustine's recollection of language acquisition. Wittgenstein does not dispute this feature of Augustine's account. My task is to assess how fragile this community is (how resilient it can be in the face of inhumanity) and its implication for politics.

As irreducible as trust is in our relations with others is uncertainty.

> "I can only *believe* that someone else is in pain, but I *know* it if I am." ——Yes: one can make the decision to say "I believe he is in pain" instead of "He is in pain". But that is all. –What looks like an explanation here, or like a statement about a mental process, is in truth an exchange of one expression for another which, while we are doing philosophy, seems the more appropriate one.
>
> Just try – in a real case – to doubt someone else's fear or pain. (1958b: sec. 303)

My daughter complains of a headache on a school day. I do doubt that she has a headache and believe the pain complaint an invention to avoid school. There is pain here, but it is not the specific throbbing pain of a headache. It is the pain of being compelled to do something one would rather not do: go to school. There is doubt, but it gives way to something deeper. Call it trust that the pain complaint is real but misdirected. This trust that, in Wittgenstein's example, another's expressions of pain are outward criteria for an inner experience of actual pain is a product of growing into membership in a language community. Trust is, no doubt, a consequence of a perception of physiological/ neurological isomorphism. The person who is, I take it, wincing before me (as opposed to responding to a foul odor emanating from a nearby garbage can) is experiencing a pain I can identify with because, first, I am shaped similarly in the general sense of head on top, arms to the side, feet on the bottom, and second, because I assume this person's nervous system is as adept as mine in producing pain signals. When a student caught his fingers in the door on his way out of class one day, I felt and watched in the faces of others true empathy and listened to moans of sympathetic pain emitted automatically from about the room. Physical or medical explanations for pain empathy or communication have proven inadequate, historically, as a basis for maintaining a political sense of equality. That is, for example, acknowledgment that the pain of another must be similar to my own because of our commonly shaped nervous systems did not prevent slavery or atrocity. Despite our capacity for empathy, there is a fundamental breakdown in the communicative dimension of pain and pain expression. What words can I combine to tell my dentist that the pain I have from a broken tooth necessitates an emergency appointment, today, *now!* ? This leaves the one in pain feeling alone, as Scarry (1985: 11–19) observes, "acted upon" by the world as a victim, or punished. Wittgenstein answers this division engendered by our inability to communicate pain with a richer account of language than the attenuated view often presented in medical language-games. This would be no help, we understand, to the person in pain. But in the next section I want to tease out the importance of Wittgenstein's view of pain for theorizing politics in an age where traumatic pain has effaced trust.

IV. Conclusion: Painful and Essential Challenges to Trust

Crary (2000) notes in her overview of the treatment of Wittgenstein's work in political thought that to assess his importance for political theory, we need to step outside the strictures imposed by questions of conservatism or radicalness (118). I agree and see Wittgenstein's work as a theorist's response to the political upheavals and shocks to morality created by the wars, genocides, terrorism, and sheer inhumanity of the world he lived in. At times, I find myself reflecting on his experiences in battle on the northern Italian front in World War I. It seems likely that Wittgenstein engaged in hand-to-hand combat. Not only must he have seen death up close, but he may have killed (to avoid being killed). In responding to this trauma, Wittgenstein tried to steer philosophy onto a new path, and his effect on political theory needs to be seen similarly. This new path can be thought of as similar to the one suggested by Lyotard when he pronounced the end of metanarratives at the edge of modernity and the beginning of postmodernism.

The usual way of presenting ideas in political theory is to develop them in critical response to what is in the literature already. In following this recipe for academic theorizing, then, Wittgenstein would be shown to oppose philosophical arguments for justification, or to expose the epistemological foundations of interpretative theory, or to appear congruent with poststructuralism and deconstructionism. Wittgenstein viewed himself as removed from various philosophical schools and circles. His writings read as if he was seeking a response to the world unmediated by the protective insularity of methodologies and philosophical approaches. He wanted to feel pain and to express it. A measure of his success is the utter improbability that he would be able to publish his work in any mainstream journal of political theory or philosophy today because he does not bother to locate himself in the literature. And so, as an effect of conventionality, we would miss a work of unconventional vision.

The problem of theorizing today is not one of coercion or imprisonment; rather it is self-imposed entrapment that is actually a form of resistance to the antifoundationalism/conventionalism of Wittgenstein by political theorists who place great emphasis on the universality of politics in the form of "the political." No doubt there are relatively invisible forms of coercion that occur in the training of political theorists, the jargon of the enterprise, and even in recognizable approaches or schools of political theory. But theorists in open societies are free to move about and experiment without much fear of persecution. The worst thing that can happen is that you do not get published, fail to gain tenure, and live the rest of your life in poverty and despair.

I want to conclude here with an important feature in Wittgenstein's view of language. This is described as "bewitchment" or "entrapment" by a phrase or representation, and it leads to a fixed perspective that, it follows, produces a static, repeatable image of linguistic reality that can held as accurate and necessary when it is neither.

The concept of "the political" is such a bewitching element in late twentieth- and early twenty-first-century political theory. It entered the discourse from its origins in Schmitt through the readings of Strauss and Arendt. From there, "the political" is a concept that unites the left and right, the post-Marxian and the neo-Straussian. It is a vague concept and that quality of imprecision leads to wide usage. From the beginning, in Schmitt, "the political" was designated as a sphere distinct from other spheres. Thus, while the aesthetic sphere was concerned with the beautiful and ugly, the economic with wealth and poverty, and the ethical sphere with the good and the bad action, the political was the sphere created by the opposition between friend and enemy, us and them. Once the political was established as a sphere, natural and necessary, it became the clear object of theoretical reflection. That is, the subject matter of political theory is "the political," as opposed to surface or supervening phenomena like "politics," "the state," or government; and this object distinguishes political theory from social sciences such as political science. Although there are significant differences in the way "the political" is conceived and employed by followers of Arendt, Strauss, and postmodernists, its place as the true object, actual or potential, of political theory is urged by all (Hauptmann 2004: 36–7).

The concept of "the political" is taken to be the preconventional or natural one behind the many versions of politics that occurs on the surface of human existence. To express this in Platonic terms, the various true and corrupt forms of politics – monarchy, tyranny, aristocracy, oligarchy, democracy – are united in that they partake in the form of "the political." Describing the relations between these forms of politics as a matter of perception, as an ability to see their "family resemblances," as Wittgenstein would contend, does not provide the firm foundational footing of "the political." For if these family resemblances are shattered, if the political forms of life are themselves obliterated by violence and mistrust and then replaced by a form of organization that requires no trust, like bureaucracy, then any turning back to politics may prove impossible except as a historical enterprise. "The political" in the modern age is a metaphysical construct as well as what passes for politics after trust can no longer be sustained.

Notes

1. This is not to say we cannot act with certainty. This is commonplace. "Certainty is a doing not a knowing," observes Zerilli (2003: 139).

2. Literary theorist Michael Bérubé in his book, *Life As We Know It* (1998), offers an evocative example of learning a new way of life in what must be called a compulsory context, in explicitly Wittgensteinian terms. This book is a perspicuous representation presented as a memoir of a family adjusting to the birth of Jamie Bérubé. Jamie has Down Syndrome and his father's loving description of Jamie's birth and first years includes a detailed account of learning and adjusting to the technology and social services necessary. The various challenges that arise are met by learning how to play the underlying language-games: the health-care game, the education game, the larger political game of being an effective advocate for the child and for the disabled in general. "My task," Bérubé writes, "is to represent James to you with all the fidelity that mere language

can afford," and this is an important task because "how we represent each other to each other . . . is both an aesthetic question and a deeply ethical one."

3. Wittgenstein saw skepticism's question as a negative form of and not an alternative to the epistemologist's question, "How do we know?" These questions lead philosophy in metaphysical and metatheoretical directions that Wittgenstein sought to prevent, but they also expose pains and fears that are, perhaps, intrinsic to what it means to be human. In this, the "craving for generality" is an understandable move to avoid pain and an expression of frustration with the limits of the human form of life (Cavell 2005: 192–212).

4. See also Stern (1995: 175–86).

5. Cavell (1976): "In confessing you do not explain or justify, but describe how it is with you. And confession, unlike dogma, is not to be believed but tested, and accepted or rejected . . . There is exhortation . . . not to belief, but to self-scrutiny" (71).

6. As with Marx and Heidegger, the division of Wittgenstein's writings between the young and the old, or the early and the latter, masks deep areas of continuity in the respective bodies of thought.

7. This relation between acquisition of language and language itself is an antidote to the reductive claim that language is (solely) for communication. Communication is a use of language that occurs within a community of language users. For a fuller description of this commerce between communication and language, Cavell turns to Foucault, who sees it in terms of the power a community exercises over its citizens. This community is thought of best as modes of power that "reaches into the very grain of individuals, touches their bodies and inserts itself into their actions and attitudes, their discourses, learning processes and everyday lives." Cavell (1996) extends this notion of power into Wittgenstein's claim about grammar (the repetition of uses) as the essence of grammar (293).

8. Here I am responding most directly to the attenuated description of Wittgenstein's view of language offered by Chambers (2003), while also admiring Chambers' careful and provocative criticism of the "as-if-objectified" (AIO) account of language that emanates from Aristotle and pervades contemporary political theory. The alternative posed by Chambers emanates from an inventive and thoughtful reading of Heidegger's late works on language (21–2).

9. "Humour is not a mood but a way of looking at the world," he (1980b) wrote. "So if it is correct to say that humour was stamped out in Nazi Germany, that does not mean that people were not in good spirits, or anything of that sort, but something much deeper and more important" (78).

10. I draw this distinction between politology and political theory from an interview with Derrida where he struggles to distinguish the political implications of his studies of friendship, Marx, and hospitality from a deconstructionist political theory. It is difficult to tell if he equates politology and political theory at points. But I take the conversation to be advancing a distinction between a view from within a particular example of politics and the attempt in epic theory to see through the particulars with a claim about possessing an elevated vantage (Bennington 2001).

11. I am thinking here of Foucault's (1980) provocation against epic theory. "Which theoretical-political *avant garde* do you want to enthrone in order to isolate it from all the discontinuous forms of knowledge that circulate about it?" (78).

12. Wittgenstein's last words were: "Tell them I had a happy life."

13. The subversion of traditional and therefore safe political images in the death camps can be gleaned from the title of Borowski's (1976) essay, *Auschwitz, Our Home (A Letter)* (98–142).

14. Here I am imagining Wittgenstein through his contemporary, Turing (Hodges 1983).

15. In this, Davidson is reflecting explicitly the view of language presented in Lewis (1975).

16. "The presence of intentions is important, since it gives content to an attribution of error by allowing for the possibility of a discrepancy between intention and accomplishment. Intention, like belief and expectation, does not require attention or reflection, and intentions are not usually arrived at by conscious reasoning. Intentions are not normally attended by any special feelings, nor is our knowledge of our own intentions arrived at (usually) by inference or resort to observation. Yet intention has an indefinitely large scope, for intentions depend on the belief that one can do what one intends, and this requires that one believe that nothing will prevent the intended action. Thus intention would seem to have just the properties needed to make sense of the idea that a speaker has failed to go on as before." This succinct and elegant description of intentions does not give way to a view of the private character of mental life. Davidson (2001) takes pains to note the surface location of intentions. We can assume that we as interpreters have access to the speaker's intentions by asking her why she said something that strikes us as unusual, a departure, or out of character (112).

17. Of course there can be a language only one person understands, Davidson claims. The example he employs is the "secret code" one might employ in a diary. Wittgenstein himself used such a code to disguise personal reflections and events as opposed to the philosophical remarks intended, at least eventually, for public consumption. The problem with the example is that the secret code remains an extrapolation of ordinary language. Its privacy is a matter of idiosyncratic usage. And so, perhaps, we should think of such an instance of privacy as a language-game among language-games, susceptible to permeation or decryption.

CHAPTER 3

Wittgenstein and Citizenship: Reading Socrates in Tehran

Theory must . . . deal with cross-grained, opaque, unassimilated material, which as such admittedly has from the start an anachronistic quality, but is not wholly obsolete since it has outwitted the historical dynamic.

T. W. Adorno (1974)

I. INTRODUCTION

The presupposition of this chapter is that the contemporary political landscape is composed of large, discontinuous areas that are difficult to see by design. In particular, the bureaucratic order and military and surveillance powers of the modern state have necessitated a transformation of dissenting politics from the sphere of public symbolism to subaltern counterpublics that value less visible and untraceable forms of action. The hard work of theorizing today is a matter of recognizing these new forms of political life, and this sort of theoretical vision requires mobility embodied by both the theorist and the citizen. Most often this work takes the form of conceiving democratic theory as flexible enough to go "outside the conventional public sphere, outside traditional 'male spaces,' partly by a radical, pluralizing rethinking of those spaces and what they can be for citizens" (Saward 2006: 407). But I am more concerned here, following a Wittgensteinian, street-level view, to see not how new spaces expand citizenship, but the way citizens create new spaces; and not how democratic theories conceive citizens, but how citizens use democracy and seams of invisibility to engage in political action.[1] Whatever else citizenship might be according to journalists and empirically oriented political scientists, for political theory it is a concept that travels through the darker political neighborhoods and conventions of the city of language.[2] Citizenship is a peripatetic perceptual vantage that permits close views to experiences of the freedoms, restrictions, and coercions of political life today. It defies the constrictions imposed by areas of specialization and corresponding jargon, and illuminates the close, traversable relations between language-games that are themselves composed of traveling concepts like citizenship.[3]

When theorists and political scientists think about citizenship they tend to offer up unitary concepts of the good or bad citizen that turn on one's duty to the state, the rights accorded the citizen by the state, and the legitimate (measurable) behaviors of the citizen where the act of voting or dissenting along proper channels (designated, fenced-in zones for protest) are exemplary.[4] Following Wittgenstein, however, we come to expect a concept like citizenship to denote an immensely complex and dynamic perceptual vantage that, like a character in a novel, illuminates even the darkest corners of the landscape. Citizenship is a concept that encourages and enables travel across the surface of political language-games, unmoored from hope in ontological stability, and potentially peripatetic enough to open new political perceptual vantages and descriptions of (strategies for seeing) political life and events. These qualities, however, serve my theoretical inquiry well. As Wittgenstein noted in regard to philosophy, theory does not add anything to the world; the task is to describe perspicuously what lies before us (1958b: sec. 122). But theorizing does enrich theorists' experience of the world by freeing us of linguistic bewitchments – and any unitary concept of citizenship can be described along these lines of fixity and entrapment – achieved through pointing out distinctive features often missed because they are so familiar. In this chapter, I want to gain an interior view of political life that is not indebted solely to the perspectives of theorists, but also that is from the perspective of one who acts in politics, a citizen. A theorist is composed of at least these two identities; but the making of a citizen (political subjectivity) has to be different than the making of a theorist. If there were no difference, then we would all be self-identifying as political theorists. In the case of the theorist in exile or in flight, she or he is indeed deprived of citizenship, but only officially.

Throughout my reading of *Philosophical Investigations*, I have conceived of the relation between political theory and politics in terms of two language-games that abut and overlap. Once I am in the language-game of politics, however, I see that the matter is more complex. Political life is itself composed of aggregations of language-games (of dissent, consensus, uses of power) bound together by what Wittgenstein called "family resemblances." Citizenship is an attribute or identity composed of and altered by travels through and memberships in the constitutive language-games of political life. These constellations of language-games are unstable, as are the conventions within language-games. That is to say, the associations and experiences informing my identity as citizen do not achieve stasis because I remain in one place as a result of linguistic entrapment, physical imprisonment, or loyalty to a place and order. There have been appeals by theorists to various ontological devices – Being, the political, Nature, multitude, vitalism, and neural networks – to show there is unity beneath the appearance of instability in what we call politics, but Wittgenstein resists such appeals.[5] They are only conventions giving political life some shape, and the indeterminacy and porosity of these conventions permit travel, engender conditions for spontaneity in political action, thwart attempts to inculcate values as regulative ideals, and promote the impossibility of a totalized view to what we call politics today. At best, citizens and theorists alike keep moving and live the provisional character of their descriptions of politics. This inter- and intra-language-game dynamic and the multifaceted notions of citizenship and politics it engenders will be studied by considering the work of two Wittgensteinian thinkers concerned with these issues, Mouffe and Norval, but for now I want to take a slightly autobiographical turn to sense the scope of the enterprise here.

Reflecting on my own life as a citizen, I grasp the complexity of the concept and see that the unitary formulations employed heuristically by empirically oriented Political Scientists are perhaps too simplistic, rigid, and static. Their empirical orientation leads them to fix upon exemplary and measurable behaviors that extrapolate and isolate single aspects of citizenship. By contrast, my sense of myself as citizen modulates (sometimes dramatically) between the responsibilities I feel toward others in my small town, the peace I know and the gratitude I feel that come with living in the Adirondack region, a place of great natural beauty and quiet, and then the larger sense of alienation from or disappointment in citizenship that comes with being a member of a political society governed by a system of representation that excludes my political beliefs in both the forums of the State of New York and Washington, D.C. Finally, there is the still larger and more tenuous connection I feel to the global order. This latter perspective is as close to Archimedean detachment as I can come, but I feel deep pain and desire to do something when I read or see reports of political violence, moral depravity expressed in terms of torture and genocide, and the aftermaths of natural disasters in foreign lands.

The citizenship I express personally most often takes the form of public dissent. I participate in vigils and marches against various policies and injustices, I speak at public meetings in defense of the local environment and against incursions by corporate concerns into our fragile town economy, and I write editorials and longer pieces pitting my political values against those of neighbors toward whom I feel genuine affection and others in positions of power who simply try my patience. My citizenship is probably more broadly active than that of my neighbors, but it remains only a part of my identity and life that I can and do compartmentalize, particularly when I step into a classroom. The size of my citizenship expands in times of crisis such as a build-up to war or when a local environmental issue arises that requires immediate attention, organization, and energy. These sorts of modulations and fluctuations in the way I see myself as citizen and exercise my political beliefs among other citizens are indeed all manifestations of the family resemblances that compose the concept of citizenship as we see it and live it in contemporary political society. These family resemblances lead us, as citizens, to talk about citizenship in the flow of political life in a fairly nontechnical, imprecise way that, by comparison, leaves empirically heuristic conceptions of citizenship that lend themselves to empirical analysis appearing bloodless by comparison.

The "family resemblances" among the self-images and public activities citizenship captures also seems to hide aspects as much as reveal them. Citizenship in modern society appears an antiquated communal quality that is much weaker than the various forces of individuation a person is exposed to through culture, economic and political forms of liberalism, and technology. Much of the communication I engage in to pursue desirable political ends is of an electronic as opposed to a face-to-face variety. I seek to build coalitions, and even revere the power of collective action, but I foster these associations from the quiet solitude of my workroom. This isolated starting point applies to local as well as international issues and organizations. Moreover, while I can conceive of my citizenship as a membership in a community of mutual respect and equality, this is an extension of the largely invisible privileges I enjoy as a result of my ethnicity, class, and gender. From the perspective of a non-citizen or an outsider who has been stripped of the protections and mobility of citizenship, the political privileges exercised by those of my ilk must strike them

69

as a source of coercion and the real story behind the illusory equality articulated in various pronouncements of human rights. Nor am I as free or equal as I unreflectively assume I am much of the time. I have never been on the winning side of any political issue or contest, for example. My candidates *always* lose, the nation is fighting a war I opposed from the beginning, and my town is getting a Walmart. This experience of political loss is a vital link, I sense, to my identity as a political theorist.[6]

The challenge of this chapter is to begin to bring the concept of citizenship back from those simplified renditions employed by empiricists, pollsters, and ontologizing theorists to the friction-filled universe of modern political life, discourse, and the lived-life of the citizen. "If we listen to Wittgenstein," notes Mouffe (2000),

> we should not only acknowledge but valorize the diversity of ways in which the "democratic game" can be played instead of trying to reduce it through the imposition of a uniform understanding of citizenship. This means fostering the institutions that would allow for a plurality of ways in which the democratic rules can be followed. There cannot be one single best, more "rational" way to obey those rules and this is precisely such a recognition that is constitutive of a pluralist democracy . . . Democratic citizenship can take many diverse forms and such diversity, far from being a danger for democracy, is in fact its very condition of existence. (73–4)

Mouffe sets out the problem of conceptualizing citizenship by foregrounding the indeterminacy of rules. Wittgenstein calls them "signposts," and they are literally sites of complex interactions that entail (possibly) seeing, blindness, rebellion, incomprehension, learning, agreement, and disagreement. The element of unpredictability as a person nears a signpost is unsurpassable. This element is what Mouffe sees and Wittgenstein (1958b) indicates as pivotal to any truly democratic conception of citizenship. "The civil status of a contradiction, or its status in civil life: there is the philosophical problem" (sec. 25).

In examining citizenship in a more directly Wittgensteinian manner, I will look at the lived-life of the citizen, that is citizenship from the political vantage of the walker in the city of language exemplified by Socrates. But woven into this description is a consideration of a difficult corner in Wittgenstein's work: the role and place of concepts. This second consideration is from a more reflective or philosophical vantage in comparison with the viewpoints of the walker, yet no transcendence or privilege should be surmised. This is the dual perspective that comes with being both a citizen and a theorist, and it has points of consonance with the still older concern with the relation of the good citizen to the good person.

II. The Concept of Citizenship

Concepts *may* alleviate mischief or they may make it worse; foster or check it. (1980b: 55)

Concepts are words; they are parts of language as opposed to the idea that concepts compose the very fabric of mind/brain, or are a privileged feature of some discernible language of thought that is prior to and the source of ordinary language (Fodor 1998; Laurence and Margolis 1999). Concepts as words therefore have a variety of uses (actual and possible). In noting this, Wittgenstein (1958b) criticizes various schools of Philosophy for reducing concepts to one use: naming (sec. 383). Learning concepts is a complicated and lifelong business, and their production occurs not just in philosophy, *pace* Deleuze and Guattari (1991). "We talk, we utter words, and only *later* get a picture of their life" (1958b: sec. 384; 209). The picture of the life of a concept is transforming, expanding and contracting, because they seem open to more uses and capture more about the world than ordinary words. Wittgenstein (1958b) explains in a footnote: "What we have to mention in order to explain the significance, I mean the importance, of a concept, are often general facts of nature: such facts are hardly ever mentioned because of their great generality" (56).

Concepts are not employed simply for naming, and concepts are distinctive kinds of words not because of their clarity or location in thinking (because they are not always clear and they exist in our shared language), but because their uses shape the way we conceive and organize large pieces of reality. "Concepts lead us to make investigations; are the expression of our interest, and direct our interest" (1958b: sec. 570). "A *concept* forces itself on one" (1958b: 204). This is the effect of citizenship on an investigation of politics, for example.

When we speak of concepts leading us, directing our interest, forcing themselves upon us and shaping the way we see, the tendency then is to conceive of concepts as fixed frames or lenses that are inescapable. But conceptual fixity, for Wittgenstein, is a matter of intellectual indolence or self-entrapment. We may not be able to view reality without the mediation of concepts (or theories), but this mediation is dynamic. It is neither hardwired cognitively, nor arrested in a linear, word to object, relation. Wittgenstein (1958b: 230) shows the concepts we use have a life that we grow into; and we can move among and between conceptual orientations to the world. In his remarks on concepts, Wittgenstein draws close

71

to the insights of Hume, who refuted the idea of autonomous reason by noting the way "Reason" is tethered to customs and traditions, and how reasoning is altered by practices. These insights give way to a dynamic version of philosophizing and theorizing, where these practices and ways of seeing are modified by what is seen or disclosed. The distinctiveness of the philosopher lies in her dedication to conceptual investigation, which Wittgenstein (and Hume) describes in terms of the inner relations between travel and seeing (Zerilli 2005: 39–40).

There is a contrast between the theorist and the artist that can be developed to clarify this relation between travel through language-games, concepts, and ways of seeing. "Compare a concept with a style of painting," writes Wittgenstein (1958b: 230). "For is even our style of painting arbitrary? Can we choose one at pleasure? (The Egyptian, for instance.) Is it a mere question of pleasing and ugly?" What I take Wittgenstein to be saying here is that there is a lot of room to move about in, and to be done with, a concept as a way of seeing. There is arbitrariness built into a style, and a painter can (and should) change styles over the course of a career. But style in painting, like voice in writing, is an orientation to the world and to work that can be explored in a variety of directions. Artists, therefore, can be thought of as resisting fixity within a language-game, perceptual vantage, and/or concept. Theorists by contrast, can resist fixity by traveling between, along the edges of, language-games, perceptual vantage points, and concepts. Through the contrast, we gain a greater appreciation of the range of possible ways of seeing even as we sense some limits in our ability to choose painting styles. Dogmatism or orthodoxy, associated with aspect-blindness, is the death of both art and theorizing, and indeed of what it means to be human and our ability to regard the humanity of others (1958b: sec. 583).

Concepts arise in the hurly-burly of language; they have many uses, their meanings are produced by their various uses, and yet they are devices in language that, for Wittgenstein, give some organization to our experience of life lived in language. Words, concepts, and meaning all compose what we call language. This all sounds vaguely repetitive, but much of Wittgenstein's treatment of language is designed to alter the way we think of thinking, and this is akin to softening and then breaking a bad habit. Of primary concern for this discussion of concepts is Wittgenstein's (1958b: 220) contention about location: Concepts are not mental attributes or occult mental properties. And, yet, concepts can lead us to think there is an inner language of thought, "a half hidden phenomenon which is as it were seen through a veil." This way of seeing inherited from the philosophical tradition rooted in Descartes is a tradition Wittgenstein wishes to break in philosophy. When we start with the claim that "thinking is not an incorporeal process which lends life to speaking," (1958b: sec. 339) and see thinking as a tool, grammar, or use of the language we learned as a child and spend a lifetime growing into, then a whole range of usually invisible lines engendering dualisms – mind/body, private/public, essence/appearance – are rendered visible and effaced by the friction created by continuous travel across boundaries once conceived as impassable. More significantly, perhaps, is Wittgenstein's effect on the way we see our relations with others and ourselves. Language is less a tool in this regard than a medium where what were thought to be private attributes previously are now made available to philosophical scrutiny, while the area for intimacy is expanded radically.

What is extraordinary about Wittgenstein's philosophical discussion of concepts is the way this interrogation leaves the reader aware of the power or hold that a concept can have. Which is stronger? Is it the hold of the Cartesian concept of the self as composed of ephemeral corporeality and an eternal mental substance joined together at the pineal gland, or the strength of Wittgenstein's conceptual investigation that leads us to see that we do not need to conceive ourselves "like an inner tube which is simply inflated by a mind?" (1980b: 11).

The power of concepts is illuminated when we see them not as "fundamental constructs in theories of the mind," but as words that capture "family resemblances" among nouns, verbs, and other features of language. "Citizenship" as a concept captures an array of activities, as well as personal characteristics, institutional expectations, and duties. Wittgenstein uses "family resemblances" as a synonym for concepts; he shows how we can move around in a concept, see reality refract in various directions; and, because some of these directions surprise – the hallmark of good metaphor – concepts are the life force of language. In this sense politics itself gives way to a view of a region of language composed of a vibrant and changing vocabulary emanating from a cauldron of constitutive language-games and practices. Similarly, citizenship leaves us noticing its relations with rights, justice, and patriotism (as the citizen expresses gratitude for, and a desire to extend to future generations, what the political order provides), but also indoctrination, xenophobia, and jingoistic blindness (where citizenship entails a severely circumscribed range of acceptable public activities and with it an attenuated view that excludes some not only from the category of citizenship, but from humanity too).

III. The Lived-Life of Citizens: Two Examples

In this section, I will focus on a particular view of citizenship as an endlessly malleable identity produced by disagreement and asymmetries in political life. The most fundamental of these divisions for Mouffe, a theorist who writes widely and inventively on Wittgensteinian themes, is that distinguishing "the political" from politics on a vertical plane. Where surface political actions and decisions are concerned with questions of the just order of humans leading collective lives, "the political" is a subterranean condition of hostility, violence, and partisanship that both informs political discourse, and arises whenever politics' differences fail to achieve resolution. The most direct consequence of the political on ordinary political life is the fracturing and pluralism I described earlier as the constitutive language-games of political life. In this section, the agonic production of citizenship and its relation to pluralist democracy noted by Mouffe (1993) will be examined and questioned through the experiences of two figures, one historical and one contemporary.

Socrates considered himself a loyal citizen of Athens. He (vis-à-vis Plato) defended his loyalty with distinct rhetorical strategies: autobiographical, religious, conceptual, and conventional. Through these defenses, Socrates becomes an exemplar of the sort of pluralistic or agonic notion of citizenship Mouffe devised with help from Wittgenstein. But his death is better grasped in terms of a clash between competing grammars or uses of justice, and between the style of philosophical life he led and the way the demands of citizenship were conceived in the charges brought by Meletus and Anytus. This is what examining an extreme or unusual event does for us, according to Wittgenstein. What breaches in the ordinary reveal is not the play of the occult on ordinary life, but rather what goes unnoticed precisely because they are so visible.

> The aspects of things that are most important to us are hidden because of their simplicity and familiarity. (One is unable to notice something – because it is always before one's eyes.) The real foundations of his enquiry do not strike a man at all. Unless *that* fact has at some time struck him. – And this means: we fail to be struck by what, once seen, is most striking and most powerful. (1958b: sec. 129)

Significantly, violent partisanship can never really be regarded as an extreme or illuminating situation in Mouffe's work. "The political" as posited by Mouffe is the "ontological dimension" beneath the surface of politics, which she describes as an underlying collective identity. As I noted in the Introduction, Mouffe (2005: 8–10) argues that liberal theories of democracy with their emphasis on what makes us individual and their expressions of concern with how to perpetuate and embellish individuality fail to comprehend this dimension that sounds like Hobbesian human nature by a different name. How this underlying collective identity manifests itself in politics is through an array of antagonisms (actual and potential). Those agonic binaries like "us versus them," "friend versus enemy," that were taken as the nature of politics by Schmitt are really only one manifestation of the political among many, notes Mouffe. What she wants us to see is that it is the dissension spawned by the political that feeds the pluralism of politics, and goads citizens into partisan action. This political action challenges any consensus arising in political life, and then serves to distinguish the realm of politics from the realm of "the social," described by Arendt in antipolitical terms as the erosion of the division between public and private life.[7] For Arendt, bureaucracy is the most social form of collective life, and its growth over the last two centuries has led to the demise of the *polis* and the political life.

Do we need this concept of "the political," presented as an extralinguistic universal, in order to understand either the plurality of political life (that range of language-games bound together by "family resemblances") or the agonic, violent character of political disagreement? My sense is that this construct is a result of the impulse to generalize Wittgenstein warned against, and it has the unfortunate effect of explaining away the injustices and violent events *in* politics as somehow natural and inevitable, and somehow deeper and more essential than professed goals *of* politics like peace and justice. In this sense, the political works as an inversion of the Rationalism at work in Habermas's God's-eye contention about the foundational role of consensus that informs his reading of Wittgenstein. Habermas (1990) writes, "language-games only work because they presuppose idealizations that transcend any particular language-game; as a necessary condition of possibly reaching understanding, these idealizations give rise to the perspective of an agreement that is open to criticism on the basis of validity claims" (199). No doubt there are idealizations or truths at work in language-games, and we can suppose that these standards transcend the practices of these games, but, for Wittgenstein

(1969), our idealizations are not prefigured by metalinguistic Reason; rather, "our talk" about reason, truth, and certitude "gets its meaning from the rest of our proceedings" (sec. 229). The political, in Mouffe's view, is also an idealization with explanatory power: It explains the dissensus manifest in and continually informing differences and conflict between language-games. Resort to "the political" by Mouffe, I will argue, is a most un-Wittgensteinian moment in her work, and an aberration that arises whenever we seek something higher (Habermas) or deeper (Mouffe) than "the groundlessness of our believing" (Wittgenstein 1969: sec. 166). My task here, then, is to examine and describe the effects of a plurality of language-games on citizenship and violence from the street-level where vision is enlarged through motion, and explanations are avoided as a matter of trying to get beyond what we can see at the core of any form of metaphysical escapism.

The story of Socrates does not need to be retold here. We have inherited an image of Socrates, old, ugly, disheveled, wandering through the *agora*, seeking to invigorate the intellectual life of his fellow Athenians by questioning them. Undergraduates tend to read Socrates, at least initially, as arrogant and suicidal. They think his questioning of respected citizens tantamount to heckling. But I believe you must take Socrates at his word that he seeks wisdom from those who claim they possess it. The enterprise of philosophy he inaugurated is a serious business that interrupts complacency in all areas of life from politics, religion, and sex, to ethics, the practical knowledge of trades, and art. Once you realize you do not know something you thought you did, then the intellect, like nature, finds it abhors vacuums and seeks to fill the hole in knowledge through inquiry, study, and conversation. The larger effect could be, Socrates hoped, an awakening of a now dormant intellectual culture in the city.

Wittgenstein does not buy into this positive spin I place on the story of Socrates. He writes of Socratic dialogues as "a frightful waste of time," and of Socrates as possessing a concept of knowledge so limited, so beholden to a unitary and metaphysical notion of Truth, it led not only to the unjust insult of those he questioned, but a denigration of what counts as knowing among humans in order to bolster an idling characterization of Philosophy (1980b: 14, 56). A critical encounter with Socrates becomes an appreciation of the complexity and liveliness of concepts:

> But that is the difficulty Socrates gets into in trying to give the definition of a concept. Again and again a use of the word emerges that seems not to be compatible with the concept that others uses have led us to form. We say: but that

isn't how it is! – It *is* like that though! And all we can do is keep repeating these antitheses. (1980b: 30)

In responding to a Socratic question such as, "What is the nature of citizenship?" Wittgenstein gives us fair warning that no answer will capture the desired essence of the concept. Even Socrates, in defending his loyalty as a citizen of the city before those who condemned him for sedition, explored an array of possible justifications. The list of these ensuing rhetorical strategies is quite long, and these too are well known. He claimed he was appointed by Apollo to help Athens return to the cultural greatness it had known in the Age of Pericles through philosophy. When defending his citizenship before the friend who would help him escape his prison cell, he turned not to a religious foundation for his argument, but the conventions of the city itself. To escape even an unjust death penalty would involve dishonoring his ancestors who, like him, obeyed the laws and served in the military. Again, in the court, Socrates defended his refusal to obey an order issued by an oligarchy to return a general to the city for what would surely be an unjust trial in the name of citizenship. Later, he would proclaim it the duty of every citizen to adhere to the terms of even unjust rulings by a corrupt mob rule.

In the lived-life of even the most famous philosopher-citizen, a person who believed the wisdom of the afterlife would include recollection of the essence of all concepts, the condition of his own citizenship could not be described in essentialist terms. In this, he articulated the complex perceptions that come with immanent theorizing. That is, he described the lived pluralism of political concepts. This pluralism includes distinctively reflective theory and philosophy language-games defended by Socrates as necessary to spur disagreement and thought on the part of citizens. This dissensus was not a product of politics' nature, but the range of perceptual vantages that are themselves the effect of the range of language-games in and around political life. Exploration of these practices and features of Athenian political life was, in the example of Socrates, enabled by his peripatetic orientation to the city.

As we enter the city of language to investigate the breadth of citizenship, what is visible immediately is the divide between citizens and non-citizens. Citizens have rights that are withheld from non-citizens (though certain social benefits like employment, education, and emergency medical services might be extended to non-citizens or obtained surreptitiously). The status of the non-citizen is always tenuous, but it becomes especially dangerous in times of war and upheaval, as Wittgenstein the émigré knew.

77

When a political society is threatened, non-citizens are often the first to be singled out for persecution. But how do we explain the trial and death of Socrates? Prosecutors never questioned his status as citizen. Yet, he died for his expansive view of citizenship. Here we confront an area of incommensurability between language-games locatable in the neighborhood of politics. What is revered as creative and critical in the activities of theorizing and philosophizing, is condemned in another of the constitutive language-games of politics. This is a danger that is only heightened by the effacement of the boundaries that permit travel. As you step from one language-game to another the different rules may not be immediately apparent. But there can be changes within a language-game either through gradual processes, as in Kuhn's (1962) analysis of new thinking about anomalies that lead to paradigmatic change from normal to abnormal to normal science, or through more revolutionary conversion, which alter the game's rules while retaining their indeterminacy. Still, adapting to these altered conventions is conditioned by punishing consequences.

These kinds of transformations in conventions leading to new forms of entrapment and liberation delineated along the lines of distinctive, yet traversable, boundaries *within* language-games can be found in Nafisi's memoir, *Reading Lolita in Tehran*. Here the factual/conceptual distinction is drawn as a politics/literature distinction. Nafisi was a professor of American Literature in her native Iran at the time of the overthrow of the Shah by the Islamic fundamentalist regime headed by Ayatollah Khomeini and the establishment of an Islamic theocracy in that country. Nafisi, herself a devout Muslim, experienced the revolution and its aftermath as a period of systematic repression. The regime sought first to create prophylactic barriers between its attenuated conception of Islamic culture, and what it considered the degenerate cultures and regimes to the West. As these barriers were erected, Nafisi quietly bought up a number of books by Western authors (Austen, James, Fitzgerald, Nabokov) in anticipation of the closure of bookstores. Next, coercion and violence were deployed to engender religious homogeneity within the society. Intellectual life was forced underground; and Nafisi participated in this movement by convening a reading group in her living room.

Despite the dangers it posed for Nafisi and her students, the state headed by Khomeini's regime appears relatively distant throughout the memoir because of more immediate dangers posed by students, colleagues, and neighbors. The agents of violence who commanded loyalty and the outward appearance of virtue were dispersed throughout the society.

There were white trucks with armed brigades who would arrest women off the streets for such transgressions as improper head coverings, the wearing of lipstick or nail polish, or walking with men other than their husbands, fathers, or brothers. But repressive power was widely disseminated: neighbors could turn in neighbors, the media was subverted to advance the goals of the theocracy, and administrators, faculty, and students alike contributed to the suppression of the very idea of intellectual freedom. Competition among ordinary citizens to appear most orthodox and intolerant of any form of dissension came to characterize the society from the street-level perspective offered by Nafisi. These elements were the immediate face of repression, even as they were understood to be effects of the theocratic state.

Reading Lolita in Tehran is only partly an account of the use of power to restrict freedoms (of women particularly) by a theocratic regime. It is also a moving memoir of the freedom that can be found in literature. There are, to be sure, important differences between the kind of linguistic and conceptual entrapment that Wittgenstein sought liberation from for himself and other philosophers, and the actual imprisonments and oppressions experienced by people like Nafisi in authoritarian contexts.[8] Keeping these distinctions clear by avoiding what Laclau and Mouffe have derided correctly as the "logic of equivalence" is an important step in discerning the relation between vision and freedom that Wittgenstein suggested. Our capacity to observe the difference between the "visual room" in a painting of a house and the physical room we may be standing in while examining that painting leaves us free to engage in imaginative flights relating the one type of room to the other. Language-games create corridors or spaces between the seams of their differences that enable us to move and see. In Nafisi's case, the seam she walked was the one created by the contrast between the world she knew on the streets of Tehran and the worlds created by the novelists she loved and taught.

The experience of literature in Nafisi's memoir is both a prelude to political dissent and the stage upon which dissent could be expressed. As a prelude to dissent, the literary worlds in the novels of Austen, James, Fitzgerald, and Nabokov, both illuminated the injustice of the actual repression suffered by the reader and offered some temporary relief through escape. Once Nafisi was forced to leave the university, she sought to create a surrogate classroom in her home with some of her favorite, most trusted, female students. This was a dangerous undertaking for all the participants. They would meet to discuss literature under the noses of authorities that condemned such works as subversive and heretical. The outward homogeneity in female fashion demanded by the regime ironically created the condition of relative invisibility on the city streets necessary for these meetings to take place. Inside the house, the women were then free to examine, as an example, what Humbert Humbert's treatment of Lolita had to say about their own victimization. *Lolita* provided a vocabulary, a set of images, and space to walk and see anew the injustices perpetrated by the Khomeini regime.

Frontal assaults by courageous citizens against an unjust modern state are recipes for bloodbaths.[9] This is the lesson of Tiananmen Square: The state, whether theocratic or secular, will use weapons against its own children to defend itself. Other tactics for political dissent therefore have to be devised. In Nafisi's (2003) memoir, the seam of difference between the Iranian theocracy and even the repressive regime imposed by Humbert on Lolita becomes the stage for articulating the dissent itself engendered by the difference because it is the only stage left: "It seemed as if, apart from literature, the political had devoured us, eliminating the personal or private" (237).

For Wittgenstein (1967: sec. 458), the equation of philosophical investigations with conceptual investigations retains space for the imagination, related integrally to our ways of seeing, to flourish.[10] Apart, slightly and nonhierarchically, we have the room to imagine alternative worlds more just, more humane, freer, than the one we walk through daily. There are two types of constraint Wittgenstein's philosophy seeks to address. The first is a constraint common to philosophers where they lose themselves in a philosophical problem or system, find they cannot go on, and experience their entanglement as a detachment from the ordinary flow of language that is reified. Wittgensteinian philosophy in this instance seeks to help philosophers "back to rough ground," where freed from their entanglement they can walk again. The second constraint affects nonphilosophers as well. Wittgenstein (1958b: sec. 115) describes this experience of limitation in terms of malnourishment as a result of a one-sided diet of examples. I think of it in terms of the world of information promised and offered by the Internet. At our fingertips now is a wealth of perspectives, but most of us apparently are using the Internet to reaffirm our own dogmatic approach to the world. We travel to the same sites every day and by force of habit close ourselves off from alternative points of view and sources of information. The task of philosophy here is to cut the tethers that affect our intellectual mobility adversely. This mobility is the measure of freedom in Wittgenstein's work. "For Wittgenstein," notes Genova (1995), "logic only facilitates life in the bottle, not escape from it. Without realizing it, we soon settle for the bottled world, transforming our ideals into idols to which we insist reality must correspond" (10). The conception of philosophizing and theorizing that emerges in the *Philosophical Investigations* is a unique way of life dedicated to obliterating the aspect-blindness of dogmatism in its various guises and to enhancing learning and seeing by inviting travel between as many of the language-games (conceived as perceptual vantage points) composing language as possible.

IV. CITIZENSHIP AND CONTINUOUS SEEING

In the previous section, citizenship was viewed as a mode and result of travel through language-games in politics that were threatened by forms of tyranny, both political and religious in character. The entrapments here were not self-induced, as in the philosophical pictures Wittgenstein studied. They were engendered by competing world views, and by asymmetries in political, social, and military power. The conflicts in their particularity did not expose a deeper source of antagonism either in the psyches of participants or in the subterranean world of "the political." Rather, from the street-level of Socrates and Nafisi, what could be seen and clarified through physical, rhetorical, and imaginative travel is the play of grammars that give rise to both stupid, unjust violence, and political creativity in the forms of resistance and dissent. Because these grammars are malleable and substitutable, the violence of political life observed in the examples of Socrates and Nafisi are neither natural nor inevitable. Politics, like all other language-games, is conventional all the way down.

This conventionalism is emphasized in the analysis of the formation of the democratic citizen's political subjectivity presented in explicitly Wittgensteinian terms by Norval. A careful consideration of Norval's work yields a sense of consonance between Wittgenstein's pluralistic conception of language and the pluralism of experiences and group memberships that compose contemporary citizenship. That is, Norval shows Wittgenstein to be a powerful lens onto the way we form ourselves over time as citizens of politics and language.

Norval's (2006) focus is twofold: First, she wants to consider the "key moments that *turn* the subject into a democratic subject" (230). Then she will study those "practices" that perpetuate, challenge, and enrich this identity over time. The context for this study is a South African political society in transition from the authoritarian and racist regime of apartheid to a representative democracy that eschews racism as a justification for inequality and segregation. To study this transition that includes the cultivation and inculcation of democratic values in citizens accustomed to antipolitical norms, the theorist must walk in for a closer view. In this study, we can surmise, the formation of the democratic subject is an autobiographical exercise. The close-up view of this personal and political transformation provided by Norval (2006) "allows us to reflect on the visibility of contingency and its role in the establishment of a democratic grammar" (242). This contingency is not unique to political language-games, Wittgenstein knew. It is the flexibility and creative impulse he sought to capture in his image of "the stream of language."

Our human tendency to avoid confronting the contingency of grammar leads to unnecessary perceptual limits, Norval notes. This avoidance is a good way to consider the role of "the political" in Mouffe's work. Refusal to see the contingency of grammar, Norval continues, leads to entrapments in rigidly defined political concepts like liberty or justice. Hypostatizing such concepts obscures their polysemic character, and in so doing we become mired in a use or language-game we take to be authoritative. Escape is secured by genealogy or perspicuous re-presentation of our truly contingent relation to rules or grammars. We learn from these moments that escape is really just a matter of turning and walking (Wittgenstein 1958b: sec. 203). These turns and horizontal movements lead to a new "*way of looking at things*" (Wittgenstein 1958b: sec. 144).

Novel ways of seeing, for Norval, lead to and are reflective of the "changes in political subjectivity," obscured by the focus on procedures in the discourse of deliberative democracy. This proceduralism evades the issue of the formation of democratic identity by contending that rules are obeyed "blindly." And, indeed, as Wittgenstein pointed out, rules are followed blindly or unreflectively. But they are also ignored, missed, bypassed for another rule in the vicinity, or followed (not incorrectly, but) innovatively. Norval sets aside the formalism of proceduralism and posits instead an image of a woman immersed in practices of democratic politics. This participation involves a "subjective assent" to the effect "I am a democrat." "This '*identification as*' (that we are to understand as the political equivalent of 'seeing as') is an embodied act, of a subject passionately involved in an activity, which structures her political life and participation in a certain way . . . Dimensions of argumentation, such as persuasion and rhetoric, as well as bodily, materialized inscriptions, are key to this process" (Norval 2005: 241).

The limit to this analysis is clear when compared with Norval's opening promise to examine the formation of a political identity in the context of a political society in transition. Here we get a model of democracy – the discourse of deliberative democracy – and a hypothetical counterexample to the model's proceduralism. A vital part of the experience of seeing aspect change, for Wittgenstein, is the ability to see a picture as a picture. I will discuss this in other chapters, but for now I will note simply that the inability to see a picture as a picture is yet another form of entrapment. Wittgenstein (1958b) illustrates this in this way:

> Think of a picture of a landscape, an imaginary landscape with a house in it. – Someone asks "Whose house is that?" – The answer, by the way, might be "It belongs to the farmer who is sitting on the bench in front of it". But then he cannot for example enter his house. (sec. 398)

Norval's example of "identification as" is illuminating in spite of this odd failure to see academic discourse on deliberative democracy as a picture of political deliberation. (It is odd because an entire section of the article is a wonderful explication of "seeing pictures as pictures" in Wittgenstein. Moreover, she proceeds to examine the importance of Wittgenstein's remarks on aspect change as a corrective to overly simplistic and static models of democracy in political theory today.) "Aspect change," she notes astutely, "allows one to notice that one is now seeing something, not just in terms of this or that picture but also *as* a picture." This insight gets to the emancipative effect of Wittgenstein's remarks on perception directly.

Lessons from moments of political dislocation or "emancipations" studied by Laclau, or strategies for breaking from pictures exemplified in Žižek's heroic politics as a challenge to Aristotle's contention regarding the continuity between ethics and politics are examined. However, as Norval notes, the focus on techniques of emancipation from one identity and the creativity involved in forging new identities may lead to an overly determinative account of grammar. For Wittgenstein, travel through the boundaries of language-games is easy. What is difficult is breaking the habitual preference for the familiar, and the sense of security, that can be bred in a language-game. Wittgenstein illustrates this as the dogmatism that leaves you feeling trapped in a room while the door to leave is just behind you. But with the escape comes a new way of seeing that Wittgenstein expresses in the phrase "Now I see it as . . ." and Norval expresses as a moment of political self-reflection: "Now I am a democrat!"

In the end, Norval presents what is described best as a democratic approach to Wittgenstein, rather than the Wittgensteinian approach to democratic identity she set out to show. This may be unavoidable. We read Wittgenstein as political theorists. Still, Norval makes a strong case for the toleration and openness to conversation that results from and encourages travel through language-games, which she labels a process of making "contingency visible." From perspective to perspective, one grows to see knowledge as provisional, education as lifelong, language's complexity as a lesson in community, and barriers to travel as occasions for rebellion.[11] In this life in motion, Norval (2005) notes perceptively, we are really assembling reminders that "politics is a visceral activity; passion, bodily practices and violence are all part and parcel of political life and grammars" (250). Noting this is the theorist's contribution to an enriched view of the complex network of paths and experiences leading to democratic citizenship.

V. Conclusion: Pluralistic Citizenship

The impetus for Mouffe's turn to Wittgenstein for a pluralistic conception of citizenship is the agreement she sees between the "diverse forms" democratic citizenship takes and the freedom implied in the variety of ways to play the "democratic game" of politics. This is part of her larger project to "democratize democracy," an enterprise that makes creative use of Wittgenstein's work. But her organization of political life as divided between the politics of the surface and "the political" of the depths seems to me a reversal of Wittgenstein's description of language. From this picture, we see dissensus and antagonism as understandable products of differences between language-games, and the distinctive life-histories of those living within language-games, which is the subject of Norval's inquiry. Beneath the surface is not a zone of essentialism; rather, there are just more conventions forming the "bedrock" of trust that marks the end of inquiry into the nature of language by showing there is no such foundation, while functioning on the surface to invite travel across language-games.

In this conclusion I would like to take the pluralistic conception of citizenship in a different direction and to show it functioning in a context of totalitarianism. Language is not essentially political or democratic. Such characterizations reveal very little about either politics or language. Moreover, they tend to so over-generalize or ontologize language as to hide its origins in the repetition of physiological capacities to vocalize and scratch out symbols. In disguising conventionality with ontology, we lose a crucial feature of language use as meaning producing: its malleability. Concepts, Wittgenstein shows, are like balls of mercury. When you try to crush them, they squirt out in different directions; fracture them and they form smaller, independent balls.

The importance of this feature of concepts becomes all the more apparent when we consider citizenship under the pressure of a coercive state to reduce what counts as good citizenship into one or two circumscribed activities, like voting or attending parades. Most will succumb to these outward appearances of homogeneity and because the freedom of citizens must be practiced to endure there can be atrophy, but there is always room (even in a theocracy with modern means for surveillance and policing), as Nafisi illustrated, for creativity and experiments in enlarged citizenship. These practices tap into the subversive potential of subaltern counter-publics, enliven democratic thought, and produce temporary spaces and spontaneous tactics that permit and encourage political dissent.

Notes

1. For a similar perspective that starts with describing what citizens do, see Geuss (2008).
2. This claim is fleshed out in the work of "difference" democratic theorists. See, for example, Hirst (1994) and Young (2000).
3. The image of a traveling idea as a way of seeing comes from Said (1983).
4. Even where citizenship is conceived more expansively, beyond the parameters of the voting booth, the political actions of citizens, if they are to count as political actions, are performed within formal and legitimate boundaries. Habermas (1996), for example, presents a fairly active account of citizens creating their own spaces in civil society, and using this space to "ferret out, identify, and effectively thematize latent problems of social integration," and having deliberated on how best to express these conflicts, they then take their complaints to legislatures "in a way that disrupts the latter's routines," but with the larger goal of embellishing the peace or integration of the order (356). There does not appear to be room for challenging injustices without this larger aim of legitimizing government by passing through formal procedures of policymaking. Actions that occur outside the bounds of formal procedure, then, cannot be regarded as acts of citizenship. The circumscribed notion of travel implied here is in contrast to the Wittgensteinian account of citizenship I will be fleshing out in this chapter. See McAfee (2000: 93–6). For an overview of what for Political Scientists count as legitimate participation on the part of citizens, see Schlozman (2002).
5. Heidegger and his followers, Hardt and Negri, Laclau and Mouffe, and Connolly posit the ontologizations of politics I am noting here. This list is borrowed from Critchley's

85

consideration of the separation of ontology and politics in Badiou and Rancière. See Van Oenen, Rosenthal, and Sonderegger (2008: 43).

6. Dumm (2000; 2008) has explored the experiences of loss and losing in political theory in aching terms.

7. There is little hope for the continued preservation of politics in the presence of the powerful instruments of consensus (bureaucracy chief among them) that epitomize the social's prominence. "The disappearance of class identities and the end of the bipolar system of confrontation have rendered conventional politics obsolete. Consensus finally reigns with respect to the basic institutions of society, and the lack of any legitimate alternative means that consensus will not be challenged" (Mouffe 1999: 3).

8. Wittgenstein conceives of the effect of conceptual entanglement on thinking, seeing, and learning in this evocative way: "A man will be *imprisoned* in a room with a door that's unlocked and opens inward; as long as it does not occur to him to *pull* rather than to push it" (1980b: 42). Nafisi's prison is her own home; and there are laws, locks, surveillance, and guards keeping her from the free public life she wants.

9. This is a fundamental lesson in the work of Wolin and I am paraphrasing his language too closely here to leave it unacknowledged. Even at his most optimistic, when, for example, Wolin described how plural interests coalesce into a victorious movement like Poland's Solidarity, the state's bureaucratic order, militarism, and antagonism toward "the political" remain undiminished and dangerous. For representative pieces on this theme, see Wolin (1982: 17–28; 1985: 217–35; 1994: 11–25).

10. Again, Deleuze and Guattari define philosophy famously as an activity involved in the creation of new concepts to reveal aspects of our lives today. For Wittgenstein, philosophy does not involve adding anything new to the world; rather, he saw philosophizing as a therapeutic activity charged with the responsibility of repairing the rigid hold we have on concepts available already. There is no doubt that he did contribute new concepts to the discourse of philosophy, and so it is more accurate to say that concept creation is not the sole province of Philosophy, but a function of a wide range of social practices.

11. Personal rebellion against barriers to travel and immersion in activities of politics can be raised to a collective level in describing recognition of one's political voice either as a member of a minority culture seeking political enfranchisement, or in defending cultural identity as an expression of political freedom. A start would be a Wittgensteinian reading of Kymlicka (1995).

CHAPTER 4

Why Wittgenstein is Not Conservative: Conventions and Critique

Where in the world constructed of language is theory, and what has become of the theorist?

Sheldon S. Wolin (1994: 582)

I. INTRODUCTION

When Wittgenstein looked at a particular neighborhood or form of life in the city of language, what he examined were surface details and activities. Activities were performed with adherence to rules that were perhaps beneath the surface, but these subterranean features could be made visible by asking the question, "What is the rule for . . .?" or by a dispute over a play in a game that requires reference to the rules, or even by a behavioral faux pas that breaches a rule or rules, resulting in embarrassment. The rules themselves were the product of the activities visible on the surface. They affect the activities with incomplete and indeterminable reciprocity. As products or codifications of activities, the rules demarcate the activity from other activities (chess from checkers, for example), but at the same time these rules have a provisional character. That is, they can be amended, bypassed (with something akin to a "mulligan" in golf or a "do over" in some referee-less street game), or dropped altogether. Indeed, language-games and forms of life come into being and die out transforming what is described best as Wittgenstein's linguistic vision in small but distinctive ways. This city of language before us is actually a palimpsest where the surface includes traces of razed structures and older districts buried over by time. Older versions of the city become part of what counts as the bedrock upon which the newer city is built.

Let me begin, then, with the image of the city of language presented by Wittgenstein the author of the *Philosophical Investigations* as opposed to Wittgenstein the flâneur that walked its pages. Wittgenstein the author is able to take the longer and wider view of the mapmaker; the walker cannot see the organizing parameters of the city from his street-level view but assumes there is a larger logic holding things together. The author's cartographic description of the city is brief and occurs early in the *Investigations* both to illustrate the complex and living or incomplete quality of language and to set the dramatic stage upon which the philosophical walker will travel. Wittgenstein begins by responding to the objection that the language-games he has explored in the first seventeen remarks consist solely of orders (that is, "Bring me a slab!"). A language composed of orders is incomplete, goes the objection. In articulating this criticism, Wittgenstein is repeating his own objection to the one-dimensional picture of language as representational advanced as complete in his *Tractatus Logico-Philosophicus*. Out of this self-criticism, then, Wittgenstein offers an image of language as more than an instrument or set of tools for the production of meaning. This "more than" quality of language is presented by Wittgenstein as unrepresentable and resistant to ontologization (as the "house of Being," for example) because of its dynamic character. The edges or limits cannot be seen from the outside (at least by humans), but they can be experienced or felt from the inside, or imagined and expressed synoptically from the God's-eye standpoint of the author.

One is a tourist even in her or his home city because of development or sprawl that alters the perimeter constantly, and because of the transformations, sometimes subtle and private, within neighborhoods on the inside. Each alteration tells a story.

> Our language may be seen as an ancient city: a maze of little streets and squares, of old and new houses, and of houses with additions from various periods; and this surrounded by a multitude of new boroughs with straight regular streets and uniform houses. (Wittgenstein 1958b: sec. 18)

At the center is the historical beginning of the city. It is largely unplanned. Buildings and streets were added on as needed, but in a relatively compressed way to maintain convenience and defense in the form of propinquity. Squares fulfilled the need for public gathering spaces where goods could be sold and speeches and pronouncements made, heard, and debated. For a long time, the city was not designed, *per se*; it grew in accord with the immediate needs of its inhabitants as opposed to some underlying principle or overarching blueprint. Houses, too, reflected this self-organizing feature. As families grew in size and/or prosperity, their homes expanded.

But at some point the mode of expansion and the architecture of new buildings changed utterly. This point is manifested in the line of demarcation distinguishing the old city from the new "boroughs." And this point and line betoken a range of other transformations. Streets become straight and regular to accommodate new modes of transportation that, in turn, alleviate the physical and economic need for closeness. In the new boroughs there is a marked end to the public square, to the public life we associate with politics, and to architectural uniqueness.

By describing the city of language this way, Wittgenstein evokes a striking juxtaposition of the spontaneity and public-centeredness of the old city with the imposed, efficient order of the new reminiscent of Levittown and Le Corbusier's ultramodern urbanism (Berman 1982: 164–71). Apparently, Wittgenstein was looking at the same urban features described by Arendt in terms of the decline of the public realm and the *zoon politikon*, and the corresponding rise of the social realm like an unchecked cancer emerging from the economy of the home. Arendt described the growth of "the social" in terms of the erosion of the traditional public/private dichotomy and the supplanting of citizenship actions by the relentless work schedule of *animal laborans* and the insatiable consumption of *Homo economicus*. It leaves me wondering about the adequacy of the philosophical explanation for why Wittgenstein did not travel the neighborhood of politics in his mid-twentieth-century city of language. Perhaps he could not walk there because what counted as his political life was now dead or moribund, and not because mathematics, aesthetics, and the psychology of perception held greater philosophical interest for him. More importantly, this description of the city suggests nostalgia for the old way of life that has been mistaken for an expression of political conservatism on Wittgenstein's part. I consider this conservative appellation "mistaken" because it hides more than it reveals, particularly the political dimension of Wittgenstein's philosophy that places him in a fairly large category of theorists beginning with Weber and Arendt, who struggle intellectually against the public hallmark or apparent *telos* of modernity: the supplanting of politics by bureaucracy. A thorough antimodernism is not to be found in these writers. Indeed, such an orientation is imaginable only in a religious community like that of the Amish or in a Luddite-type movement. Wittgenstein's opposition to modernism occurred from within the throes of modernity. And it was directed at the soporific effects of the authority assigned to scientism by various philosophical schools or circles. It was expressed only occasionally as nostalgia for old, active political forms of life.

In responding to those who consider Wittgenstein's reflections on the conventional basis of language and life, and his conception of philosophical activity as descriptive, as indications of sympathy for politically conservative (read: antidemocratic) politics, there are three interrelated questions I want to answer in this chapter: Does conventionalism eliminate criticism by undermining the absolute standards upon which philosophical judgment relies? Is there an antipolitical philosophy of language behind bureaucracy that Wittgenstein helps theorists to analyze and respond to critically? Is the motion celebrated in his work the public criterion of an inner freedom at odds with forces of conformity?

II. LANGUAGE AND CONVENTIONS

To call a philosopher or theorist "conservative" is more than a heuristic matter of ideological categorization. It can be a kind of reputation assassination that eliminates the voice of the so labeled from the discourse of political theory.[1] I will examine this rhetorical tactic as various theorists have applied it to Wittgenstein. But the main thrust of my argument is designed show the spurious quality of the charge as well as the radical character of Wittgenstein's antifoundational view that human life occurs in a linguistic medium shaped by irreducible conventions. At the heart of Wittgenstein's view that the forms human life takes are predicated on habits and customs is the contention that what is does not have to be. When facing ethnic strife, sexism, totalitarianism, and other forms of violence and injustice, the utopian dimension of theorizing politics can be emboldened by the idea that change toward justice is not a matter of contravening metaphysical absolutes or rewriting the book of nature; rather, it is a matter, difficult still, of breaking bad habits, altering consciousness, eliminating oppressive institutions, denaturalizing domination, eliminating laws (recognizing they can be eliminated) that disenfranchise traditionally subjugated groups and writing laws that are inclusive and promote democratic participation (Patterson 1992).

For example, we know there is one single, unified biological category called the human race. Yet even the best intentioned divide humanity up into various races. We have devised a whole vocabulary of "race relations" to heal the breaches between "races." Talking about races in the plural gives biological or natural credence that perpetuate divisions expressed better in terms of ethnicities. Ethnic divisions, themselves sites of xenophobia and violence, can be healed and coexist peacefully through mutual recognition, respect, and communication. Biological divisions require a far slower, evolutionary process we cannot control. But there are no biological divisions between blacks and whites other than obvious secondary features like melanin content. Yet this belief in human races and the lexicon that supports and expresses it prove recalcitrant. Speaking of race as though there is more than one among humans is a convention that needs to be and can be broken. This reform of the way we describe the world is based not only on a desire to express human biology accurately, but also on recognition that this convention is oppressive.

The happy side of conventionalism is that it nourishes the idea of human perfectibility while eliminating the inhumanness of perfection as a goal. There is, as I noted above in the race example, a dark side too. Wittgenstein saw the world he knew and believed stable (in the *Tractatus*) prove all too malleable. We are reminded of the fluid character of human identity with each photograph or description of what Primo Levi called the "drowned" or "walking dead" of the concentration camps. Whatever civil, religious, or cultural bulwarks were in place to prevent atrocity and inhumanities, they were shown to be all too conventional in Wittgenstein's Europe. He lived long enough to see that even those rules that gave shape to what it means to be human could be so distorted that the very capacity for trust Aristotle considered the fragile bedrock of political life could be effaced almost completely.

Are we talking about the same thing when we examine the apparently entrenched vocabulary of races among humans, on the one hand, and the fragile conventions supporting political institutions and our ideas on what a human being is on the other? Are some conventions closer to the surface of daily life than others and therefore more exposed and vulnerable to change? Wittgenstein (1958b) indicates that the answer to both questions is yes by introducing a range of distinctions between surface and depth grammars, framework conditions that undergird language-games, and the perceptual distinction between those things so familiar they remain invisible to us and oppose temporarily the idea that "nothing is hidden" in language (secs. 111, 112, 126, 129). These distinctions do not lead Wittgenstein (1958b) to advance a series of philosophical techniques for cutting through the illusory surface to get to some more truthful core (secs. 92, 126).[2]

Even features of depth grammar, frames, and invisibles are available for view. What we are looking at, then, is akin to the problem Socrates faced in his trial. There were two distinct categories of charges against him: first, the specific charges of atheism, religious unorthodoxy, and corrupting youth. But then there was the deeper background charge or belief, repeated for two generations by parents fearing for their children's reputation and future in public life, that Socrates was a dangerous influence. The specific claims, though articulated by voices of influence and power, were refuted easily; but the background claim was plastered thickly enough upon the city's culture that it could not be effaced sufficiently by a single speech on a single day. By bringing the invisible charge to view in the courtroom, however, Socrates set in motion his exoneration – the new set of background beliefs fashioned memorably by Plato that shape our reverence for his teacher. Wittgenstein illuminates the relation between surface and depth in his metaphor of the riverbed:

> It might be imagined that some propositions, of the form of empirical propositions, were hardened and functioned as channels for such empirical propositions as were not hardened but fluid; and that this relation altered with time, in that fluid propositions hardened, and hard ones became more fluid.
>
> The mythology may change back into a state of flux; the riverbed of thoughts may shift. But I distinguish between the movements of the waters on the riverbed and the shift of the bed itself; though there is not a sharp division of the one from the other . . . And the bank of the river consists partly of hard rock, subject to no alteration or only to an imperceptible one, partly of sand, which now in one place now in another gets washed away or deposited. (1969: secs. 96–9)[3]

There are large chunks of reality that we agree upon unquestioningly and that impose physical limits on the way we live (1969: 211).[4] Think of the laws of Newtonian mechanics and the physiological isomorphism among humans and higher primates in this light. In Wittgenstein's work where meaning is a product of use, the question we confront consistently is, "How is communication and agreement (or disagreement) achieved given the infinite number of possible word combinations, contexts, and uses of utterances?" The regulative effect of the framing conventions supporting language-games is one answer. The medium through which these largely unarticulated agreements are questioned and perpetuated is language and the loci of these agreements are forms of life and language-games. This is to say two things in Wittgenstein (1958b): There is a reality outside of language expressed by grammar *in* language (secs. 371–4); and we only concur on what it looks like and compose this concurrence through the mediation of language. In this manner, Wittgenstein evades linguistic idealism while striking the conventional and psychological bedrock of this complex weave of language-games we can only assume forms a coherent, dynamic, and edgeless whole we call language.[5]

Wittgenstein employs the word "convention" (*Abmachung, Übereinkunft*) in three distinct ways in *Philosophical Investigations*. Two of the three involve criticism of a sort of essentialism that supports and justifies privileging certain claims to knowledge that occur in philosophy. All three also show the intimacy of conventions and the surface activities they shape. That is, the later Wittgenstein renounces his earlier participation in the search for invisible worlds – the "realm" of logical form lying beneath propositions that resembles outwardly Freud's discovery of the Unconscious or the Platonist's conception of an external source of truth. What Wittgenstein presents in his post-*Tractatus* works is a world where "nothing is hidden" even though some features may escape notice because of familiarity, routine, or the limitations of a particular perceptual vantage point.

The first use of convention occurs in a remark that harks back to a simple language-game where tools were given proper names (Wittgenstein 1958b: secs. 15, 41). Of particular interest is a tool called "N." What Wittgenstein wants us to see is the conventionality of the supposed symmetry of word to object in the activity of naming. Worker A gives her assistant B the sign for N. But tool N has been broken. What must B do? Wittgenstein (1958b) shows in this remark the synonymous relation between convention and rule, but he also questions the contention that meaning derives from the symmetry of word to object exemplified by proper names (sec. 41). Here meaning can be said to derive not from the use in worker A's utterance, but in the wider context of the language-game itself. N continues to mean something, continues to "be given a place in the language-game" even though it has ceased to exist as a tool for a designated purpose (and it is apparently a one-of-a-kind tool). Convention, in this remark, reveals an improvisational flexibility that can be said to oppose the regulative effects those deeper conventions or frames contribute to the shapes our forms of life and language-games take, but what we are seeing is a fine example of the polysemic or indeterminate character of rules. Conventions also take on a spatial connotation. They combine or form patterns that, in turn, come to be seen as specific contexts – the sentence, the language-game, the form of life – where meaningful performances occur, disclose aspects of the world, communicate to and affect others, and unify and/or rend communities. Moreover, these spaces are traversable. We come to a language-game with a notion of how to play developed from life in and travel through other language-games. Traces of memberships in language-games combine uniquely and construct what we have come to call our individual identities, as I observed earlier in Mouffe's (2000) consideration of the democratic citizen.

In the second use of "convention" Wittgenstein examines the privileging of sense-impressions as sources of knowledge that also possess the power of prediction. Our usual way of regarding sense-impressions is to afford them depth and inner privacy. But we know and use sense-impressions through their outward criteria. What Wittgenstein shows here is the language or criteria of sense-impressions are in a continuum with or identical to the sense-impressions themselves. The implication is that different languages have different sensations or at least express them differently. In this way the occult or inscrutable character of the sense-impressions are made visible, and, more importantly, this language of sense-impressions "like any other is founded on convention" (Wittgenstein 1958b: sec. 355).

Remarks like this have contributed to Wittgenstein's reputation as a behaviorist. This is an inaccurate label. Wittgenstein is an anti-Cartesian who opposed systematically the mind/body duality and the conception of identity as residing in an ineffable mental substance. Wittgenstein held that we do indeed have (what we take to be) an inner life, but the medium for this range of activities including thinking, judging, dreaming, intending, and so on, is the very same language we use to converse. The language of our inner life has no claim to greater truthfulness or closeness to a methodical absolute like Descartes's *cogito*. Yet, the availability of the language of our inner life to others gives rise to deep experience of the integrity or humanity of others. If the erosion of trust that occurred in the twentieth century can be reversed, then this conventional language that dissolves solipsism in its various philosophical and psychological guises is where the remedy resides.[6]

The third use of convention is similar to the first, but takes on a truly rich existential cast. Where the first posits an identity between rules and conventions, and the second between conventions and criteria, the third exposes the sublime in conventional seeing and description (Wittgenstein 1958b: 172).

In this use of convention, Wittgenstein (1958b) embarks on a discussion of the perceptual performance he calls "seeing as." We look at a painting of a triangle. "A triangle can really be *standing up* in one picture, be hanging in another, and can in a third be something that has fallen over" (171). To see a triangle as standing, or hanging, or as having fallen over, is to experience a change of aspect in the painting. Clearly, nothing has changed in the pictures of the triangles in question. The change is in the perceptual experience expressed as "Now I see it as . . ." "Could I say what a picture must be like to produce this effect?" Wittgenstein (1958b) asks. "No. There are, for example, styles of painting which do not convey anything to me in this immediate way, but do to other people. I think custom and upbringing have a hand in this" (172).

Failure to see the triangle *as* something, in this example, therefore, is not an indication of the pathology Wittgenstein describes as "aspect-blindness," which is the visual equivalent of tone deafness or humorlessness. We might not notice a change of aspect for a number of reasons. There are paintings, and here I am thinking of René Magritte's work, that seek to produce the effect of an aspect change. The juxtaposition of an image of a pipe with the sentence "*Ceci n'est pas une pipe*" is a particularly famous example that challenges the representationalism of the upper half of the canvas and, indeed, of art. Is this a pipe? No. It is an image of a pipe. Or, no, there are many different types of pipe. Or, perhaps, this is a philosophical example of a self-referential sentence where the word "this" is certainly not a pipe. And so on.

There are more difficult Magritte works that correspond to Wittgenstein's insight that to see an aspect change or to not see an aspect change in a painting boils down to "custom and upbringing." In one picture we see a bedroom with simple furnishings drawn to scale in relation to the rest of the room. On each piece of furniture, however, is an enormous ordinary object – a comb, a razor, a shaving brush. What do I see this as? Well, nothing, at first. I did not understand the painting at all, but given Magritte's reputation I could only assume I was missing something. As a creature of habit the tools of my daily life – pen, pencil, brush, keys, fork, and so on – are all placed carefully so I can find them when needed. Then came a time when I could not find my keys. For three days I could not rest or concentrate on anything other than searching. My eyes would flitter off the page or newspaper to search out corners of the room for the lost keys. On the third day my neighbor came to my door with my keys in hand. After losing days of work, along with my sense of security, I felt profound gratitude and surprise at what an ordeal this had become. Then I understood, at least partially, the Magritte painting, as I saw now how large ordinary objects could loom when they are lost. Their rearrangement, and here this was accomplished by playing with scale and an act of misplacement, brings this commonplace to notice.

> What does it mean to say that I "see the sphere floating in the air" in a picture?
>
> Is it enough that this description is the first to hand, is the matter-of-course one? No, for it might be so for various reasons. This might, for instance, simply be the conventional description. (Wittgenstein 1958b: 172)

Conventional in this remark might be a synonym for "normal" and "ordinary," or even pejoratives like "hackneyed" or "trite." But Wittgenstein has noted earlier the creative or idiosyncratic effects of custom.

Can description ever be "simply" conventional? Yes, in the sense that I might produce a description that provokes no challenge from any reader or listener. This is the sense of convention critics employ when contending that Wittgenstein's philosophy is conservative. But in Wittgenstein's world, conventional description turns on the larger movement he calls for within philosophy away from the abstract icy frictionless of metaphysics and toward the walk-able world of ordinary language and usage. This ordinary language is mainly a therapeutic idea that Wittgenstein applies to philosophers to give them a sense of direction toward the human and inexpert.[7] The image of the relation between metaphysics and ordinary language is unfortunately and infelicitously dualistic. Elsewhere, Wittgenstein cautions against conceiving the possibility of ideal and private languages. Whether we are speaking of symbolic logic, mathematics, or the eccentric communication that occurs between long-married couples or identical twins, these languages are extrapolations of ordinary language. And, so, because of the impossibility of stepping out of language into something else, all languages are, in effect, grounded in the ordinary. Their relations to one another are rhizomic rather than hierarchical. When Wittgenstein (1958b) writes, "what we do is bring words back from their metaphysical to their everyday use," he is describing his own critical project that aims to reform philosophy (sec. 116). He seeks to re-think philosophical activity as an enterprise that accepts the inescapability of ordinary language and tries (but never achieves) to "*command a clear view of the use of our words*" (secs. 122, 125).

To attain this "clear view" (a physical impossibility that serves nevertheless as a goal) is not an epistemological project that results in a privileged knowledge of the essence of language and language use. Nor is it a matter of transcending the prejudices, inaccuracies, and uncertainty of everyday language to achieve an Archimedean vantage. The clear view of uses that produce meaning involves travel into the plurality of language-games that compose what we think of as language. Because this plurality is not reducible to some underlying, unifying grammar, what might be termed a "conventional description" of a painting, an action, a book, or anything that requires understanding might be orthodox in one language-game and viewed and responded to as novel, provocative, humorous, or absurd in another.

The descriptions Wittgenstein (1958b) conceives as issuing from the philosopher's concern with "seeing connexions" and "finding and inventing *intermediate cases*" involve critical discernment and peripatetic action (sec. 122). Recognizing the perceptual activity and legwork that lead to philosophical descriptions is the beginning of a response to those who regard Wittgenstein's work as conservative and therefore outside the province of political theory. Generally, the conservative charge against Wittgenstein's philosophy emerges from a static or even aspect-blind reading of our ordinary relation to language-games.

III. CALLING WITTGENSTEIN A CONSERVATIVE

Political theory as an activity begins with the question that exposes an inner affinity with anarchism: Are politics and government necessary? Once the question is raised, what was invisible, the conventionality or historicity of politics as a form of life, is made visible. Also brought to view is theory's critical regard for tradition. Human beings are not hardwired for politics; the *polis* is not natural or necessary; rather, political life and government are recognized as convenient, traditional, and relatively just ways of organizing ourselves collectively. But it was not always so. And it might not always be so. Aeschylus's *Oresteian Trilogy* is a dramatic re-presentation of the emergence of political society in an explicitly juridical form from the collapse of an older tribal order founded upon and animated by an increasingly untenable definition of justice as vengeance. Plato's *Republic* articulates an argument for the necessity of a Noble Lie to hide the convenience and arbitrariness or untruth at the base of any political order. The veil of illusion produced by the lie works to impose the stability of absolute truth on a conventional order, here a city, which undergoes change with every birth and death. As Plato shows, this works well for the citizens of this political society, but philosophers and theorists cannot sustain the inner logical contradiction of a truth *polis* founded upon deception. The *kallipolis* is less a victim of eugenic miscalculation than a logical implosion that illuminates the essential tension between truth and politics. This becomes the reason for philosophers and theorists to step outside the city: Truth must be protected from the corruption of politics.

For our purposes it is enough to see and acknowledge the historical origin of politics. The consequence is equally clear: If politics has a historical origin, then it could have (or has had) a historical terminus. Wittgenstein provides insight into the consequences of this temporality for the activity of theorizing politics in the twentieth century. Broadly, the argument I will cull from Wittgenstein is that if politics has ceased being the predominant form of order and has become a mode of resistance against bureaucratic formalism and statism, then the activity of theorizing politics has to be similarly transformed from a fixed perceptual stance to a traveling perceptual performance.[8]

One reason Wittgenstein is not accepted as anything more than an "underlaborer" or clarifier of language in the discourse of contemporary political theory is because both detractors and sympathetic readers have labeled his philosophy "Conservative."[9] The charge of conservatism drives the thought and thinker so categorized to the periphery of the activity of theorizing politics. "The truth of political theory is political freedom," wrote Neumann (1957) in a statement that is emblematic for those identified as critical theorists. "From this follows one basic postulate," he continues. "Since no political system can realize political freedom fully, political theory must by necessity be critical. It cannot justify and legitimize a concrete political system; it must be critical of it. A conformist political theory is no theory" (162). There are two points to be made here in response to Neumann. First, his characterization of political theory's relation to political freedom is eloquent and accurate. This is true also of the conclusion that "a conformist theory is no theory." But, second, this identification of theory and political critique gives rise to the rhetorical tactic plied against Wittgenstein. What I will show is that Wittgenstein's theorizing is not conservative; his descriptivism entails and even demands a life devoted to nonconformity; and the conventions he exposes at the base of all human languages are the source of political and critical freedom.

The charge of conservatism has been cast against Wittgenstein in both existential and philosophical terms.[10] Often these terms are employed indiscriminately so that an anecdote about Wittgenstein's personal conservatism is read into his remarks on what a philosopher can do (describe the world) and should avoid trying to do (providing theoretical explanations for phenomena). I tend to disagree with both applications of conservatism to Wittgenstein, but I stage a more energetic defense of his philosophy.

For some critics of Wittgenstein, his philosophical worldview is dominated by a nostalgic and ideological desire to return to the Vienna fin de siècle that encouraged his industrialist father's financial and assimilative successes. It has been argued by the cultural historian Nyíri and the philosopher von Wright, for example, that Wittgenstein's aristocratic upbringing, his family ties to the Hapsburg Empire, education, friendships, and his readings of Spengler, Dostoyevsky, Tolstoy, and the anti-Semitic misogynist Otto Weininger, reveal a deep affinity for or consistency with conservative tradition and thought. However, similarly anecdotal evidence pertaining to Wittgenstein's friendships with a number of Communist thinkers and activists, his avowed indebtedness to the radical economist Piero Sraffa, along with his never realized plans to move to the Soviet Union to become a laborer or field hand, could lead to a far different conclusion about his personal politics, as Janik (1989) has observed in response to Nyíri's work.

What I wish to account for is the vituperation and slander that often accompanies the charge of conservatism directed at Wittgenstein. The malicious quality of the claims about Wittgenstein's personal politics serves to hide the thinness of the scholarship employed for substantiation. Full biographical studies produced by Ray Monk and Brian McGuinness, as examples, come to no conclusion about Wittgenstein's political views (although Monk tends to highlight radical trends in Wittgenstein's philosophical and occasional remarks). Most often the evidence adduced to back an assertion about Wittgenstein's political and religious proclivities is biographical, circumstantial, associative, and extremely selective.[11] Moreover, these sorts of arguments about Wittgenstein's personal politics, whether approving or disapproving, are as insignificant for shedding light on his philosophy as they are unsubstantiated. They reveal little or nothing about Wittgenstein and conservatism; rather, they are expressed usually as part of a larger claim – about philosophy's intrinsic radicalness or conservatism, the political trends that originated in Vienna fin de siècle, or the nature of modernity, postmodernity, sexuality, and so on – or an *ad hominem* attack on Wittgenstein's "temperament."[12]

Finally, the suspicion bred around Wittgenstein in the circles of political and social theory breaks down the ideological line separating Conservatism from Fascism and Nazism. Often, Wittgenstein is made to look more sympathetic to Hitlerian politics than disciples like Heidegger, Carl Schmitt, collaborators like Paul de Man, or attempted accommodationists like T. W. Adorno and others.[13] A particularly vivid example of this tactic of tying Wittgenstein's philosophy (and here the early philosophy of the *Tractatus*) to Hitlerian politics is included in a study of modernism.

> In the early Wittgenstein of the *Tractatus* we see that curious phenomenon of a *depersonalized subjectivism* that underlies so much of twentieth-century culture. He thought he had achieved the "final solution," as he said in his preface, to the problems of philosophy, just as, though it is extremely doubtful he ever read the preface of the *Tractatus*, a certain failed Viennese painter and would-be architect, Adolph Hitler, later thought he could achieve a German radical "foundationalism" through a "final solution" of genocide. (Rochberg-Halton 1986: 242–3)

Though the author goes on to distinguish the "diabolical" Hitler from the "ethical" Wittgenstein, the latter's nominalism is held up as an exemplification of the twentieth-century culture that replaced the active subject capable of political and moral dissent with a passive subject, prone to silent spiritualism, who is incapable of being anything more than a victim of or spectator to atrocity.

For political and social theorists (and here Marcuse and Gellner figure most prominently) the descriptivism and conventionalism of Wittgenstein's philosophy is held suspect as a relativistic, politically disengaged, passive and uncritical support for the mutilated language of the status quo. At base, Marcuse and Gellner offer a defense for universal foundations supporting theory's claim to judgment. They contended that effective political criticism – philosophical criticism of politics, especially the politics of totalitarianism – is engendered from the epistemologically or dialectically elevated perspective of the epic theorist. Marcuse describes the origin of philosophy in terms of the tension between truth's universality and the fact it is apprehensible by only a privileged minority. This minority of philosophers then seeks to translate this truth into practice. That is, philosophical thought, characterized as abstract, unfolds as a political discourse critical of existing institutions revealed to be oppressive. We are to see abstraction as the source of universality any critical judgment requires to stand apart from the ephemeral and corrupt political realm. "Paradoxically," Marcuse (1964) continues, "it is precisely the critical intent in philosophic thought which leads to the idealist purification – a critical intent which aims at the empirical world as a whole, and not merely at certain modes of thinking or behaving within it" (134–5).

For Marcuse, the hostility of the political world of advanced industrial capitalism to philosophy necessitates an epistemological retreat that both establishes the primacy of thought, and preserves its purity and critical-ness from corruption and co-optation. A necessary retreat from politics by philosophers, the lived experience of émigré thinkers like Marcuse, engenders the ideal purity that then becomes the epistemologically privileged foundation of political theory's critical relation to politics. This foundation anchors theory as it turns toward the relativism and fetish-ism of facts that characterize politics. To weaken this foundation, which is what Marcuse claims Wittgenstein is doing quite intentionally, is to naively replicate the antiphilosophical tactics of totalitarianism.

What philosophers, political theorists, and historians focus upon when they label Wittgenstein's philosophy, and by implication his personal politics, "conservative" is this remark from the *Philosophical Investigations*:

> Philosophy may in no way interfere with the actual use of language; it can in the end only describe it.
>
> For it cannot give it any foundation either.
>
> It leaves everything as it is. (1958b: sec. 124)

In this, these critics are missing the critical tenor of the remark: It was directed against forms of epistemological hubris embraced by philoso-phers. To argue that philosophy cannot give language a foundation, nor discover or uncover one, certainly does not leave "everything as it is" for practicing philosophers.[14] The very idea of a First Philosophy, for one, would be affected and transformed. Wittgenstein's remark needs to be contextualized as part of a sustained dispute, within the language-game of philosophy, against the idea that ordinary language can be somehow transcended, purified, or have its underlying logical or pre-Babelian form revealed by philosophers and theologians armed with special techniques or a privileged stance outside of language.

Neither Wittgenstein's personality and his personal history nor his phil-osophical efforts to break the epistemological and metaphysical escapist habits of philosophers are intrinsically conservative. That Wittgenstein's philosophy "leaves everything as it is" would be thought impossible to take literally if not for the example of Marcuse. In the remark, Wittgenstein signals a transformation of the practice of philosophy to respond to the events of the twentieth century that distorted the justness of Western collective existence and shattered the culture. Although it is true that Wittgenstein tended to express these transformations using the imagery of Spengler – that is, the decline of a vibrant, creative culture marked by great music and art toward an increasingly tame civilization beholden to the authority of science – versions of these views taken to be proof positive of conservatism were shared by many of his critics, including Marcuse, with radical political pedigrees.

IV. WITTGENSTEIN'S NON-CONSERVATIVE THEORIZING

My contention is that Wittgenstein's challenges to the fixed and privileged perspective so central to the self-image of the epic theorist is one strong reason behind attempts to exclude his work from social and political theory. As I have noted, a common element animating the charge of conservatism is the "passive subject" he purportedly created. To me, this criticism is a form of projection. Wittgenstein is accused of fixing people within the confines of language-games and their traditions. This condition, so the criticism goes, renders them hopelessly relativistic and incapable of making judgments and criticisms of perceived injustices that occur both within their particular language-game and in other language-games or cultures. This criticism of Wittgenstein is a kind of projection because it is designed to preserve the putative and privileged fixity of the epic perspective. That is to say, the entrapment of theorists to their fixed, epic self-image is expressed in the inability to see the motion or horizontal freedom of the Wittgensteinian theorist. From the other direction, the travel between language-games enjoyed by Wittgenstein in the pages of the *Philosophical Investigations* serves to illuminate, by contrast, the orthodoxy of the epic theorist wedded to a selective and overly romanticized historical tradition that might appear conservative to some.

Wittgenstein signals a return to the Socratic. This new take on the pre-Platonic is necessary if the activity of theorizing politics is to survive as something other than a historical enterprise. The Socratic image of theorizing is immanent. That is, it occurs within the city with no pretense to a transcendent or untimely perspective apart from the life of other citizens. It is peripatetic. The fixed Olympian height presented by Plato as a way of preserving the Truth of philosophy is traded in for a mobile existence that accentuates the perceptual basis of theorizing.[15] And, finally, the Socratic image of theorizing is critical. The task is to provoke thought in others and reawaken their intellectual powers. For Wittgenstein (1980b), the sleep inducer of the twentieth century is Science and the notion of ineluctable progress associated with science's authority.[16]

102

If there is a neglected aspect of Wittgenstein's work, then it must be the place of science in his philosophical and cultural perspective. Wittgenstein trained as an engineer prior to coming to philosophy. When he first met Bertrand Russell he identified himself as an "aeronaut." The relationship between science and philosophy was a theme that united the *Tractatus* and the *Philosophical Investigations*, the early and latter Wittgenstein.[17]

Indeed, one way of gauging the turns in Wittgenstein's thinking between the *Tractatus* and the *Philosophical Investigations* is by foregrounding the remarks on science. While under the influence of Spengler's *Decline of the West*, an influence exhibited in the remarks from the early 1930s, Wittgenstein conceived of philosophy's role in relation to science as one of writing "the synopsis of trivialities." These trivialities were any new facts discovered by scientists that were then reported to the public in simplistic, journalistic form. For Wittgenstein, following Spengler, a sure sign of culture's degeneration is when the importance of the arts and the idea of cultural genius were defined reductively in terms of their service to science, mechanics, and mathematics (Monk 1990: 298–301). It is important to note that Wittgenstein never accepted the scientism of Logical Positivism. He contended consistently that although philosophy may serve to set the logical limits of the world of facts and offer a coherent picture of reality useful to scientists, philosophy could never adopt the methods of science. Nor should it. Science seeks answers to questions like: "What is the specific gravity of hydrogen?" Philosophy is concerned, by contrast, with grammatical investigations of the sort presented by Augustine in his reflections on the nature of time. "Something that we know when no one asks us, but no longer know when we are supposed to give an account of it, and is something we need to *remind* ourselves of" (1958b: sec. 89).[18] Over the two decades of work that culminated in the *Philosophical Investigations*, Wittgenstein turned away from this conception of philosophy as the logical clarifier in service to science and toward an ethical attack on the alliance between the scientific establishment and the military. His hope was that the realities attending the development and use of atomic weapons might break the public's quiet and unquestioning romance with the promise of science (1980b: 49). If science were to remain on a pedestal free from ethical and political scrutiny, humanity would be left with a "truly apocalyptic view of the world" (Monk 1990: 484–8).

Significantly, Wittgenstein conceived of science critically as a conservative force in the culture.[19] Its conservative character, he believed, had large and dangerous consequences. In a remark from 1930, Wittgenstein observed, "Man has to awaken to wonder – and so perhaps do peoples. Science is a way of sending him to sleep again" (1980b: 5). For philosophy to diagnose this danger, it had to remain free from the seductions of science. Resisting science is an element common to the *Tractatus* and the *Philosophical Investigations*. The *Tractatus* was a work honored by members of the Vienna Circle as a model of how philosophy should function to divest science of any metaphysical tendencies. But Wittgenstein maintained a clear division between science and philosophy throughout the *Tractatus*; they were presented as logically distinct orders of discourse where philosophy, a second-order enterprise, perceives the limits of natural science. Philosophy does not affect or circumscribe the actual activity of science; rather, in a claim reminiscent of Kant, what philosophy does is observe the logical disjunction between the propositions of science, on the one hand, and the metaphysical realm "whereof one cannot speak," on the other (Wittgenstein 1922: 6.53–7).

Where the later Wittgenstein refers to natural science it is to distinguish it from other language-games (ethics, aesthetics, and so on). Science is demarcated as a neighborhood in the city of language whose effects bleed across its edges and color the entire culture in dark hues. For Wittgenstein, science is a coercive, pacifying force in the culture. The Socratic tenor of Wittgenstein's work is especially pronounced here. If science puts us to sleep, then philosophy must serve to wake us up. But first philosophy must resist the sedating cup offered by science.[20]

Philosophy's relation to science remains diagnostic in the *Philosophical Investigations*. Philosophy can distinguish between good science (represented by Faraday's *The Chemical History of a Candle*) and bad science (works that popularize and simplify scientific discovery, acknowledge and make visible science's inner conservatism, as for example in the historical pull of science away from the "abnormal" and toward the "normal" observed by Kuhn), but cannot reform the activity (1980b: 42; Glock 1996: 341–5). Although philosophy possesses neither an epistemologically privileged nor culturally authoritative vantage in relation to science, it can make visible science's limitations and the conventional foundation it shares with all other human practices. The leveling effect of this idol destruction is unmistakable. The critical character of philosophical observation and description is exposed in this relation between philosophy and science. It is a point of convergence between the philosophical project of Wittgenstein and that of his harshest critic, Marcuse.

V. The Language of Bureaucracy

There is a relation between science and bureaucracy that Wittgenstein addresses critically, though indirectly. This relation is achieved through a common attenuation of language and meaning. That is, all that is language is reduced to communications establishing clear ties between words and objects. There is also a common goal or consequence of scientific and bureaucratic activities and that is the acceleration of the pace of everyday life. The word–object relation that is the focus of the philosophy of language animating science and bureaucracy facilitates this speeding up of things. That is, language is conceived in science and bureaucracy as a tool designed to re-present and communicate features of the physical world. The sinews of definition accomplish the attachment of language to reality: The meaning of a word is derived from the object it re-presents. Meaning is only obscured and distorted when language is used creatively to express things not found in physical reality. Expressions pertaining to time, God, or love, as examples, lead science, philosophy, and organizations away from reality and toward metaphysics, away from things and toward chimeras, and away from the straight line from sign to signified and toward inefficient meandering. As we know from Arendt's analysis of Eichmann's language and its dearth of categories and room for ethical reflection, the distance between word and object, and the speed of life, are not a benign feature of an "objective" or "professional" science and bureaucracy; rather, they are malignancies that efface the ethical regard for others and then create the conditions necessary for efficient killing by factory methods or by the flash, heat, and fallout of nuclear weapons.

There is no space to recount the analyses of bureaucracy and science presented by Weber, Arendt, Marcuse, Habermas, Levinas, Bauman, and others. What I need to show here is Wittgenstein's critical powers at work against a view of language and philosophy that can lead to and justify inhumanity by degrading thinking and obscuring vision with distance. Bureaucracies supplant the transparency of conventions – a quality that permits travel through language-games – and posit in their place formalized, opaque rules. As a consequence, paths to thought, sight, and wisdom are closed off. Hermeticism prevents the wider view sought by Wittgenstein through travel by enforcing regulated paths to defined goals that enhance speed and efficiency, the core values of modernity. Bureaucracies, then, can be thought of best as language-games that succeed by reducing improvisational play within their boundaries and mobility to an outside where the value Wittgenstein thought central to the philosopher's way of life, slowness, could be cultivated and serve as a contrastive perspective.[21] The creeping of bureaucracy into philosophy is an undercurrent of Wittgenstein's critical responses to the stultifying effect of Logical Positivism's program to disenchant philosophical language by reducing meaning to the logical symmetry of word to object relations. In this, "philosophers use a language that is already deformed as though by shoes that are too tight" (1980b: 41).

A second point to be raised, then, is that these critical encounters between Wittgenstein and science and bureaucracy can be framed as an exercise in self-criticism. But such exercises have themselves been taken as indication of Wittgenstein's conservative proclivities. In condemning the soporific effects of faith in the inevitability of scientific progress and the values of speed and efficiency attendant to bureaucratization, Wittgenstein also encounters the simplistic, static picture of language presented in the *Tractatus*. As mystical as portions of that work were, it was nevertheless held up by proponents of Logical Positivism and Empiricism as an exemplar of the worldview they embraced. As noted, many of the criticisms of Wittgenstein expressed by those who see him as conservative turn on the remarks that feature individual transformation and improvement as conforming responses to forces in the world. The changes I make, according to this view, are designed to make myself fit in and become more acceptable to the world. The self-criticism Wittgenstein performs in the *Philosophical Investigations*, together with his desire to have the new book published with the *Tractatus*, is not an act of conformity, however; rather, it should be read as part of a defense of eccentricity philosophy must embrace and live. This defense is similar to the argument of J. S. Mill, but Wittgenstein conceives it as a mode of awakening from a sleep induced by science that occurs both personally in the philosopher opposed to the pandering to science by fellow (Positivist and Empiricist) philosophers, and also in a newly enervated civilization that creates a culture.

How does bureaucracy, described by Weber as the embodiment of goal-oriented rationality, use language? The language of bureaucracy gives shape to and then reflects discipline and hierarchy. It engenders distance as a tool for administrative efficiency (and here we think of the distance between state bureaucracies and citizens, between professionals and clients, or even in the clinical gaze of the physician).[22] Bureaucracy's language as the expression of instrumental reason, for Marcuse, turns citizens into "objects of administration." It feminizes the public realm by cultivating "qualities of dependence, submissiveness, and attentiveness" in men and women, bureaucrats and clients (Ferguson 1984; Hartsock 1997). The goal of bureaucratic organizations is to create a stable and efficient state in service to a capitalist economy. For Arendt, following Weber, this stability is achieved by a rational-legal system that eliminates the unpredictable element of tradition or convention-based political life with organizations designed to enforce laws. The police and legal professions designated as their enforcers, in turn, distinguish laws from conventions.

Bureaucratic language is performative and the effect is to eliminate public space and domesticate or tame what counts as public action. In this, bureaucracies possess linguistic mechanisms that render occupants, even political theorists, blind to their pervasiveness and insensible to their coercion. As Ferguson (1984: 81–2) has noted, bureaucracies in the form of administrative discourse disarm political theory by attacking speculative thinking as time consuming and unremunerative, eschewing the language of critical self-reflection as an antimanagerial lexicon and activity, and "rebuffing" political change by making its own conventions appear natural, necessary, and scientific. Marcuse accuses Wittgenstein and ordinary language philosophy in general of complicity in achieving the bureaucratic goal of emasculating the public and leading philosophy into political quietism. Marcuse characterized this silence memorably as a brand of "academic sado-masochism, self-humiliation, and self-denunciation of the intellectual."[23] However, as in the area of criticism of the authority of science in the contemporary age, there are points of deep affinity between Wittgenstein and Marcuse that escaped the notice of the latter. The effect of bureaucratic language on citizens/clients is immobilization by formalized domination and the regulation and reduction of the space available for action. The thrust of Wittgenstein's work is to show philosophy to be an antibureaucratic language-game and a way of life that is a marked contrast to the disciplinary constraints and objectifications lived by bureaucrat and client alike. But therapy needed to be performed for this contrast to be fully realized by philosophers trapped in a conception of language and truth as merely representational. Most often in treatments of Wittgenstein's work, his criticisms of metaphysical philosophy as "a house of cards," his willingness to abandon philosophical problems to achieve personal peace, and the advice he gave students to resist the temptation to become professors of philosophy are emphasized. But the larger effect of these insights and admonitions of Wittgenstein for philosophizing and theorizing is that they evince or disclose language as a varied, traversable, changing landscape that can be neither transcended nor burrowed into.

These criticisms, therapies, and the enlarged conception of language they presume give way to a deep passion for the freedom or antidogmatism and the humanizing effects the philosophical style of life afforded the practitioner. This point can be developed through remarks that feature what Wittgenstein approved of in philosophy and what, we can surmise, drew him back to his philosophical writings even as the hope to publish the *Philosophical Investigations* faded.

"Philosophy, as we use the word, is a fight against the fascination which forms of expression exert on us" (1958a: 27). As we travel through the city of language, we confront inequities among conventions. Some conventions are, for us, more rigid than others; still others are presented as authoritative and contain elements of coercion. There are language-games that restrict mobility and hold us captive. Bureaucracy can be taken as such a language-game, but we also need to see the effect of bureaucracy on other games. The stability and instrumental rationality celebrated in bureaucracy colonize or have resonance in other language-games. This force of homogenization across the language landscape is difficult to measure, but it can be gleaned in the postmodern/poststructural response that emphasizes play and the indeterminacy of conventions (rules regarding signification, for example). If we take postmodernism as a philosophical expression of resistance to bureaucratization, one effect is to highlight Wittgenstein's role as a progenitor of this orientation and the antibureaucratic tenor of his remarks on conventions.[24] Indeed, the ability to travel and to cultivate disagreement not only runs against the goal of bureaucracy, but it is the very form of politics today.[25]

There are an internal and an external dimension to Wittgenstein's response to the bureaucratic spirit of the age. The internal response is coordinated with remarks critical of the limited view of language as propositional in form and representational in effect. Here Wittgenstein presents a more expansive and active view of language as composed of various uses and games. The external response is perhaps described best as the antibureaucratic character of philosophy itself. Philosophy/theory stands as an alternative to the static, regulated form human life takes when bureaucratization is successful. To retain the character of this alternative style of life "our only task is to be just. That is, we must only point out and resolve the injustices of philosophy, and not posit new parties – and creeds" (Wittgenstein 1993: 181).

VI. CONCLUSION

Wittgenstein's critical assessment of the role of science, and, by extension, bureaucracy, in contemporary culture does more than signal the non-conservative character of his philosophy, and, by implication, the non-conservatism of his impact on theorizing politics. It also raises the question: Where *in the world* (since there is no stepping out of it, no transcendence from it) does criticism come from? Those like Nyíri claim that Wittgenstein's conservatism is of both the existential and philosophical variety. That is, the argument goes, Wittgenstein was personally predisposed to, and philosophically invested in, the avoidance of criticism, the acceptance of what is before us, and an overemphasis on the agreements that underlie and give shape to forms of life. This focus on agreement, then, renders Wittgenstein's philosophy blind to disagreement and incapable of conceiving of criticisms of social practices while we are engaged in them.[26]

Wittgenstein locates himself and humanity in the hurly-burly of language. Philosophers have been unique in their mistaken belief that they have a privileged place hovering above language, but all they have actually managed to do is extrapolate static pieces of language and equally static examples to illuminate the putative stability of these pieces. Since the source of criticism cannot be the contrast between the absolute and the relative, the general and the particular, the privileged and the unprivileged, the truthful and the opinionated, and since criticism does exist in the world, the source must lie elsewhere. Wittgenstein finds it in motion among language-games. This motion is made conspicuous by its absence from the philosophical views of those who claim Wittgenstein conservative.

The charge of conservatism leveled against Wittgenstein's philosophy relies on an image of the philosopher as existing within a language-game that resembles a prison. Criticism is considered inconceivable because, so the charge continues, Wittgenstein eliminates those higher levels of conceptualization that distinguish philosophical heights from the ordinary. This is accurate only if a philosopher finds herself or himself anchored in one language-game for a lifetime, and this is not the world Wittgenstein describes. He posits a plurality of language-games, themselves expanding and contracting, abutting and overlapping, whose rules – even those that distinguish one language-game from another – are permeable. The peregrinations of philosophers, as well as others, engender notice of differences between language-games. These differences among the constellation of language-games one travels throughout life are both the source of criticism and what we might call individuality.

The implication of Wittgenstein's perspective for political theory is that he exposes conservatism, a celebration of a form of nationalism or disciplinarity, in the fixity of the political theorist. Of course the image of the theorist on the mountaintop, on society's periphery, as an exile, as well-fed and clothed *Homo sacer*, is a metaphor or allegory for the uniqueness of the theorist's perspective in comparison with that of the citizen. Wittgenstein's criticism of the epic self-image of the theorist responds to the ethical blindness encouraged by the fixity and transcendence this image rests upon. He counters with a traveling image that is immanent and distinctive. This peripatetic counterimage, so important for theorizing in the twentieth and twenty-first centuries, is the subject of the next two chapters.

Notes

1. There are many ways to measure the absence of Wittgenstein in Political Theory. One I will mention here is the neglect of Wittgenstein in a chapter devoted to ordinary language philosophy by the usually thorough Dallmayr (1984) in his survey, *Language and Politics: Why Does Language Matter to Political Philosophy?*

2. Despite Wittgenstein's remarks leading us to see the surface character of both language-games and forms of life, surface and depth grammar, Hilary Putnam, for one, contends that in Wittgenstein you find a philosopher who is dismissive of the importance of conventions for understanding language and action. What *is* important, according to Putnam's reading, is the older and deeper regulative and logical role played by the natural limitations on human life embodied in the very idea of a form of life. My response to Putnam is that his is a reading of the *Philosophical Investigations* is overly influenced by the *Tractatus*'s search for the logical form underlying all propositions. Here, in Putnam (and other analytic philosophers responding to Wittgenstein's later work), logical form is presented as synonymous with form of life. As I will show, forms of life have a multiplicity and relative impermanence and fluidity when compared with logical form. See Putnam (1981) and the response by Shusterman (1986).

3. Cited in O'Connor (2002: 33). What we are looking at when we get to the hard riverbank are the "frame conditions" of language. These "include (a) general regularities concerning the world around us (b) biological and anthropological facts about humans, and (c) sociohistorical facts," O'Connor notes. Frame conditions are features of our language, life, and world that are so familiar and general they go unnoticed, much less questioned. "The *facts* of human natural history," writes Wittgenstein, "that throw light on our problem, are difficult for us to find out, for our talk *passes them by*, it is occupied with different things. (In the same way we tell someone: 'Go into the shop and buy . . .' not: 'Put your left foot in front of your right foot etc. etc., then put the coins down on the counter etc. etc.'" Cited in O'Connor (2002: 31–2). Frame conditions have been observed as the area of affinity between Wittgenstein

and Phenomenology where the latter seems to be arguing for a philosophical method that would permit philosophers access to this deep, underlying bedrock of *things themselves*. See, for example, Gier (1981). But Wittgenstein's remarks on how to see what is ordinarily so familiar as to be invisible are a simple matter of "rearranging particulars." This is accomplished not through phenomenological processes of bracketing and reduction, but through ethnomethodological "breaching experiments" that lead us to reflect on what we assume when we say something or engage in the "artful techniques for creating meaning" in ordinary circumstances like the breakfast table. See Garfinkel (1967).

4. O'Connor's treatment of this material is quite good (2002: 29–34). As O'Connor notes, Glock's (1996: 135–9) entry on "framework" is essential reading.

5. The idea that Wittgenstein evades idealism is a contentious point in the literature that cleaves into two readings of his *Philosophical Investigations*: the transcendental/Kantian reading and the conventional/post-Kantian reading. I fall into the second camp that contends that the institutions, behaviors, language uses are not regulated by rigid, underlying "hardness of the logical must" (1958b: sec. 437); rather, these features of our world are shaped by an interaction between arbitrary and contingent conventions, lessons of upbringing and natural history, and our very human need and agreement for order. "It is in language," after all, "that an expectation and its fulfillment make contact (1958b: sec. 445).

6. "Solipsism," notes Sass (1994), "was one of Wittgenstein's most central examples of a metaphysical or philosophical disease, a disease born not of ignorance or carelessness but of abstraction, self consciousness, and disengagement from practical and social activity" (8–9).

7. Through the therapy of returning to ordinary language, Wittgenstein "combats the professionalization of philosophy, that is, its reduction to the technical (that is, positivist) discourse of a specialty. More generally, he rejects the purifying process that, by eliminating the ordinary use of language (everyday language), makes it possible for science to produce and master an artificial language ... He attacks the presumption that leads philosophy to proceed 'as if' it gave meaning to ordinary use, and to suppose that it has its own place from which it can reflect on the everyday." What philosophers lose in expertise (the illusion of domination over language) they gain in mobility (a freedom from fixity). See de Certeau (1984: 8–12).

8. Theory, in Wittgenstein, is a problematic term that I will address further. At this point, however, I want to note that conventionalism or antifoundationalism in Wittgenstein is a liberating prelude to critical political thought. Once the order of things is revealed as artifact, then structural or behavioral change is neither unnatural nor humanly impossible. To be sure, one of the great difficulties of describing a conventional world, Wittgenstein shows, is capturing the malleability of order while avoiding the seductions of static representations. A vocabulary has to be fashioned for this work that needs to be sufficiently ordinary to avoid becoming another excuse for philosophical hermeticism in which "language goes on holiday." I think Wittgenstein succeeds in this therapeutic project by carefully combining technical vocabulary – "perspicuous representation," "changing aspects," "continuous seeing," and so on – with a healthy diet of examples. For theory, the Wittgensteinian effect is one where the activity is released from epic fixity by severing its onto-theological moorings and heroic self-image as earthly surrogate for the Divine. Theory becomes theorizing, and it is freed to do things other than try to uncover

111

hidden sources of unity beneath the surface of political orders. See the discussion of the theological roots of theory offered by Taylor (1991).

9. Ball (1997), for example, sees Wittgenstein's significance for political theory as "more meliorist than conservative," but his characterization of ordinary language philosophy in general and Wittgenstein in particular emphasizes the sanguine or "humble task" of clarifying the language of politics. And this task leads political theory in an apolitical direction. "This narrowing not only blinded political theorists to the fact that meaning and usage change from one age and generation to the next, but it also led them to believe their enterprise to be a politically neutral one" (32–3).

10. Gellner (1959; 1998); Nyíri (1976; 1981; 1982; 1986); Marcuse (1964). See the assessments developed in: Wertheimer (1976); Lyas (1982); Lugg (1985); Schulte (1986); Jones (1986); Hymers (2000); and Cerbone (2003).

11. See, for example, Moran (1972); Levi (1978–9); Eagleton (1982); and in a parody of this sort of scholarship, Janik (1989).

12. This name calling that then degenerated into amateur psychological evaluations of Wittgenstein was begun by Bertrand Russell who called Wittgenstein "mad," but in an admiring way. Later, after the friendship between Wittgenstein and Russell deteriorated, Russell settled on "schizophrenic" as the apt descriptive term. More recently, in an interesting and insightful article on creativity and obsession, Oliver Sacks speculated on Wittgenstein's "autism" and Gellner then adopted this designation, though with far less neurological insight.

13. There is a book by Cornish (1998), touted as "historical research," that claims the anti-Semitism leading to the Final Solution was the consequence of a schoolyard squabble between Hitler and Wittgenstein. The work goes on to claim that Wittgenstein was a Stalinist spy, and that both Hitler and Wittgenstein shared a common philosophical interest in occultism. As absurd and conspiratorial as this argument is, I think some of the assertions are unvarnished renditions of claims put forth by various scholars regarding Wittgenstein's philosophy and politics. This particular line of argument is built upon one historically accurate anecdote: Hitler and Wittgenstein were both born in 1889, and attended the same high school.
On Adorno, see the discussion of a review he wrote for the monthly journal, *Die Musik*, that Hannah Arendt and Karl Jaspers (1992) described as part of "his unsuccessful attempt to align himself with the regime in 1933 . . ." (633–46).

14. See Shusterman's (1997) useful comparison of Dewey, Wittgenstein, and Foucault on "philosophical living as somatic" (47). The effect of the comparison is a highlighting of Wittgenstein's remarks on philosophy as a style of life where the goal is the freedom of the philosopher, as opposed to some notion of Truth. Also see the Wittgensteinian shape of Hadot's (1995) reading of ancient philosophy. Hadot describes the influence of Wittgenstein on his reading and thinking in the volume's "Postscript."

15. It is worth recalling that Wittgenstein was taking this Socratic path without the philo-tyrannical ambitions that arose with what Arendt described as Heidegger's temporary "change of residence" from the philosopher's mountaintop to the ranks of the Nazi Party. Wittgenstein's example is, at the very least, an antidote for the tendency of theorists and philosophers to "tarry with the negative" of Heidegger's example by reifying the putative purity of epistemological heights in relation to the corruption of politics. Arendt is guilty of this kind of mirroring response to trauma described by Hegel. See Žižek (2001: 47).

16. "The truly apocalyptic view of the world is that things do *not* repeat themselves. It isn't absurd, e.g., to believe that the age of science and technology is the beginning of the end for humanity; that the idea of great progress is a delusion, along with the idea that the truth will ultimately be known; that there is nothing good or desirable about scientific knowledge and that mankind, in seeking it, is falling into a trap. It is by no means obvious that this is not how things are" (56).

17. The consideration of philosophy's critical relation to the cultural optimism invested in science's promise ("scientism") unites Wittgenstein with his predecessor Nietzsche and his contemporary, Heidegger. Like Nietzsche, Wittgenstein believes philosophy can expose "the unshakable faith that thought, using the thread of causality, can penetrate the deepest abysses of being, and that thought is capable not only of knowing being but even of *correcting* it" (Nietzsche 1967: 95). See also Bearn (1997: 23–4).

18. "In the natural sciences, the nature of one's subject is often not expressed by grammar," observes Brenner (1999). "For example, when a science teacher asks about the nature of gold, she wants to be told not about how the word *gold* is used, but rather about the hidden atomic structure of the stuff called 'gold.' In philosophy, however, the subject in question will never be a kind of stuff. Never hidden, the essences investigated by philosophy will always be expressed by something already in plain view, namely the 'grammar' (as Wittgenstein calls it) of the language we speak" (5).

    We can also conceive of the difference between philosophy and science logically and in their respective relations to reality. Gunnell (1998) provides a careful taxonomy of the differences between "first-order practices" like science, and "second-order" practices like the philosophical reflection on science.

19. As his friend Rhees (1981) recalled, Wittgenstein contended that "nothing is more *conservative* than science. Science lays down railroad tracks. And for scientists it is important that their work should move along those tracks" (202).

20. "Philosophers constantly see the method of science before their eyes, and are irresistibly tempted to ask and answer questions in the way science does. This tendency is the real source of metaphysics, and leads the philosopher into complete darkness" (1958a: 18).

21. Wittgenstein's (1980b) celebrations of slowness take the forms of advice to prospective philosophers and those who will try to read his works. "In philosophy the winner of the race is the one who can run the most slowly. Or: the one who gets there the last" (34). "Sometimes a sentence can be understood only if it is read at the *right tempo*. My sentences are all supposed to be read *slowly*" (57). "This is how philosophers should salute one another: 'Take your time!'" (80).

22. "Citizens entitled to services relate to the state not primarily through political participation but by adopting a general attitude of demand – expecting to be provided for without actually wanting to fight for the necessary decisions. Their contact with the state occurs in the rooms and anterooms of bureaucracies; it is all unpolitical and indifferent, yet demanding. In a social-welfare state that above all administers, distributes and provides, the 'political' interests of citizens [are] constantly subsumed under administrative acts" (Habermas 1992: 211).

23. "In the totalitarian era," writes Marcuse (1964), "the therapeutic task of philosophy would be a political task, since the established universe of ordinary language tends to coagulate into a totally manipulated and indoctrinated universe. The politics would appear in philosophy, not a special discipline or object of analysis, but as the intent

113

of its concepts to comprehend unmutilated reality. If linguistic analysis does not contribute to such understanding; if, instead, it contributes to enclosing thought in the circle of the mutilated universe of ordinary discourse, it is at best inconsequential. And, at worst, it is an escape into the noncontroversial, the unreal, into that which is only academically controversial" (199). One could imagine Wittgenstein accusing Marcuse of a similar kind of metaphysical escapism.

24. This tenor or spirit can be seen in Wittgenstein's work as early as the pivotal year of 1930 when, as Stern (1995) has noted, the turn away from logical form internal to language and toward the way meaning is produced was realized. In that year, Wittgenstein produced a "sketch for a foreword" for his *Philosophical Remarks*. This short essay emphasizes Wittgenstein's antipathy toward the "main current of European and American civilization" that is "manifest in the industry, architecture, and music of our time, in its fascism and socialism." Reflecting Spengler's influence, Wittgenstein goes on to note how this spirit of the age is one where civilization tames culture, leading to a denigration of the arts as a form of human expression. "High" culture is replaced by "low" culture. This is where Wittgenstein finds himself: He is responding to a civilization where what passes as culture resembles a bureaucracy and the role of the artist or philosopher is not one of producing great works of expression, as the role would be in high culture, but of producing friction, the visible consequence of resistance. "A culture is like a big organization which assigns each of its members a place where he can work in the spirit of the whole; and it is perfectly fair for his power to be measured by the contribution he succeeds in making to the whole enterprise. In an age without culture on the other hand forces become fragmented and the power of an individual man is used up in overcoming opposing forces and frictional resistances; it does not show in the distance he travels but perhaps only in the heat he generates in overcoming friction" (6).

25. Janik (2003) explores this characterization of politics as conceptual conflict in his Wittgensteinian reading of Connolly's *The Terms of Political Discourse*. As Weber (1978: v. 2) observed, "Politics means conflict."

26. Cavell (1976: 44–72) labels this kind of reading of Wittgenstein's forms of life as "Manichean." See also Scheman (1996: 386–7).

CHAPTER 5

Aspect-Blindness in Religion, Philosophy, and Law: The Force of Wittgensteinian Reading

> There are times in life when the question of knowing if one can think differently than one thinks, and perceive differently than one sees, is absolutely necessary if one is to go on looking and reflecting at all.
>
> Michel Foucault (1985: 8)

I. INTRODUCTION

Aspect-blindness is a condition that Wittgenstein posits in order to create a contrast to the experience of changes in aspect. We cannot be sure if Wittgenstein is describing an actual condition – as tone deafness, or lacking a sense of humor are actual conditions likened to aspect-blindness – or if he is merely presenting the conceptual negation of seeing something as something else, a painting of a cube as a cube, for example. If it is the latter, then the matter of aspect-blindness could be settled by speculating that an aspect blind person can, when observing the Jastrow drawing of a duck/rabbit, see a duck or a rabbit, but not both; nor, and more importantly, could the person experience the paradox that comes with the expression of changing aspects, "Now I see it as . . ." This is not, in Wittgenstein's rather short series of elucidations, a fatal condition. But in comparing aspect-blindness to tone deafness and humorlessness, Wittgenstein wants us to see that the enjoyment of life is impaired by this deficiency. Literally, aspect-blindness robs the afflicted of an ability to perceive the uncanniness of the ordinary, to use Cavell's phrase, or respond to the world playfully.

Wittgenstein's project for Philosophy can be compared profitably to Kierkegaard's project for Christianity in this respect. As Kierkegaard worked to show the compatibility of Christianity with the human world, so Wittgenstein worked to show the compatibility of philosophical activity with other human activities. The result in both instances is a less grandly metaphysical Christianity and Philosophy. Yet, also in both instances, the vitality of Christianity and Philosophy were heightened as they were shown to contribute to the richness of ordinary existence. The same result can be achieved, as I have been arguing in earlier chapters, for political theory. But this would require illumination of the contributions theorizing could make to our appreciation of ordinary political existence at the expense of the epic self-image of political theory. To get to this point requires breaking from the aspect-blindness expressed in the fixity of the epic stance.

Wittgenstein suggests there is more to aspect-blindness than the service it performs in elucidating the experiences of aspect changes and continuous seeing. "The importance of this concept," Wittgenstein (1958b) writes, lies not only in its pathological quality in comparison with the healthy ability to perceive change, but also "in the connexion between the concepts of 'experiencing the meaning of a word'. For we want to ask 'What would you be missing if you did not *experience* the meaning of a word?'" (214). Mulhall (1990) has termed the linguistic equivalent of perceptual aspect-blindness, "meaning blindness" (35). I think the term suggestive, but it has the consequence of creating and perpetuating a distinction between using language and seeing that Wittgenstein was seeking to eliminate. This intimacy can be gleaned from Wittgenstein's remarks on criteria, his critical engagement with the claim that meaning is a psychological attribute as opposed to a creative achievement of language use, and his observation that playing a language-game entails a particular kind of seeing. Language-games are perceptual vantages, and the only path to enhanced perception available to humans is through travel across a range of such vantages.

Where travel is restricted, where one is wedded to one definition of "seeing," the resulting condition is aspect-blindness, the inability to experience the paradox of seeing something as something else that Wittgenstein (1958b) has called a form of entrapment. "What would a person who is blind towards these aspects be lacking? It is not absurd to answer: the power of imagination" (207). Aspect-blindness marks an inability of a philosopher or theorist to see "a conventional picture of a lion *as* a lion." A picture of a house would be viewed as an architect views a blueprint. You would not get the impression of motion when looking at

116

a photograph of a person running (1980a: 483). "The aspect blind person's failure . . . to express his awareness of an aspect change," observes Mulhall (1990), "must be seen as having a double function: it manifests his incapacity to have a specific visual experience and thereby reveals that his general relation to pictorial symbols is not that of continuous aspect perception" (32).

Aspect-blindness can be compared to a religious fundamentalist's encounter with what she or he regards as sacred scripture. No experience of the work's poetry would accompany the reading; passages that inspire reflection in others would be regurgitated faithfully as literal, uninterpretable truth. It is a passivity that probably would not continue into other perceptual events. "One doesn't 'take' what one knows as cutlery at a meal *for* cutlery," writes Wittgenstein (1958b: 195; 1967: secs. 344, 411).

Wittgenstein's concern with the experience of aspect change and, conversely, the lack of experience accompanying aspect-blindness, is viewed best as an effort to de-emphasize the certitude that arises when you mistake the language-game you are in for the entirety of language. This fixed perspective can be surmounted by walking through other language-games, or, as in the example of Nafisi's *Reading Lolita in Tehran*, with imagination inspired by reading. In travel, the embodied perceiver walks to and around objects, filling in areas of imperceptions with imagination. Seeing is not a passive, but a creative endeavor. De Certeau (1984) describes these perceptual activities in terms of "the procedures of everyday creativity," and, for Garfinkel (1967), they are "artful techniques for creating meaning." These ordinary perceptual activities are tied intimately and historically to the activity of theorizing. For the theorist or perceiver, the personal effect is measurable, for, as Wittgenstein (1980a) observed, a change in aspect involves a change in life. Most such alterations are minor, but even so they contribute to the vitality of life, and this is awe-inspiring, or should be. "What is incomprehensible is that *nothing*, and yet *everything*, has changed" (474). Aspect change, continuous seeing, and the dynamism of the world they reveal is the focus of the next chapter.

What I want to investigate in this chapter is the relation between language-games and aspect-blindness. Can some language-games be so rigid they curtail linguistic creativity extensively enough to induce aspect/meaning blindness, and vice versa? Does the experience of aspect-blindness, an experience of the onlooker and not the afflicted, give us an intimate view of the effect of ideology on perception? Here, ideology is defined in Marxian terms as a super-structural or cultural effect that masks reality and directs vision away from the social sources of pain and leaves the sufferer, a person or a class, with no recourse other than seeking relief in religion or stoicism.[1] This investigation will take the form of a reading of Plato's early dialogue, "Euthyphro," and Antonin Scalia's opinion in the case of *Michael H. v. Gerald D.*

II. EUTHYPHRO AND PIETY

"What would you be missing if you did not *experience* the meaning of a word?" There are words used daily and conventionally in our utterances and practices that involve no special sense of experience. We use them thoughtlessly, except when we are misunderstood and called upon to clarify what it is we just said. Every language-game seems to have a list of words that count as "technical jargon," or are special enough to inspire scrutiny each time they are used. "Politics" in the language-game of Political Science might be an obvious example.[2] "Holiness" or "Piety" in religious language-games are equally illustrative of words with meanings that are so contested that scrutiny is not merely employed but experienced each time they are used.

Euthyphro is an actor in a religious language-game wherein "piety" is not contested, apparently.[3] He is a prophet and an acquaintance of Socrates (Nails 2002: 152–3). When he meets Socrates at the court of the King Archon, Euthyphro has filed an indictment against his own father. The story behind the charge is that a slave or laborer in the house of Euthyphro's father killed a servant. Euthyphro's father has the slave bound and thrown in a ditch while another slave is dispatched to the Oracle for advice on how to proceed in this case. Before the slave can return, however, the murderer dies, probably of exposure, in the ditch. For this reason, Euthyphro is determined to prosecute his father for a capital offense, inviting the displeasure of not only the rest of his family who accuse Euthyphro of impiety and insanity, but momentary disbelief on the part of Socrates too.

Euthyphro's conviction that the man who died at his father's hand deserves justice, even though he is a slave and murderer, is admirable. But Socrates' questioning leads quickly to a deep problem in Euthyphro's thinking. Socrates asks, in effect, how Euthyphro has resolved the conflict he must feel between the dual obligations to his family and to his city or sense of justice. Surprisingly, Euthyphro experiences no conflict; he is possessed of a certitude that Socrates, under the circumstances, does not know whether to admire or to fear. Euthyphro's certitude rests on what we recognize today as his religious fundamentalism. He *knows* the will of the gods in this instance; he has no doubt about the piety of his action to prosecute his father for this offense, even if it leads to his father's execution; the meaning of "piety," like the meaning of Scripture or the Constitution of the United States for strict constructionists, is plain and incontestable when you lay claim to privileged knowledge of the mind of God, the Prophet, or the minds of the founders. Socrates professes a lack of such certainty in his own thinking, and so he asks Euthyphro to become his teacher.

That piety is the prosecution of wrongdoing is the first lesson offered by Euthyphro the teacher. Just as Zeus imprisoned and castrated his father for eating his children, so Euthyphro prosecutes his father for the offense of leaving his servant to die of exposure. The imitation of Zeus, the most just of all the gods, is pious. For Socrates, Euthyphro's first lesson is a failure. The form behind all examples of pious actions was not reached. All Euthyphro managed was a description of one pious action among many possibilities. The next lesson, a result of revision by Euthyphro at Socrates' request, is no better. "What is dear to the gods," asserts Euthyphro, "is pious." By implication, impiety is determined by what the gods hate. Socrates responds by observing the discord between the gods described by the poets. The gods, then, cannot be the source of unity in the definition of piety or in the universe.

Socrates tries to lead Euthyphro beyond the realm of the gods for the source of pure piety and pure impiety, but Euthyphro seems trapped, physically and conceptually, in the religious picture of reality to which he has dedicated his life, staked his reputation, and appealed to for justification for his legal action against his father. He cannot experience the conflicting meaning in his use of piety; his aspect-blindness takes on an auditory cast as well since he cannot really hear the challenges articulated by Socrates.

The path of the exchange between Socrates and Euthyphro is well known. Socrates asks for a definition of piety, and Euthyphro replies with an example that Socrates will consider inadequate.[4] What Euthyphro offers is a series of what might be taken as instantiations of piety, but they contain enough contradiction to implode logically and indicate that the essence or truth of piety has not yet been uncovered or (in Socrates' epistemology) remembered. The path will lead to *elenchus*, the eventual silencing of Euthyphro. In eristic competitions this silence would signal the victory of Socrates over his opponent. But this is no competition for Socrates; he is engaging in Philosophy. The silence of Euthyphro will be a disappointment, even though Euthyphro promised more than he, or any mortal, could possibly deliver.

But silence on Euthyphro's part is not achieved at the end. Convinced still of his grasp of piety, he leaves the conversation with Socrates to, we assume, continue his legal activities against his father. His aspect-blindness – the utter inability to "see" and feel the dual obligation Socrates and readers alike see and feel – remains not as a conviction to be admired, but as a malady in need of therapy. Following Wittgenstein, aspect and meaning blindness are experienced as entrapments in a picture not by the victim, but by the aspect- and meaning-sensing interlocutor. What the "victim" experiences is a place of intellectual rest. Critical reflection has come to an end, and the result is contentment expressed as arrogance that resists the encroachments of fear and shame emanating from outside sources. Euthyphro evades these sentiments associated with *elenchus* by parting company with Socrates.

III. Socratic Blindness

There are multiple areas of agreement between Wittgenstein and Socrates. They belong to the same tradition of peripatetic philosophers for whom the intellectual journey is not only a metaphor, but also a way of life (Hadot 1995; Shusterman 1997). However, there is a significant difference between the Socrates we know through Plato, and Wittgenstein. The *Philosophical Investigations* can be read profitably as a sustained resistance against the intellectual contentment that attends aspect-blindness. His (1958b) philosophical goal is "*complete* clarity," he writes.

> The real discovery is the one that makes me capable of stopping doing philosophy when I want to. – The one that gives philosophy peace, so that it is no longer tormented by questions which bring *itself* in question. (sec. 133)

At no point in the remarks composing this book does Wittgenstein describe "*complete* clarity" as having been achieved. The philosophical struggle against aspect-blindness is never final. Where clarity is attained it appears provisional. The struggle to see more clearly is best regarded as an integral condition of the philosopher's way of life.

There is a resting point in Socrates' orientation to philosophizing. Most often, Socrates describes this rest in terms of death and the afterlife. In death, we return to the source of unity and wisdom we left and forgot as part of the process of being born into life. If the Socrates of the dialogue "Crito" seems a bit suicidal, this can be explained by the certitude he expresses in what the afterlife has to offer. Yet, there are moments in other dialogues where speculation about the afterlife ends because glimpses are afforded by questioning in this life. Such a moment is pivotal in "Euthyphro."

The line, in the form of a question that itself distinguishes the aspect-blind Euthyphro from the meaning-sensitive Socrates, is well known. "Is the pious being loved by the gods because it is pious, or is it pious because it is loved by the gods?" The question remains a great subversive moment in the history of Philosophy because it implies in its very grammar a realm of truth and unity higher and older than, and epistemologically superior to, the realm of the gods. Priests, like Euthyphro, have settled too early and on too low a rung of the ladder of intellectual development, the question by Socrates suggests.

In the context of the dialogue, the question is asked to coax Euthyphro away from the effects of piety to piety itself and the tactic fails completely. The religiously based aspect-blindness of Euthyphro thwarts the travel required to move from his theological language-game to the perceptual vantage and change of Socrates' philosophical game. But the parameters of this game, conceived as the ultimate source of meaning, are as rigid as Euthyphro's religion. In this eidetic realm achieved by Socrates through dialectical play, the playfulness that comes across in "Euthyphro" is resistance to dogmatism. Aspect-blindness, evaded heretofore, is now embraced by Socrates. For all their differences, a deep similarity in Euthyphro the priest and Socrates the philosopher is revealed. Both conceive of language as originating in pre-linguistic ideas or thought. Fixity is therefore inevitable once the path back from the multiplicity of words and meanings is believed to be complete and culminates in the one behind the many. As Euthyphro and Socrates experience it, the source is a place of rest, of blindness rather than clarity, but also a reason to die or kill.

The record on Socrates is immensely complicated. It is difficult, for example, to reconcile the terminus of the dialogue "Euthyphro" in the true meaning of piety with the larger Socratic project, defined as ongoing even in death in the "Apology," "Crito," "Meno," and "Phaedo," of interrogating and comprehending the Oracle's claim that "no man is wiser than Socrates," or the related claim by Socrates that "all I know is I know nothing." This philosophical journey is rendered moot by the underlying belief that wisdom and truth, if they exist, are outside the province of mortals. This image of a lifelong philosophical journey requires what Wittgenstein called the "rough ground" of language use for the ground and friction requisite for walking. Yet, in his desire to establish the conceptual uniqueness and superiority of Philosophy in relation to religion, Socrates renounces the rough ground of travel and is entrapped in aspect-blindness. He says to Euthyphro, from an apparently ethereal vantage they share, "I am so desirous of your wisdom, and I concentrate my mind on it, so that no word of yours may fall to the ground."

This reflection on the exchange between Euthyphro and Socrates leads to two entwined questions: Is aspect-blindness an actual condition? Can it be reversed? The answer is "yes" to both, and we can know because Wittgenstein's philosophical work exists. From the entrapment or aspect-blindness of the picture theory of language fleshed out in the pages of the *Tractatus Logico-Philosophicus*, Wittgenstein could pronounce Philosophy's endgame had been attained, the underlying logical code of all philosophical problems discovered, the journey launched by the Oracle of Delphi had reached the shores of its Ithaca. Blind and content, Wittgenstein sat in a prisoner of war camp on the Italian border. His release from this enclosure would parallel his release from Philosophy. But he was too young, too imaginative, too traumatized, and the world around him too shattered to sustain the contentment. The opaque little corner of language in which he had encased himself gave way and the travel resumed.

IV. The Law is Blind

In a law court, for instance, the question might be raised how someone meant a word. And this can be inferred from certain facts. – It is a question of *intention*. But could how he experienced a word – the word "bank" for instance – have been significant in the same way? (Wittgenstein 1958b: 214)

The very existence of the field called Bioethics signals some remarkable transformations occurring in the world as a result of scientific and technological advancement on the one hand, and the loosening or disintegration of older forms of human organization and social roles for various reasons, on the other. The fields of philosophy and law must, to remain vital, respond to these transformations imaginatively and with the fluidity of Socrates' wanderings in the Athenian *agora*. Against the backdrop of new reproductive technologies flowing and reshaping conventions regarding sexuality, parenthood, and family life, ideological or concept-induced aspect-blindness is especially pronounced.

The 1989 Supreme Court decision in the case of *Michael H.* v. *Gerald D.* is a fine example of aspect-blindness expressed in terms of nostalgia and conservative ideology and religious values.[5] The facts of the case are fairly complicated, but they are not, as Justice Antonin Scalia described them, "extraordinary." Carole and Gerald D. were married, and Carole was having an affair with Michael H. when she became pregnant. Gerald was listed as the father on the child's birth certificate, but Carole suspected that the baby's genetic father was Michael. A blood test confirmed this. Carole left Gerald, and she and the baby girl, named Victoria, moved in with Michael. Carole then left Michael, moved in with Scott K., and prevented Michael from seeing his daughter.

In response, Michael filed a filiation action in California to establish paternity legally and gain visitation rights. The court initiated investigations to discover the child's best interests. A cross-complaint was filed on Victoria's behalf, claiming that she had more than one father and was entitled to relationships with both. By this time, Carole had moved back in with Gerald and requested a summary judgment from the court. Before this judgment could be issued, however, Carole left Gerald and moved back in with Michael. She then asked that her request for judgment be rescinded; Carole and Michael filed a motion requesting that Michael be recognized legally as Victoria's father. Before the motion could be ruled upon, Carole and Michael split up, and Carole asked that this motion not be filed. She and Victoria returned to Gerald; their marriage continues; they have two children in addition to Victoria.

The California Superior Court heard the case and ruled that Carole be awarded sole custody of Victoria, but they also permitted Michael visitation privileges *pendente lite* ("while the litigation is taking place"). Gerald responded with a request for a summary judgment on his paternity. He claimed that the California Evidence Code stipulates that paternity is presumed when a wife is living with her husband, and he is shown to be neither sterile nor impotent. Such a presumption can be challenged by blood tests, but these tests must be filed with the court within two years of the child's birth. The blood tests establishing Michael's genetic paternity were never filed. Carole and Gerald then submitted affidavits showing they were living together at the time of Victoria's birth and establishing that Gerald was not sterile or impotent. Gerald's motion for summary judgment was accepted; Michael's challenge was rejected. Michael was then denied continued visitation privileges to protect "the integrity of the family unit."

The question that came before the Supreme Court was whether Michael's right to companionship with his biological daughter, Victoria, outweigh the State of California's interest in preserving the integrity of the marriage unit. The reason for reciting the case facts at length is to show that the integrity of the family or marriage unit could be rescued only by obstinate, risible blindness on the part of the Court in reference to not only this specific case, but also to larger social trends toward greater conceptual flexibility regarding families and parenthood.

Blindness prevailed in the plurality decision authored by Justice Scalia. He begins his reasoning in support of the Superior Court's decision to deny Michael a relationship with his daughter by observing, "California law, like nature itself, makes no provision for dual fatherhood." However, had the blood test establishing Michael's paternity been filed almost ten years earlier there would be no case. The liberty interest of companionship with one's child under the Fourteenth Amendment would extend, without question, to Michael, as Victoria's father. Victoria would have, like many other children across the country, *de facto* multiple parents. The need for such expansiveness in the way we see and recognize parents is apparent in technologies that create reproductive conditions where there may be five participants in a child's birth: the egg and sperm donors, the birth mother, and the adoptive parents.

The "family unit" that Justice Scalia wishes to preserve in this case is recognizable by any fan of 1950s television or a traditional Roman Catholic or Baptist. It is husband/father/male, wife/mother/female, and their genetic/birth offspring united by state law and religious ritual. There is no room in the picture for same-sex couples, single adoptive parents, stepparents, or surrogacy arrangements. Scalia assigned himself and the courts the role of defending the family against the challenges posed by Michael H. whose sole motivation, as far as can be ascertained from the court records, was to continue his fatherly relationship with his daughter. "Whatever the merits of the guardian *ad litem*'s belief that such an arrangement can be of great psychological benefit to the child," Scalia argues in rejecting Michael's parental assertion, "the claim that a State must recognize multiple fatherhood has no support in the history or traditions of this country."

The justifications for the decision proceed on three distinct grounds that compose willful or ideological aspect-blindness: lexical, traditional, and constitutional. On the lexical front, as Justice William Brennan observed in his dissenting opinion, Scalia succeeded in attenuating Michael's liberty interest in maintaining the companionship of his daughter, an interest afforded constitutional protection to parents traditionally, by substituting "fatherhood" for "parenthood," and examining the minute range of precedents for the recognized interests a father may express when his child's mother is married to another man. Regarding the role of the Court in protecting the marriage and the family, Scalia asserts, "our traditions have protected the marital family (Gerald, Carole, and the child they acknowledge to be theirs) against the sort of claim Michael asserts." From this "marital relation," a phrase that implies an intimacy and hermeticism that flies in the face of the facts, the legitimacy of children emerges. Finally, there is constitutional support for the conceptual rigidity claimed here in reference to "the family." The liberty interest of the Fourteenth Amendment must, as Scalia reads it, accord with basic social values, history, and tradition. Such a rendering contrasts markedly with other Court rulings that have rendered the Fourteenth Amendment Due Process and Equal Protection clauses expansively to establish a right to privacy, as in *Griswold v. Connecticut*, procreation in *Skinner v. Oklahoma*, and abortion in *Roe v. Wade*. Brennan responded to this argument as well, contending that Scalia's tactic of reading the provisions of this Amendment as protecting only those liberty interests already accepted by society as one that "mocks those who, with care and purpose, wrote the Fourteenth Amendment" to execute the emancipatory effects of the Thirteenth Amendment and protect those citizens formerly held as slaves.

In exchanging "parenthood" for an overly rigid concept of "fatherhood," Justice Scalia reveals a form of dogmatism that might be taken for willful aspect-blindness. His opinion is suffused with values he derives from his Catholic religious and cultural beliefs. William Brennan was also a practicing Catholic, but he was able to put personal beliefs aside in order to issue rulings and opinions fair to people of all religious and nonreligious beliefs.[6] What we are seeing in the reasoning of a decision like *Michael H. v. Gerald D.* is the imposition of the grammar and standards of certitude of one language-game upon another. This type of conflict has been the object of analysis by Wittgenstein's student, Stephen Toulmin.

For Toulmin (and Jonsen 1988), language-games are particularized, concrete contexts, and the resolution of conflicts within these contexts are resolved best by attending to the details of the conflict in its particular context rather than appealing to thin, generalized moral theory. The context of legal reasoning, observes Toulmin, is fairly problematic because of its pervasiveness. He (1979) writes, "almost all of us have some

125

familiarity with the general rules and patterns of legal reasoning" (203). We grasp that legal arguments must be constructed with care and persuasiveness, and we possess a general idea about what the law is designed to protect, and how lawyers and courts pursue these protections. But the specifics of the language-game of law, while it abuts and overlaps with other language-games we may be familiar with, and while other practices have adapted aspects of legal reasoning, we "do grasp one fundamental feature of our procedures of legal reasoning, that trained advocates present the arguments on behalf of clients and that we are not obliged to defend ourselves" (Toulmin et al. 1979: 204). Questions of law, as distinct from questions of fact, are best left to practitioners – the denizens of the legal language-game. There is comfort in the fact we are not handing conflict resolution over to a small band of experts. Very few of our societal disputes find their way into courts of law.

The grounds for Justice Scalia's decision in the case of *Michael H. v. Gerald D.* are not testimony, medical evidence, or law. The reasoning rests solely on the circumscribed definition of "fatherhood," conceived by Justice Scalia in his attempt to defend the integrity of the family. That is to say, the grounds for this legal decision exist not in the language-game of law, but in the practices and beliefs of Roman Catholicism in the language-game of religion. An area of imbrication between two language-games is not a symptom of aspect or meaning blindness necessarily, but engendering such an area without an experience of conflict or paradox is. For Socrates, in his confrontation with Euthyphro, the conflict between one's loyalties to family, to the gods, and to the laws of the city, must at least be acknowledged. Euthyphro and Justice Scalia each partakes in the inability to acknowledge such conflict. They may walk into a court of law, but the grammar of their thinking revealed in the construction of their arguments show them to be trapped in an overly dogmatic conception of religion. This entrapment, again, is reflected in the fixed character of aspect-blindness.

V. ASPECT-BLINDNESS IN PHILOSOPHICAL ACCOUNTS OF READING

The *Philosophical Investigations* open famously with Wittgenstein examining Augustine's memory of how he learned language by seeing and memorizing connections between objects and the words the adults used to label those objects. This examination of the *Confessions* gradually gave way to a critical reckoning with Wittgenstein's own earlier view of language as propositions conceived as logically atomized pictures of reality. The older Wittgenstein had come to see such propositions as one language-game among many, and he moved forward to examine some of the language-games within traveling distance from the game he had previously mistaken for the whole of language. The bulk of these researches converged on issues in the philosophy of mathematics, and most of this work was not included in the *Philosophical Investigations* (Monk 2007). But travels through the philosophy of mind, psychology, and perception were included in the work. Thus we find a series of remarks and examples on pain, intention, meaning, reading, thinking, judging, and perceiving, which, taken together, have the effect of eliminating traditional dualities of mind and body, inner and outer, by presenting views of language from many angles that effect an effacement of physical and conceptual lines separating inner and outer processes. Wittgenstein (1958b) regards such lines as inventions of philosophers designed to partition language so thoroughly that the discipline has to be retrained to perceive language as flowing. These partitions are "like a pair of glasses on our nose through which we see whatever we look at. It never occurs to us to take them off" (sec. 103).

What is revealed when the glasses are removed is not reality as it truly is, but the limits of the philosophical point of view hypostatized by imagining it as external to language, and the subsequent (aspect) blindness of the philosopher (Levin 1999: 99–100). This point is fleshed out in Wittgenstein's remarks on reading.

These remarks follow a series of investigations of language learning and philosophy as a descriptive enterprise. Taking up the issue of reading feels initially like a radical change of direction, but there are lines of continuity between these areas. Thus Wittgenstein can open his consideration of reading with descriptions of some of its multiple meanings when perceived across language-games. But he is not so much interested in defining "reading" as examining what takes place when people read. This examination occurs over a span of more than twenty remarks.

We begin with the assumption that the person "has learned to read in his native language." What counts as reading is "the activity of rendering out loud what is written or printed; also writing from dictation, writing out something that is printed, playing from a score, and so on" (1958b: sec. 156). In offering such a wide-ranging version of reading, Wittgenstein is seeking to challenge and skirt the idea that "reading is a special conscious activity of the mind." As Feyerabend (1968) observed in his own consideration of these remarks, Wittgenstein is showing the limits of a philosophical analysis of reading, while also indicating that no vocabulary or mode of explanation – religious, psychological, neurological, and so on – is more privileged or complete than any other. We can infer that much of what we know about reading has come from aspect-blindness that is expressed by practitioners in a form of disciplinary or language-game chauvinism. In reading Wittgenstein on reading, therefore, we are participating in a journey across language-games, a journey mirrored in the act of reading itself.

In confronting a philosophical analysis of reading in particular, Wittgenstein attacks the idea of an a priori mental capacity or category for reading (or, more generally, for language) by re-describing the differences between the adult and novice reader, and between the states of reading and not reading. Philosophers, Wittgenstein observes critically, wish to explain away these distinctions by resorting to general rules the mind must follow or by employing the occult and general vocabulary of unconscious mental processes. Wittgenstein sees these tactics as evasions from the hard work of describing particular instances of reading.

For Wittgenstein, the states of reading and not reading are neither static nor categorical. Upon closer examination, we see that there are transitional states uniting the two poles. This is conceived as an important starting point for philosophical description. "A perspicuous representation" is, for Wittgenstein (1958b), the goal of walking and seeing (the activities that compose immanent theorizing), and it "produces just that understanding which consists in 'seeing connexions'. Hence the importance" for the theorist "of finding and inventing intermediate cases" (sec. 122).

At what point on this continuum of intermediate cases, Wittgenstein wonders, can a person be described accurately as a reader – one who is able to read? It cannot be simply when an appropriate sound is applied to a symbol on a page because, in the example of reading music, a player piano can manage this. Or, more broadly, a correct or anticipated sound could be produced by accident. There must be an observable alteration in the person's behavior, posits Wittgenstein. This is an evocative point and illuminating strategy. Until now, the prevailing image of reading I have employed while thinking through this constellation of remarks is that of a person, in a comfortable chair, next to a bright lamp, reading a book in isolation. Ancillary to this image is the silence of reading; it is an essentially private matter occurring within the reader. Now I must see reading as an activity performed in public.

In the transitional states between reading and not reading are instances where a person is merely pretending to read. In Wittgenstein's example, he imagines one who tries to trick us into believing he can read Cyrillic script by memorizing a sentence in Russian and then repeating it as his eyes move across the appropriate line of printed symbols. Wittgenstein offered similar examples in his descriptions of pain states. What is the difference between being in pain and feigning pain? The answer is humbling if you are seeking certitude. Wittgenstein showed that you can pretend to be in pain, but you cannot feign the criteria for (the behaviors associated with) pain states. There is no immediate difference between pain and the report of being in pain. The authenticity of pain simply cannot be established philosophically (or medically often enough). This is the limitation built into our consideration of the state of reading. We can say that the person who pretended to read is a liar: she or he "will have none of the sensations that are characteristic of reading and will perhaps have a set of sensations characteristic of cheating" (1958b: sec. 159). Wittgenstein continues on to consider instances where apparent acts of reading are something else because the person involved is under the influence of a drug or dreaming that she is reading. With each case, Wittgenstein has complicated the heretofore neat division between reading and not reading, and has shown the transitional states or games between similarly permeable. Each such state should be regarded as an opportunity to break the hold of aspect-blindness.

Yet, there is an activity called reading that is conventionally agreed upon, and only rarely noticed or questioned by practitioners or onlookers. This activity can be described in terms that render it distinct from other activities, and Wittgenstein sets out to perform this task. As we can say there are criteria for pain and consciousness, so too can we speak of criteria for reading. Describing criteria entails a move away from philosophical accounts of reading as a species of mind activity and toward an examination or perspicuous re-presentation of the social rules associated with reading. However, while there can be said to be rules for reading, these rules are not determinative. The activity of reading cannot be reduced to a set of underlying rules that govern it. Wittgenstein (1958b) illustrates this crucial point by noting that while there are rules "governing" the application of letters of the alphabet, a person will employ these rules when presented with the letters A B O V E and read them. But "now we shew him the same marks in reverse order and he reads E V O B A; and in further tests he always retains the same interpretation of the marks: here we should certainly be inclined to say he as making up an alphabet

129

for himself ad hoc and then reading accordingly" (sec. 160). Can he be described as reading in both rule-governed instances? If letters are not mentally, genetically, or grammatically inscribed, then nothing we can describe as part of language can be called "rule-governed."

Wittgenstein (1958b) pushes this insight further by experimenting with the following rule: "You are reading when you *derive* the reproduction from the original" (sec. 162). The rule is convincing initially because it causes a repeatable behavior – deriving "the sound of a word from the written pattern" by following the general instruction – and because it posits a general and deeper characterization of language as divided between speaking and writing. Wittgenstein's investigation exposes the aspect-blindness at work in this rule in both the regions of language it presupposes.

We want to say something deep about the activity of reading. We want to be able to ascertain the reality of an internal transformation that distinguishes reading from the mere articulation of sounds of words. This cannot be shown philosophically. Wittgenstein moves in another direction with an investigation of what it means "to derive" sound from the printed text. What Wittgenstein reveals is that the use of "to derive" in the language-game of philosophy, and the corresponding desire on the part of philosophers to expose the essence of deriving, leads to a false picture of the act and another manifestation of aspect-blindness. There is no essence of reading or deriving; they must be seen and appreciated as a "family of cases." "And in different circumstances we apply different criteria for a person's reading," and for a person's deriving sound from a word (1958b: sec. 164).

After working through this series of exceptions, Wittgenstein (1958b) wonders aloud if his method of deriving a general rule of reading is at all helpful in our understanding of the activity. The answer is no. "And if you say that reading is a particular experience, then it becomes quite unimportant whether or not you read according to some generally recognized alphabetical rule" (sec. 165). The task now becomes one of how to go about describing the activity of reading. What "manner of speaking," as Wittgenstein described Freudian psychoanalysis, does one use to give a perspicuous re-presentation of what occurs when one reads? All we can say so far is that describing reading as a special kind of mental image tells us nothing about what is unique in the activity.

Wittgenstein walks away from the focus on the reader and turns to the symbols, the lines on the printed page, comprising the object of reading. The symbols are described in terms of their familiar appearance and sound. Although, as we may now say, reading is "a quite particular process," we note "our eye passes over printed lines differently from the way it passes over arbitrary pothooks and flourishes" (sec. 168). We experience comfort in this terrain. Disturbances occur when we come across a misspelled word, but this only underscores the conventionality of the arrangement of symbols in words and words in sentences. Does this particular arrangement "cause" us to read? Is there a causal connection between symbol and sound?

To answer these questions, Wittgenstein sets up a comparison between the sensation one feels when reading a sentence and reading a line composed of an arbitrary set of symbols. In reading the sentence we may hear the words resounding apparently from within. There is no similar transition from printed symbol to sound in the arbitrarily conceived line. "It would never have occurred to us that we *felt the influence* of the letters on us when reading, if we had not compared the case of letters with that of arbitrary marks. And here we are indeed noticing a *difference*. And we interpret it as the difference between being influenced and not being influenced" (1958b: sec. 170).

Reaching this point on reading has been a long, even tedious process, involving attention to detail and countering generalizations with specific cases. Wittgenstein considers the implications of his investigations on reading at this point. For one, no one vocabulary, discipline, or language-game can offer a comprehensive account of reading. For this kind of account, we must be willing to walk through and along the borders of various language-games and make use of the perceptual vantages they offer. To remain in one is to fall victim to self-imposed aspect-blindness. Second, to seek out ground exterior to language in metaphysical heights or unconscious occultism is understandable. Again, our relation to the page as readers is ordinarily expressed in terms of absorption, stepping into an alternative reality, engaging in an internal conversation, and so on. We want to acknowledge the profundity of this relationship. Third, when we read, normally, we do not reflect on the effect the words are having. Even so, we can be moved to tears, laughter, and rage in the act of reading. Finally, to reflect on reading, Wittgenstein shows that we need to go to the activity itself, and not to what we can see from the distance of theoretical generalization, the most consistent product of epic theorizing, nor can we substitute occult processes for the activity as it is performed in public.

The observation regarding the sensation of influence when reading familiar symbols is not to be confused with the answer to the questions: What is reading? How is reading different than not reading? In both questions we begin by observing that the word "reading" has no essence, fixed meaning, parallel mental process, or definite object. What we can say about reading is a product of close perception and travel, the antitheses of aspect-blindness and the entrapped, fixed perspective of epic theory. But our understanding and descriptions can always be improved.

VI. Conclusion

The quality of willfulness was presented by Wittgenstein in his various accounts of seeing or noticing aspects. Thus, he writes, "One wants to ask of seeing an aspect: 'Is it seeing? Is it thinking?' The aspect is subject to the will; this by itself relates it to thinking" (1958b: 213; 1980a: 544). Wittgenstein was interested in presenting his philosophical remarks as "a new way of seeing." That is, he hoped the effect of his work on students and readers would be to alter their perceptual orientation to the world by loosening the hold of stability or fixity both on our way of seeing and on our descriptions of what we see. Seeing an aspect can therefore be willed, but within certain parameters. "It makes sense to say, 'See this circle as a hole, not as a disc,' but it doesn't make sense to say, 'See it as a rectangle,' 'See it as being red'" (1980a: 545).

In this chapter exploring possible forms or manifestations of aspect-blindness, the willfulness of this perceptual malady has been exposed. Making this dimension visible, however, does not lead to immediate remedy through instruction. As the cases of Euthyphro, Socrates, Scalia, and the picture of reading as a mental process suggest, aspect-blindness contains both ocular and otic walls of resistance. Their experience of words central to their respective enterprises – piety, the good, the family – were either reinforced so thoroughly in the language-game or social practice they occupied that any sense of play, of further intellectual travel and imagination, was eliminated, or aspect-blindness is a physical or cognitive condition.

In the following chapter, aspect-blindness will be investigated further in the context of political theory, and as a contrast to the vocabulary of seeing presented by Wittgenstein that ties him to theorizing. These terms are not merely significant to theorizing. Expressing them is itself a performance of theorizing as seeing.

Notes

1. This is the negative variant of "ideology" in political and social theory. For Skinner, Tully, Ashcraft, and others who see themselves as communitarian in their orientation

to political theory, "ideology" does not induce blindness, but rather is conceived as the ground where political theorists have and do engage in actual political problems, and the context in which the texts of political theory ought to be placed and read. See Vincent (2004: 64–80).

2. See Vincent's (2004) discussion of "essential contestability" (95–104).

3. I will restrict this discussion of Euthyphro to the dialogue "Euthyphro." There is also a Euthyphro featured in "Cratylus." The uncontested character of "piety" in Euthyphro's definition of piety is the result of satisfaction with the use of the word as referring to the relation of gods to the shape of human morality. This reference remains stable even in a context that should pit Euthyphro's filial loyalty against the injustice of leaving a murder go unprosecuted. In this, Socrates' tactic of attempting to destabilize Euthyphro's definition of piety is correct. Euthyphro grasps that letting go of his linear conception of the relation of gods to moral righteousness would involve a break from tradition and resists. In this sense, Euthyphro should be considered one of Socrates' most enlightened and reflective interlocutors, in spite of his entrapment in an overly constricted religious worldview. See Irwin (1992: 51–2).

4. Wittgenstein (1980b) read such exchanges as revealing a problem in Socrates rather than his interlocutor. "But that is the difficulty Socrates gets into in trying to give the definition of a concept. Again and again a use of the word emerges that seems not to be compatible with the concept that the other uses have led us to form. We say: but that *isn't* how it is! – it *is* like that though! and all we can do is keep repeating these antitheses" (30).

5. *Michael H.* v. *Gerald D.*, 491 U.S. 110 (1989).

6. It might be argued that Brennan failed to put personal religious beliefs aside when it came to the question of obscenity, which he conceived as outside the protections of the First Amendment in the 1957 case, *Roth* v. *United States*. He came to regret this decision that sent the Supreme Court down a two-decade-long path of trying to determine the essence of obscenity.

CHAPTER 6

Seeing as it Happens: Theorizing Politics through the Eyes of Wittgenstein

> What determines our judgment, our concepts and reactions, is not what *one* man is doing *now*, an individual action, but the whole hurly-burly of human actions, the background against which we see any action.
>
> Wittgenstein (1967)

1. INTRODUCTION

Much of what has been written on Wittgenstein by political theorists is concerned with how his work fits into the array of contemporary orientations to theory.[1] From this literature we learn there are two great obstacles to incorporating Wittgenstein into political theory: His stated antipathy toward theory and the absence of concern with politics in the body of his writings. Despite these barriers, a number of political theorists have sensed that Wittgenstein has something important to offer their enterprise and have sought to graft his ideas regarding meaning, language-games, *Lebensformen*, the character of language, and its relation to the world onto their various takes on the discourse.

My thought is that grafting Wittgenstein onto political theory, seeing him as merely "significant" to political theory, or considering his work as a kind of therapy for, or underlaboring clarifier of, perceived maladies in the activity are inadequate, although such efforts have yielded some interesting results (Pitkin 1972; Danford 1976). What Wittgenstein demands of political theory is a reconsideration of the pictures of the theorist and the relation of the theorist to politics that guide practitioners, shape their attitudes toward the world, and give them a sense of identity. The process of rethinking these relations is also an opportunity to analyze the discipline as a social practice composed of people with varying senses of what theorizing entails and what being a political theorist means. I will develop this critical and therapeutic reflection first, and then I will turn back to connect Wittgenstein's philosophy to political theory on the ground I think most firm and definitive: their common concern with how we go about seeing. A focus on seeing both illuminates the perceptual basis of theorizing (Embree 1972; Gunnell 1979; Taylor 1991; Gadamer 1998; Sandwell 2000), while it eliminates a lot of the temporal and spatial conceptual abstraction in our consideration of the relation of political theory to politics. Such abstraction was the subject of my critical analysis of the discussion around Isaac's (1995) "The Strange Silence of Political Theory," in Chapter 1.

II. WALKING

I am struck by the lack of autobiographical works or essays by political theorists in the late twentieth century that disclose how they go or have gone about theorizing politics, all the more so because of the considerable amount of metatheoretical reflection in the discourse of contemporary political theory. Even in volumes and special journal issues dedicated to reflection on the enterprise, forward-looking theorists manage to eliminate themselves from the field of vision.[2] To be sure, there are writings devoted to methods of reading texts, of teaching, and expressions of frustration with political theory's estrangements from Political Science and political society, but I find no works that help me understand why I should think of political theory as a vital, improvisational activity as opposed to an academic profession, a discipline, a settled style of writing, a set of texts, an emulation of classical approaches to theorizing, and a subfield. Moreover, it is difficult to discern arguments for why political theory needs to be vital and improvisational. There appears a general acceptance that the canon presents all the conceptual tools necessary to theorize politics today (Kateb 2004). What I feel I am lacking is some insight into what must be the unique character of theorizing political life in the late twentieth and early twenty-first century. Our tendency as political theorists is to conceive of our agency as an abstraction. That is, we speak of political theory and the political theorist as ideal categories that can incorporate an eclectic range of intellectual interests and approaches embraced by political theorists. But the lived-life of the political theorist is missing from view. To start with the activity of theorizing is to confront the obstacles to perception unique to the forms political life takes in the early twenty-first century. Wittgenstein conceived the description of obstacles to close examination of the details of life a key feature of philosophizing (1958b: sec. 52). These are forms that may not be at all recognizable from the standpoint of the "Great Tradition" of Political Theory. The resulting blindness to new political developments and conventions is akin to the inability of artists trained in the history of art to recognize new styles of painting. Philosophers have been comparatively far more reflective about what might be called their contemporary "philosophical style of life" than political theorists.[3] What keeps theorists from engaging in this form of self-reflection?

To paraphrase a remark from Wittgenstein (1958b), political theorists are trapped in a picture whose static character is revealed by the paucity of investigations into the difficulties of theorizing as a contemporary activity (sec. 115). Wittgenstein himself sheds some light on the difference raised here. He was very proud of being perhaps the only professor of philosophy who had never read a word of Aristotle (Monk 1990: 496). Wittgenstein was not interested in Philosophy *per se*; rather, he was concerned with philosophizing and eliminating the encumbrances – personal, linguistic, conceptual, perceptual, social, and disciplinary – philosophers confront when engaging in the activity. This direction of Wittgenstein's philosophical remarks has been described as "therapy" (Peterman 1992). What I see in this aspect of his writings, particularly in the *Philosophical Investigations* and its range of preliminary studies, is understood best as an interior or personal (modulating) view of philosophizing/theorizing in action, as it happens or as it is produced.

How do we show Wittgenstein walking among the language-games that compose his *Philosophical Investigations*? Patterns form in his travels through the pages of the text. Wittgenstein picks up a problem on the relation of naming to description, or on the apparent interiority of the language of thought, and he follows it. The pattern ends, usually abruptly, either because he has come to an end in his thinking for now (he may pick it up again later), or because the path of the problem has sent him into an adjoining language-game or problem. A longer pattern in the book concerns the traveling philosopher's relation to Philosophy, and this runs from remarks 109 to 133. If philosophy is a language-game, then it is a unique one for its lack of shape. Rather, for Wittgenstein, the role of Philosophy in philosophizing is "a battle against the bewitchment of our intelligence by means of language" (1958b: sec. 109). Philosophy is a call to the philosopher to move through and around problems to seek their dissolution. There are three errors or illusions to be avoided in the instruction to keep moving: the illusion of transcendence (rising above language to see it as a whole), the illusion of depth (burrowing below language to discern its essence), and the illusion of captivity that arises from a failure to recognize the permeability of the language-game's borders (1958b: secs. 109–15). To break the hold these illusions exercise over Wittgenstein's philosophizing, he warns himself away from succumbing to various forms of fixity and to embellish his perceptual apparatus with motion. In the end, Wittgenstein suggests that complete clarity is attainable once all the problems of philosophy have been dissolved through perceptual acuity. This state where the need for philosophizing as a form of travel is eliminated is never realized in the *Philosophical Investigations*, of course.

What is produced in this philosophizing/theorizing is a description of a world in pieces. But, again, there are two levels or aspects at work here: There is a description produced by the author of the book; and this description is also a lexical imaginary traversable by the walker *in* the book (Cavell 1979). This inner perspective is, I argue, of profound interest to the contemporary theorist because from this peripatetic vantage Wittgenstein presents faithfully the conditions of theorizing politics in a world where (his) political life has been shattered. The political life of Wittgenstein has to be surmised because he was rarely explicit about this aspect of life. Indeed, he was more forthcoming about his sexuality in some respects. We are left with scattered remarks from correspondence and the memoirs of students to glimpse how Wittgenstein adapted to the transformations exerted upon him by war, Fascism, and anti-Semitism.[4] Since Wittgenstein's political life cannot be reassembled, it must be understood in new, "damaged" terms that include moments where inner connections and likenesses are perceived and explored. Thus, Wittgenstein travels the language-games that compose his "city of language," but he knows there is no perimeter that gives it shape. Nor is there a standpoint that permits a view of such a totalizing perimeter if it existed. The language-games themselves abut, crisscross, and form patterns, but they do not cohere in any necessary or permanent way (1958b: secs. 66, 130, 132). Like neighborhoods in a city, these language-games can expand and contract or, over time, fade from view and memory. Wittgenstein's world is in pieces and the theorist as walker cannot see everything to pull it all together, but must presume or create some sense of solidity to continue walking from one language-game to another. His critical remarks concerning "theory"

137

are understood best as admonishments directed toward those who seek to retreat from the disorder of the world into a nostalgia evinced as an abstract grand metanarrative mistaken as a product of epistemological or metaphysical privilege. By contrast, Wittgenstein is a theorist for a fragmentary world; he resists the temptation to weave a grand narrative or vision that reduces the anxiety that disorder produces.

As noted, this disorder or splintered ontology is of at least two interrelated sorts. The first is a reflection of Wittgenstein's own world. The Hapsburg Empire he was born into, the respect his family was accorded, and even the sense of personal safety and order he described in both logical and religious terms collapsed under the weight of two world wars and virulent anti-Semitism.[5] Second, this shattering of Wittgenstein's life is captured in the piecemeal quality of the world as it appears to the walker in the pages of the *Philosophical Investigations*.[6] Problems arise and are walked through or evaded just as obstacles to a clearer view of the street ahead can be surmounted by sidestepping fellow pedestrians or craning one's neck to see above buildings and around parked vehicles. Philosophical problems take the form of "I don't know my way about" (1958b: sec. 123). We travel with the faith the road will continue, beyond what we can see for now. This faith, or what Wittgenstein addresses as modes of "the phenomena of hope" is the distinguishing feature of humanity (1958b: 174).

The entrapping self-image of the theorist is an amalgamation of heroic or epic accounts of theorizing politics from Plato onward. The common thread uniting these accounts is the theorist standing at a fixed, privileged point on the periphery of the city looking downward (or, in Plato's and Machiavelli's case, looking upward).[7] Whether this static perceptual vantage is the result of a philosophical claim to truth, a pronounced utopian imagination, or persecution and exile, it offers a panoramic perspective that sets the political theorist's vision of politics apart from that of the citizen, journalist, and politician who is involved in constitutive practices of politics. Communitarian variants on the place of the theorist in relation to a more specific political society efface the distance associated with the epic perspective, but they too tend to present theory as the product of immobile, encumbered, or what Fish (1995) has termed "professional" theorists while neglecting reflection on the process or "life-practice" of theorizing (Cornell 1993). Even though these static images do not correspond to the lived-lives of working political theorists today, most of which are mainly academic, they endure. More importantly, this

138

epic self-image produces sanguinity that precludes any competing, less heroic, self-images. As long as this sanguinity takes the form of resistance to critical encounters with how theorizing politics is performed (or if can still be considered a performance rather than an act of retrospection), Wittgenstein will not appear to fit.

I take Wittgenstein's work to be an investigation into theorizing (as a form of life). The form of the investigation is episodic and expressed in patterns of ultimately unsystematic remarks. This form resists the "grand" formulations we who are trained in the epic tradition are accustomed to seeing, but the fragmentary and disjointed quality of the Wittgensteinian remark also enables us to see more clearly the contemporary character of politics, as it would appear in Wittgenstein's work had he traveled into this form of life. I will return to this point regarding seeing and the contemporary character of politics presently.

We start then with the image of a traveler that Wittgenstein offers in the "Preface" to his *Philosophical Investigations*, a book he describes as "really only an album." Our journey opens with the recognition that Wittgenstein examined neither Political Theory nor Politics. We may find direction from him; but our paths divert immediately. He embarks from the perspective of a child learning first, primitive language-games and graduating to an appreciation of the complex dynamic quality of language. We begin in Political Theory and notice the messiness or porous quality of the line distinguishing theorizing politics and politics. Within Political Theory, on the surface, there are numerous approaches and problems, various schools of thought, central figures with followers and detractors, continental divides, organizational memberships, and ranges of loyalties that attach some to Political Science, others to Philosophy, Literary Theory, the Social Sciences, and still others to a conception of Political Theory as autonomous. Yet there does appear to be something discernible about Political Theory as a way of life.

Once again I notice a perceptual tension in this enterprise of traveling through political theory and politics. I am practicing political theory and yet political theory is one of my objects. This tension mirrors the two Wittgensteins we find in the *Philosophical Investigations*: There is the Wittgenstein who offers first-hand accounts of what he sees as he journeys through various language-games; then there is the Wittgenstein who reflects philosophically from a distinctly more general or detached perspective. He engages and reflects on the engagement nearly simultaneously. The crowd and pace of the first, lower vantage is demanding, absorbing and exhausting. It gives way to the second vantage that expresses frustration and a desire to find a way to "stop doing philosophy." What I described as a "tension" is dissolved at this point because what Wittgenstein is acknowledging is that we can walk out of political theory and into another form of life that permits reflection upon political theory. It is not a quantum matter of being in two places at once; rather, theorizing politics and reflection upon the contemporary conditions of theorizing are achievable by walking from one perceptual vantage to another. There is an ethical dimension to this kind of walking: The inescapable immanence Wittgenstein describes in emancipatory terms takes us to the edges of consensus marked by language-games. The dissensus at the edges remind us of the contingent and creative qualities of language use. Theorists who walk these edges assemble reminders that descriptions are not static representations, but emergent and provisional accounts of journeys. Conceptual tension, the reification of various binary arrangements, is eliminable by physical and existential circumstance and freedom.

What is the nature of the line between theorizing politics and politics? The view from the street offers few landmarks indicating that I have traveled from one neighborhood to another. Perhaps this is expressed best in existential rather than perceptual terms. Up close, what counts conventionally as political talk – talk about events, issues, candidates, elections, and so on – permeates everything else. Politics does not feel like a distinct area of life; it bleeds into my theorizing (just as it might bleed into a discussion about sports). I think, for instance, about the relation between politics and bureaucracy in the worldview of Arendt. That is, I see how politics as a form of order and collective decision-making has been all but replaced by a more rigid and formal bureaucratic order that is a more contemporary form of what Arendt described derisively as "the social." Maybe I am overly enamored of romanticized accounts of ancient politics, but they offer a source of contrast between politics then and now that, in turn, serves to remind of the provisional character of the forms politics takes over time. As I think this through, I seek out examples and I am handed one from a recent news report on the series of debates between the presidential candidates from the two main parties. The idea of a debate captures something of the spontaneity and contentiousness of political life, and so the idea of two candidates going head to head on the issues excites me. Yet, spontaneity and contentiousness have been eliminated from the structure of presidential debates by the creation of the Commission on Presidential Debates (CPD) – an organization devised by the Republican

140

and Democratic Parties for the precise purpose of creating a forum where the two candidates avoid confronting one another on the issues, and control the questions asked by the press and the public. This strikes me as a fairly good example of Arendt's contention that the social sphere composed of bureaucratic organizations like the CPD has, since Marx, functioned to domesticate political life. How do I then tease apart the activity of theorizing politics from engaging critically an issue of general political interest without repeating the work of a political journalist?

In the lived-life of the political theorist, the language-games of theory and politics are side-by-side, with an area of overlap. But this arrangement precisely because it is so familiar remains largely invisible. Even when made visible in projects dedicated to elucidating the relation between these distinct language-games, it is difficult to escape the picture of theory hovering above politics; the temptation to conceive the difference between politics and political theory in terms of privilege (privileged knowledge, privileged perception) is markedly strong. But following Wittgenstein, transcendence is an illusion that serves to take theorizing out of the "hurly-burly" of activities where it can do its most useful work. In philosophizing, transcendence disguised as a liberating burst leads instead to frozen self-congratulations and reverence that Wittgenstein described derisively as "Philosophy." In theorizing politics, transcendence is largely an expression of distrust for disorder and leads to the creation of a surrogate for the unpredictability of politics: a stable, fixed version of "the political" discovered in the equally stable, fixed body of Political Theory. To avoid the inactivity produced by freezing, Wittgenstein replaces the picture of verticality with a flattened plane that resembles a complex mosaic.

When I step back in the direction of the "untimeliness" of theory, the perceptual vantage is altered and I see there is a logical, albeit blurry, line to be drawn; when I step toward the political form of life, I see what I might call a political distinction that should be drawn. On the logical front, my view to politics is actually mediated by various texts, questions, and metaphors. I am not seeing politics *per se*; I am shoehorning aspects of contemporary political life into categories of classical political theory. Moreover, because I am examining the accuracy of a set of concepts that I use to theorize politics, my perceptual vantage is describable as metatheoretical or in the province of the philosophy of social sciences. I need to disclose these distinctions between politics, political theory, and metatheory, to avoid the temptation of equating my perceptual distance from political life for privileged knowledge of politics. I say "I need" to draw these lines because I am in some way adhering to the rules of the activity of political theory that demand scrutiny of one's epistemological claims. What I need to be clear about is the distinction between "political" as an adjective that describes an action that occurs in political society, and "politics" as the object of theoretical investigation. This is not always an easy distinction for a theorist to draw because theorizing is not an extra-terrestrial activity; theorizing is performed physically in political society. These discernments, however, are retrospective. "Upon reflection" is really a way of saying that I step back to see differently, to notice aspects of the terrain that are not visible because of their closeness. From this vantage I notice details in the landscape such as lines distinguishing forms of life that escaped attention earlier.

The line distinguishing political theory and politics is both a heuristic device, and a convention distinguishing two distinct games and two modes of play where the former is drawn more starkly than it is experienced in the latter. We understand that we cannot engage in political practices and the practice of theorizing politics simultaneously, just as we cannot play checkers and chess at the same time. Any hybrid form of the two games would be a new game altogether. Lines like this pervade language, as Wittgenstein observes. From our ordinary perceptual vantages we cannot be sure there is language *per se*. That is, there is no Archimedean per-spective that allows us to perceive synoptically language-games hanging together somehow to form a coherent, stable thing called language. What we can know are those aspects of language that we travel through, see, and remember. They are conventional, but they are also real in the sense that travel includes friction. This lifelong travel can be viewed as the con-stellation of memberships and disagreements that compose our identity, as explored in Chapter 3.[8] We are political theorists not only by training, but also by our membership or participation in a language-game played with others who identify themselves similarly. Training is modified by such face-to-face play.

Travel among language-games is considered by Wittgenstein to be a vital source of visual acuity and critical reflection. We grasp the similari-ties or "family resemblances" shared by various games by playing or walking though them. The boundaries of language-games are often blurry, but this quality is not seen as a disadvantage by Wittgenstein (1958b); rather it is something of an advantage in that blurriness is freedom to travel through ways of seeing that, in turn, permit unorthodox perspectives (sec. 71;

Osborne 2004). This is a key point in Wittgenstein: When we wonder how criticism might arise from within a language-game, we often conceive the language-game mistakenly as hermetic rather than a part of the constellations of language-games members travel over the course of their lifetimes. Indeed, travel is the source of what might be regarded as our individuality or personal uniqueness.

There are rules to language-games that distinguish them from other language-games and guide participation within their parameters. These rules do not determine participation, however. That is, we participate differently even in language-games that contain many carefully drawn rules (as in chess) even as we agree to play by the rules. By the time a person comes to political theory they have traveled through many such games and bring those experiences to bear on the enterprise of theorizing. An answer to the question of how criticism emerges from within a language-game turns on the constellations of language-games that abut political theory or influence political theory as part of the backgrounds of some (or even one) who call themselves political theorists.

The lived-life of political theorists entails walking between political theory and politics, then. This is not another way of describing the theorist's role as one of speaking truth to politics; rather, for example, the theorist experiences the acceleration of daily life through technological means like others citizens; and, in a related way, the theorist lives the consequences of the consolidation of military and political power in the unitary executive as a Republican, Democrat, or Independent. Yet, the walk from politics to political theory is one marked by slowness or untimeliness that permits critical reflection that is unique to the theorist's language-game, and produces equally unique and rich descriptions of these political phenomena. The path between these differently paced ways of life is worn well enough, the line distinguishing the two is porous and fuzzy enough, that theorists can be guilty of conflating the two, and often are. How do these two language-games remain distinct even as the friction of practices alters the conventions distinguishing them? The answer turns on and illuminates the perceptual underpinnings of theorizing.

III. WHAT NOT SEEING ILLUMINATES ABOUT SEEING

Wittgenstein describes aspect-blindness as an inability to experience the paradox of the Jastrow duck becoming a rabbit or vice versa (Mulhall

2001). The question, "What changes?" is indicative of the experience of "aspect dawning." If you are not curious about the cause of the duck becoming a rabbit, then you are displaying a symptom of aspect-blindness. You might see the duck first, then the rabbit, and then the duck again. But either you would see this as a series of discrete snapshots or you would not be impressed by a sense of mystery or paradox. Does the object of perception change? Or is it a change of mind? No doubt there is a neurophysiological or cognitive answer to the question of what changes in the experience of aspect change, but, for Wittgenstein, such an answer is outside the province or interest of philosophy (Hoffman 1998). Describing the experience and acknowledging the accompanying sense of strangeness is what is of philosophical concern here. There is also philosophical interest in the way we do not answer the question of what we see. Wittgenstein (1958b) notes that a person would not answer ordinarily a question of what they see when looking at the duck/rabbit with, "Now I am seeing it as a picture-rabbit," for some of the same conventions I would describe a picture of a man on a staircase as "climbing the stairs" and not walking backward "down the stairs" (194; Pylyshyn 2003).

This distinction between philosophy as a form of life and those forms of life concerned with causal or phenomenal explanations for aspect seeing is important in Wittgenstein's work. Within the distinction lies Wittgenstein's contention about philosophy's descriptive orientation to seeing, and the philosopher's intimacy with surroundings that eschew dualisms – inner/outer, mind/body, percipient/perceived – that act as abstract barriers to the world or support arguments about philosophy's privileged access to knowledge about the world.[9] What I want to note is that the epic self-image of political theorists relies on a conceptual duality that serves a similar epistemological and ego-inflating function by conceiving distance and height as components of superior views to politics. Instead, Wittgenstein would show, distance and height contribute to aspect-blindness (as well as insensitivity to the pains of others). This blindness is definable as a state of being incapable of perceiving political change and experience the sense of paradox that comes with it. "We find certain things about seeing puzzling," observed Wittgenstein (1958b), "because we do not find the whole business of seeing puzzling enough" (212). With increasing distance, difference and fragmentation give way to unity; the limits of the perceptual field are mistaken easily for totality.

The aspect-blindness Wittgenstein is most concerned with pertains to an incapacity to see the other as human being, as discussed in the last chapter (Levin 1999). It is an incapacity to "believe that he is suffering," "that he isn't an automaton," or to grasp that "my attitude towards him is an attitude towards a soul. I am not of the *opinion* that he has a soul" (1958b: 152). The source of this aspect-blindness (conceived now in ethical and skeptical terms) is the dualisms employed to explain perception that fix the product of looking either in a picture of the object as external or as an internal, occult, mental picture. The relation of the mental object to the physical object, like the relation of a word to a thing, gives what is perceived meaning. Wittgenstein contends, to the contrary, that these static images of perception and linguistic meaning are distortions produced by disembodied philosophical abstraction. His emphasis on the experience of "seeing-as" is a break from Cartesian accounts of perception. "'Seeing as,' Wittgenstein (1958b) writes, "is not part of perception. And for that reason it is like seeing and also not like seeing" (197). Wittgenstein is concerned not with the passive side of apprehending reality by perception, but the active side where we see connections by *creating* them. In noticing the likenesses between a series of faces, for example, I am not seeing the faces themselves but rather creating connections between them.

I want to go one step further here and make the connection between the creative and paradoxical experience of "seeing as" and theorizing.

IV. SEEING POLITICS AS DISSENT

Political Theory is rooted in perceptual activities that Wittgenstein illuminates and describes with a thickness that no other theorist can match.[10] Unpacking this assertion will take up much of the rest of this chapter. I defend the idea of Wittgenstein as a theorist in the Introduction and Chapter 1. Here I will examine Wittgenstein's remarks on perception and their implications for theorizing politics.

When Wittgenstein (1958b) steps out into the city of language and describes what he sees, the general impression is one of fragmentation (secs. 18, 203). One reason for this is physical limitation. You can see only so far. This range is limited by obstacles confronted on the streets of the city – the bodies of others, buildings, and so on. These obstacles can be overcome partially with motion. There is no fixed view in Wittgenstein. The perceptions he offers are the perceptions of a person in motion, and he conceives of others similarly. But the fragmentation is also a reflection of the world Wittgenstein knew. The old order of his childhood had been

145

dismantled by two world wars. The ethical and political order in which he had been inculcated was shattered by the violence of battlefields and atrocities in the concentration camps. Wittgenstein does not make this post-Holocaust context explicit in his work. But his philosophical remarks bear family resemblances to the more explicitly political insights of Adorno, various "postmodern" philosophers, and writers like Borges, Musil, Canetti, and Bernhard. Moreover, Wittgenstein's writings have been a source of inspiration, solace, and insight for a wide range of intellectuals seeking to make sense of the postwar world.

In some respects we do well to think of Wittgenstein as the first philosopher to recognize that the fixed and privileged perceptual vantage claimed by theorists is no longer supportable epistemologically or ethically. The ladder to epic sight has been kicked away and we can no longer pretend to scale it. The immanence philosophers and theorists have sought to transcend is now the only position available (at least ethically). We can acknowledge this once we see the illusory quality of the epic stance and heed Wittgenstein's call "back to rough ground!" Horizontal movement is the only tactic available to achieve, in a piecemeal fashion, the wider view offered once by vertical pretense. In this, Wittgenstein serves to remind us of a second, countervailing set of images related to theorizing that oppose the fixed heroic separation of theorist from political society. These images foreground travel and an eye for comparative differences. The term *theoreos* was applied to the representative of the city assigned the task of journeying to the Oracle of Delphi or to other cities on diplomatic or anthropological missions. In this etymological strand, writes Wolin (2001),

> *theoria* took the form of a story told by a traveler who had recently returned from a voyage to a distant and hitherto unknown land. Such travels should be considered not as 'trips' but as an intimate part of the structure of a theory and so closely connected as to have the status of metaphor for theorizing itself. A theoretical voyage imparts an element of action to theorizing that contrasts sharply with the equally ancient conception of *theoria* as contemplation, as the attempt of thought to imitate the unmoved mover god of Aristotle (35).

It is this tradition that Arendt drew on when she described theory as a "divine spark" that travels between the mountain peak of philosophical truth and the city. It is this tradition of traveling *theoria* identified most closely with Herodotus and Tocqueville that I draw on in proclaiming Wittgenstein a theorist.

The view of the street is a product of continuous seeing and motion. Theorizing from this vantage is an ongoing performance of inquiry and

146

description; theory is inseparable from the practice of theorizing; theorizing politics supplants grand political theory.[11] Wittgenstein's remarks on perception can be thought of as an examination of the outward criteria of the inner process of theorizing, what happens as a theorist sees politics as it happens (inner here does not mean "mental").

Describing perception involves, as Mulhall (2001) notes, an unusually technical vocabulary in Wittgenstein's work. There is "seeing that," "seeing as," "aspect dawning," "aspect-blindness," and "attention." At the heart of Wittgenstein's remarks on perception is the experience of perceptual change that he considers a paradox of "aspect dawning" expressed in the form "Now, I see it as . . ." Jastrow's "Duck-Rabbit" gives rise to this experience of seeing differently without being sure of what has changed. A second example comes from the mundane experience of looking at someone. "I contemplate a face, and then suddenly notice its likeness to another. I *see* that it has not changed; and yet I see it differently. I call this experience 'noticing an aspect'" (1958b: 193). The capacity to experience this strangeness of "seeing as" is then contrasted with the incapacity to experience perceptual paradox in the condition of "aspect-blindness" discussed earlier. Through this contrast, from the perspective of one struck by aspect dawning, Wittgenstein's investigations into the activity of seeing take us into a street-level view of the experience of theorizing as it happens. "Never stay up on the barren heights of cleverness," he writes, "but come down into the green valleys of silliness" (1980b: 76).

Wittgenstein's initial reflections on seeing are tied to "the concept of perspicuous representation," which he considers "of fundamental significance for us" (1958b: sec. 122), and the primarily descriptive task of philosophy that "puts everything before us . . . open to view" and so "there is nothing to explain. For what is hidden," and here we might mention the neurological or cognitive component of changing aspects, "is of no interest to us" (1958b: sec. 126; 212).

What is not open to view, what is hidden, is again taken up by Wittgenstein two remarks later. The quality of being hidden from view this time *is* of interest to the philosopher. "The aspects of things that are most important to us are hidden because of their simplicity and familiarity. (One is unable to notice something – because it is always before one's eyes.)" (1958b: sec. 129). Here the visual acuity of the philosopher might be of help to others by drawing notice to what might otherwise be missed. The source of this visual acuity is not epistemological privilege but freedom from "regimentation" and "dogmatism" (1958b: secs.

147

130–1). The philosopher's capacity to see what could be missed, observes Wittgenstein, is enhanced by the multiplicity of language-games that can "throw light on the facts of our language" by acting as "objects of comparison" to one another. One might surmise from this conception of the way language-games can be compared and traveled that political theory (as language-game) can function to "throw light on" the language-game of politics (and vice versa). This may be the case, but Wittgenstein (1958b) includes the proviso that one language-game does not compare to another "as a preconceived idea to which reality *must* correspond" (sec. 131). And here he is saying two things: First, language-games are independent perceptual vantage points that are not related by some underlying, irreducible logical structure or foundation. Second, Wittgenstein is arguing for a kind of linguistic realism: We conceive of or perceive reality through the mediating lenses of our language-games, but there remains a space between language and a reality we cannot get to without the tools language offers (Diamond 1996: 13–38). Nietzsche famously conceived this space in terms of the fundamental duplicity of language.[12] Wittgenstein conceives the space in terms of the irreducible conventionality and instability of language and, by implication, of perception. The dynamic relation between seeing and language is illuminated by Wittgenstein's remarks on "perspicuous representation" as a report on the instability of seeing.[13]

> The concept of "seeing" makes a tangled impression. Well, it is tangled. – I look at the landscape, my gaze ranges over it, I see all sorts of distinct and indistinct movement; this impresses itself sharply on me, that is quite hazy. After all, how completely ragged what we see can appear! And now look at all that can be meant by "description of what is seen." – But this just is what is called description of what is seen. There is not one genuine proper case of such description – the rest being just vague, something which awaits clarification, or which must be swept aside as rubbish. (1958b: secs. 291, 292; 200)
>
> A main source of our failure to understand is that we do not command a clear view of the use of our words. – Our grammar is lacking in this sort of perspicuity. A perspicuous representation produces just that understanding which consists in "seeing connections". Hence the importance of finding and inventing intermediate cases.
>
> The concept of a perspicuous representation is of fundamental significance for us. It earmarks the form of account we give, the way we look at things. (Is this a "Weltanschuung"?) (1958b: sec. 122)

Wittgenstein is saying a great deal about the perceptual problems faced by theorists who have renounced the privileged perceptual stance of the epic theorist. Because there is no synoptic vantage point onto the city of language, the enlarged vision we have is produced by piecing together information from our walks through language-games.

The place of politics in Wittgenstein's work is small, avoidable, fragmented, and sporadic. Where politics could continue to dominate the world view of theorists in the twentieth century; Wittgenstein signals something different and distinctive. I want to describe this in Arendtian terms as the eclipse of politics by more regulated or "social" forms of statism that fit into the broad category of "bureaucracy."[14] This requires, then, a new way of seeing politics. Where politics exists is at the edges of bureaucratic order, in contrast to its formalism, and as a place to defend threatened liberties. This defense is a lexical performance; in arguing for freedom from bureaucratic formalism, the dissenter creates space for freedom's enactment.

Traditional or epic political theory's incapacity to see the transformation of politics from the form of order to an expression of antibureaucratic freedom in the twentieth century is a function of the putative distance it claims from politics. Wittgenstein eliminates the ladder to this epic stance that leads to a form of "aspect-blindness" discussed in the previous section.

Within this patched together, enlarged perspective is at least the potential to acknowledge politics as an "intermediate case." When we inquire as to where politics is today, an answer is somewhere between the idealized conceptions we cull from ancient sources and its transformation into indistinctness by the pressure exerted by bureaucratic formalism. This transformation entails dislocation: politics is not where we expect it to be, nor does it perform functions associated with the creation and perpetuation of just orders. Rather, as noted in reference to aspect-blindness, politics erupts into visibility as a critical response to historical and bureaucratic strictures on perceptual acuity and creativity. Etymological moorings tying politics to descriptions of earlier forms of collective order are as much a hindrance as an aid because these moorings tie us to pictures that may no longer apply.

Our task as theorists is to observe how politics is used today. From what activities does politics draw its contemporary meaning? This inquiry defies perceptual clarity and ontological stability. Moreover, it reveals the obfuscating limits of training in the "Great Tradition" of political theory. And herein lies a second reason for this blurriness in vision and it lies in the limitations of immanent, traveling perspective of the Wittgensteinian theorist. As Wittgenstein confessed:

149

It is . . . enormously difficult to discern [one's own] limitations, i.e. to depict them clearly. Or, as one might say, to invent a style of painting capable of depicting what is, in this way, fuzzy [Unklare]. For I want to keep telling myself: "Make sure you really do paint only what you see!" (1980b: 68)

In this manner of "painting only what you see," the theorist resists the clear, synoptic view promised by epic theory, or what Wittgenstein (1958a) labeled "our craving for generality" that is an outward symptom of aspect-blindness (17).

Wittgenstein's philosophy of perception, which issues from his account of language as composed of various perceptual vantage points or language-games, gives theorists conceptual tools and a peripatetic self-image that enables them to see politics in its contemporary cast or casts. There is no reason to believe that "politics" is a unitary concept that represents the manifold forms of political life. This sort of conceptual or category error pervades political theory. Norton, for example, in a work that seeks to redirect political science research, offers this commonplace unitary conception of politics: "Language is political." By way of explanation, Norton (2004) notes that language is conventional or shared, and then employs Wittgenstein as an authority to bolster this equation of conventionality with politics (13–14). But Wittgenstein would oppose such a generic definition of politics with an observation on the particularity of conventions and language-games that compose what we mean when we describe something as political. At best, we can say something like, "politics is a neighborhood in the city of language," or that we share these uses of the word politics. That is, we use "politics" for today to capture something of the "family resemblances" between political phenomena (actions, institutions, and so on).

In sum, politics today is hard to see, firstly, because it does not occur where we might expect it most – the institutions of government, the modern state, have been thoroughly bureaucratized. Politics in this context is an ordinary usage, but for theorists who observe changes in political life and concepts over time, this usage is anachronistic. In a society of modern armaments, large and diverse populations, and thick codes requiring enforcement, politics has proven apparently too unpredictable to stand as the predominant form of order. Politics today, then, is found (if at all) outside of government, and outside of any unitary or exclusive representation of politics as the province of governmental administration or government as the representation of politics (1958b: 198).

The second problem with seeing politics as dissent is that it is episodic (usually for strategic reasons of garnering media attention or escaping surveillance by agents of the state). Political life emerges in as an expression of disagreement or in response to a local need for collective decision-making, and it may just as quickly disappear again. Politics is best conceived today not as a form of order, but as an expression of freedom, "a scene of emotional contestation," in opposition to the kind of rationalized conformity demanded of a public especially when a state feels threatened (Berlant 2005: 47). The Wittgensteinian theorist is well situated conceptually and existentially to glimpse and recognize the drama of politics as it is performed in contemporary street settings, beyond the perimeter of the frame or picture imposed on the theorist by the epic tradition.

This is the critical component of Wittgenstein's accounts of seeing and language, and, remarkably, it is described in the *Philosophical Investigations* as a self-criticism, the breaking of a bad habit following acknowledgment that aspect-blindness is self-imposed:

> (*Tractatus Logico-Philosophicus*: 4.5): "The general form of propositions is: This is how things are." – That is the kind of proposition that one repeats to oneself countless times. One thinks that one is tracing the outline of the thing's nature over and over again, and one is merely tracing round the frame through which we look at it.
>
> A picture held us captive. And we could not get outside it, for it lay in our language and language seemed to repeat it to us inexorably. (1958b: secs. 114–15)

If the activity of political theory is to be the theorizing (read: investigation) of politics, then the mode of activity must possess the mobility and perceptual sensitivity to pursue its subject.

V. Conclusion: It's Like Starting Over

On a recent birthday I received the world's most annoying card. It was not one of those tasteless cards that make fun of you because you are getting older, or that remind you of all the things you can no longer do or have; rather, the card's annoyance stemmed from the question it asked. Simply: "How old would you be if you didn't know your age?"

Like a bad piece of elevator music that you cannot get out of your head, this question has haunted me since that birthday. How do I answer?

What this card does is remove a central category, chronological age, from our identity. You are no longer permitted to use this simple number that apparently says so much in an abbreviated way in any self-description. The result is you have to think of yourself anew – literally from the ground up. This is what Wittgenstein's philosophy means for

151

political theory. He eliminates, in effect, the epic self-identity of theorists and the corresponding image of a privileged perceptual vantage that offers a detached and synoptic view of political life.[15] Then he rethinks critically the vocabulary, expressions, and experiences of seeing as they occur in the way we philosophers, psychologists, and theorists use them in our work as opposed to the way we use them in our daily nontechnical speech. Following him through this process of rethinking entails noticing things that lie before us yet remain invisible because of familiarity. From the epic perspective, the demands of keeping truth safe from politics, of keeping philosophy pure, blunt our capacity to observe changes in what count as political phenomena by retaining a putative distance that has become disciplinary.[16] Focusing upon the ideals of universal human rights discourse and the static picture of the individual as moral agent, notes Robin Holt, blinds us to the unique needs of humans as language-users existing amid power relations and material conditions that defy generalization (Holt 1997). We come away from these Wittgensteinian inquiries seeing (as a type of recalling) the rootedness of theorizing in the activity of seeing; political theory, we understand, is a way of seeing.

Finally, Wittgenstein places himself on the streets of the city of language. The *Philosophical Investigations* are a record of his travels. This accounts for his use of the philosophical remark to express what he sees. While for Benjamin or Adorno, the aphorism betokens the fragmentation of the world and our vision in the twentieth century by forces of fascism, genocide, anti-Semitism, and technology, for Wittgenstein the remark form also suits the peripatetic character of his vision and imaginative response to the political reality of his day, analogized in his city of language, ordered and disordered by conventions.

Theorizing is a performance thought best as describing what one is seeing as it happens, while in motion. "We want to walk," says Wittgenstein (1958b), "so we need *friction*. Back to the rough ground!" (sec. 107). The flight of the theorist or philosopher is distinctive because it is consciously ongoing. Language-games are traversed; retreats into the safe hermeticism of metaphysical or historical dogma are recognized as a form of aspect-blindness. Wittgenstein's descriptions of theorizing are produced as he walks. We follow him on this difficult, episodic, yet spirited, journey. This provisional character of Wittgenstein's immanent theorizing is captured in his observation: "The philosopher is not a citizen of any community of ideas. That is what makes him into a philosopher" (1967: sec. 455).

NOTES

1. See, for recent examples, Crary (2000); Duran (2002); Pohlhaus and Wright (2002); Gunnell (2003); Heyes (2003); and Lane (2004).

2. This is an especially extensive literature remarkable for its consistent affirmation of the academic distance perceived as necessary for theorists to discuss theory and politics. See Freeman and Robertson (1980); Miller and Siedentop (1983); Nelson (1983); Vincent (1997, 2004); Frank and Tambornino (2000); and O'Sullivan (2000).

3. Borradori (1991); Shusterman (1997); Hadot (1995); Watson (1999); Tobias et al. (2000); Ragland and Heidt (2001); Upham (2002).

4. Here is a tantalizing hint that was part of Wittgenstein's larger confession of past transgressions that he related to friends and family in 1936. Wittgenstein is writing to a friend he had known since they fought together on the Italian Front, Ludwig Hansel. "I lied to you and several others back then during the Italian internment when I said that I was descended one quarter from Jews and three quarters from Aryans, even though it is just the other way round. This cowardly lie has burdened me for a long time . . . Until today I have not found the strength to confess it" (Wittgenstein 2003: 281).

5. For autobiographical material by and biographical reflections on Wittgenstein, see: Bartley (1973); Janik and Toulmin (1973); Wittgenstein (1980b, 2003); Quinton (1982); Conant (1990); Monk (1990); Hintikka (1991); Szabados (1992); John (1998); Janik (2001). There is also a large body of memoirs and correspondence from former students, friends, and family members.

6. Wittgenstein (1980b) acknowledged the autobiographical character of his philosophical work. "Working in philosophy," he wrote, "like work in architecture in many respects – is really more a working on oneself. On one's interpretation" (16).

7. "Political theory is theory: its disciplinary status consists in observing, seeing, and imagining. Inaugurating it, Plato constrained political theory to look upward, that is, to free itself from the proprium of politics to remedy its constitutive contingency with the security of order." For Plato the order is noetic in nature; for Machiavelli, the founding Prince personifies order (Cavarero 2004: 528).

8. Identity in this conception is dynamic, malleable, and resistant to the homogenization Hannah Arendt, for one, associated with the demise of politics, and what Mouffe sees as the constitutive elements of "democratic individuality". See Arendt (1958: 198); Honig (1992); and Mouffe (2000: 11–12). For explicitly Wittgensteinian explications of identity, personhood, and gender, see Zerilli (2005); and Norval (2006).

9. Luntley draws on Mulhall's reading of the remarks on changing aspects and aspect blindness and offers an elegant account of Wittgenstein's criticism of bipartite or phenomenal models of perception. There is a negative and a positive component to the argument. The negative is the criticism of the division between the object and the "inner picture" of the object that is then taken for the experiential content of the act of perception. The positive point is the account of paradox we experience in seeing the duck as a rabbit, or a drawing of a cube as a three-dimensional object. For Luntley (2003), "the positive point is the endorsement of a unitary model of content for perceptual experience can explain the puzzling phenomenology regarding our perception of ambiguous figures" (155–6).

10. The project of revealing theory's perceptual roots using Wittgenstein is comparable to Heidegger's account of theory. Heidegger examines the way modern science employs theory and notices a distortion. "Theory is the viewing, the observation, of the real." But, Heidegger (1977b) asks, "what does observation mean? Theory, in science, means something more than 'meditation' on or 'beholding' the real. It also contains the activity of 'striving' after, the refining and entrapping of the real." This activity runs counter to or undermines science's identity as "disinterested" or "objective" (163–70). Similarly, Wittgenstein proclaims that philosophy's perceptual orientation "leaves everything as it is," and, yet, for the philosopher, everything is changed.

11. At this point it is necessary to address Wittgenstein's critical remarks regarding theory. "For me," said Wittgenstein early in his philosophical career, "a theory is without value. A theory gives me nothing" (Waismann 1979: 117). The argument supporting this statement against theory marked a turning point in Wittgenstein's philosophical development, according to his biographer, Ray Monk. What the early Wittgenstein sought was to reveal the underlying logical structure of language. This logical structure was understood to be the metarules reflected in the grammar of ordinary language. His claim that "a theory gives me nothing," signals a turn away from the logic of language and toward the way we use language ordinarily. The playing of a chess game by players applying the rules for moving pieces, as Wittgenstein noted, is sufficient and does not require further justification from a theory of games or metarules. "The deed, the activity, is primary, and does not receive its rationale or justification from any theory we may have of it." See Monk 1990: 305–8.

12. In this gap between language and reality is the result of an aesthetic performance. Truth is "a mobile army of metaphors, metonymies, anthropomorphisms: in short a sum of human relations which have been poetically and rhetorically intensified, transposed, adorned, and after long usage seem to a nation fixed, canonical, and binding; truths are illusions of which one has forgotten that this is what they are; metaphors which have become worn out and lost their sensual power; coins which have lost their pictures and now are no longer of account as coins but purely as metal" (Nietzsche 1964: 184). This is one of those moments where the similarities between Nietzsche and Wittgenstein are most striking.

13. See the connection drawn in Havercroft (2003). Havercroft's argument is really quite specific. The experience of changing aspects is likened directly to noticing multiple meanings of "freedom" among political theorists. Missing is the associated sense of paradox noted by Wittgenstein.

14. The battle of bureaucracy against ambiguity is mirrored and accentuated in Legal Formalism. "Formalism, is the thesis that it is possible to put down marks so self-sufficiently perspicuous that they repel interpretation; it is the thesis that one can write sentences of such precision and simplicity that their meanings leap off the page in a way no one – no matter what his or her situation or point of view – can ignore" (Wolcher 2006: 111). Wolcher goes on to note "such a formalist would suffer from an almost congenital failure of imagination that is analogous to aspect blindness."

15. I take this critical direction as akin to Arendt's interesting distinction between political philosophy and political theory. In drawing this distinction, Arendt (1994) notes that she has said "goodbye to philosophy" because of its "enmity toward politics." She concludes, "I want to look at politics . . . with eyes unclouded by philosophy." The therapeutic effects of Wittgenstein's *Philosophical Investigations* can be described

154

similarly as an unclouding of the eyes by eliminating the inhuman or otherworldly demands of logical or metaphysical perfection.

16. Honig's (1993) analysis of the taming of political conflict by bureaucracy and law is also, in part, a study in how fascination with Machiavelli's dramatic, masculine, and unpredictable concept of virtue blinds the contemporary theorist to the domestication of the public sphere through administration.

CHAPTER 7

Bare Life: Comedy, Trust, and Language in Wittgenstein and Beckett

A philosophical problem has the form: "I don't know my way about."

Wittgenstein (1958b)

We cannot listen to a conversation for five minutes without being acutely aware of the confusion. It is all around us and our only chance now is to let it in. The only chance of renovation is to open our eyes and see the mess. It is not a mess you can make sense of.

Samuel Beckett (1961)

Dear incomprehension, it's thanks to you I'll be myself in the end.

Samuel Beckett, *The Unnamable* (2006: vol. 2, 318)

I. INTRODUCTION

Unless you accept a generic definition of politics as, for instance, "power" or "the personal," the idea that you can step out of politics – literally walk away from the conventions that give political language-games their contours into another area of existence – is uncontroversial. I have worked in earlier chapters to explicate the importance of this kind of horizontal movement for perception and creativity, two components of theorizing, in Wittgenstein's work. This is not the only kind of motion I want to talk about here. In this chapter, I want to focus on the vertical drop below the conventions constitutive of politics into the bedrock of what Agamben has described as "bare life," *Homo sacer* (life doomed to die; the sacred outlaw of Roman law that anyone was free to kill). This fall from politics is not voluntary; it is, rather, achieved by force and coercion, components of the relation between sovereignty and the body, and the corresponding erosion

156

of superficial trust that exposes what Wittgenstein conceived as the narrow space between surface and depth grammars also described in terms of trust.[1] This deeper space does not entail, I will show, any ontologization of language. That is, language, for Wittgenstein, remains a moving mosaic of patterns and games that do not add up to anything coherent or permanent. But his presentation of language as possessing thickness makes room for an image of linguistic activity where inhumanity, oppression, and poverty co-exist with fecundity, friendship, and safety.

Wittgenstein could be said to present an ontology of language only if the foundation of trust he conceived as language's "bedrock" was shatterproof, and it appears to be so under ordinary conditions. This chapter offers an exploration of an extreme situation that plumbs the depths of trust and assesses its durability. For now, we can say that ordinary circumstances show that the trusting foundation of Wittgenstein's conception of language might qualify for what White (2000) has termed "weak ontology" in that even a stable trusting relation experiences strains and moments of doubt that gives pause for reflection. Since language-games come into existence in time, and fall out of existence with disuse in time, we can describe such instances as enactments of these critical reflections on trust on a small scale. Such enactments are the marks of weak ontology. Rorty offered supportive examples of phrenology and paleontology as language-games that fell out of the larger conversation in science, or were absorbed by other, more useful language-games.

But trust can be shattered in extreme situations and weak ontology proves at these moments to be an inaccurate categorization of Wittgenstein's view of language. We are reminded in the figures of Euripides' Hecuba, the *Muselmänner* of the concentration camps, or in the trauma-induced muteness of survivors of Cambodia's killing fields, that language is, at base, nothing. This deathly, subhuman void is exposed when the bedrock of trust is effaced by systematic and sustained inhumanity. The void serves to underscore trust's character as the unsurpassable ground of human life.

In his *Philosophical Investigations* and in his advice to students, Wittgenstein suggested an end to philosophy as a discipline in order to free the living philosopher to pursue, embrace, and relish the proliferation of meaning offered by ordinary language. In eliminating the disciplinary boundary around him, Wittgenstein lived the life of a philosophical traveler on the landscape of language and literature (among other social practices). In describing a theory of meaning as unencumbered by some notion of a reality external to and represented by words, Wittgenstein eliminated ontological or categorical obstacles conceived often to distinguish philosophy as a kind of writing from literature as another kind of writing. Language is composed of a horizontal and vertical array of trusting relations that demarcate limits to suspicion. "Giving grounds . . . justifying the evidence, comes to an end" (1969: sec. 204), and the friction of trust permits walking within and between language-games.

Similarly, from the direction of culture and literature toward philosophy and theory, Samuel Beckett labored not to break down boundaries separating philosophy, but to show the falseness of such a separation by creating a philosophical literature that could, with felicity, illuminate the meaning of the meaninglessness on a landscape darkened by war and inhumanity.[2] This required the sort of roving perception Wittgenstein strove to liberate in philosophy, but also a use of the porosity of language observed in Gertrude Stein, and the dissolvability of "the word surface," an insight Beckett employed to nourish the imaginative openness of his literary enterprise.[3] Where, for instance, Wittgenstein was opposed overtly to Cartesian conceptions of the mind as some occult space accessible through privileged introspection and posited in its place a shared language and shared criteria for exposing inner processes, Beckett's anti-Cartesianism was imbued with a desire for the kind of inner sanctum posited by Descartes. He could explore this desire fully by conceiving the journey of his characters as something occurring on visible inner and outer planes. The idea of privacy extolled in Descartes's conception of the self is probably something Beckett, who equated exposure with "the mess" of this life, thought in terms of rest and safety. What troubled Beckett most about the Cartesian mental substance was the putative character of its immortality. Mind was a construct, common in the literature and philosophy, Beckett regarded as an inheritance that should inspire skepticism, for it serves to distract us from the central feature of human existence – we are all dying (Josipovici 1999). Given the barrenness of Beckett's dramas, we are left wondering if his characters are mere shadows of a now extinct humanity.

A second area of comparison between Wittgenstein and Beckett is historical. Both were innovative thinkers during and in the wake of a violent century that shattered many features of the old European order and culture. Both grasped the centrality of religion's decline in this shattering and its aftermath. Both showed enormous courage in battle (Wittgenstein) and resistance (Beckett). And, finally, their adult lives were lived as émigrés, and so they knew the estrangement and dispersed existence of bare life intimately.[4]

A third area of comparison is in the apparently shared ambivalence Wittgenstein and Beckett harbored toward trust. Wittgenstein regarded human trust as the irreducible "bedrock" of language. Yet, his presentation of language emphasizes its contingency and the multiplicity of its parts that do not add up to a coherent whole. Wittgenstein would never describe language in Heideggerian terms as "the house of being," for instance. Language is better conceived as a landscape that must be walked with great care lest you fall into a crevice that has yawned open from bedrock to surface. For Beckett, hero of the French Resistance, member of the "Gloria SMH" cell, the espionage work he did involving translating documents on Nazi troop movements and communicating them to Allied forces was possible only because of the trust between cell members (Perloff 1996: 122–7). I will show that this experience of trust, below the surface in most of Beckett's writings, is exposed anew in his play, Catastrophe. But, as Beckett noted in an interview, the existence of trust must not be regarded as an underlying organizing principle. This is also a good way to conceive of the consequence of trust on language in Wittgenstein. Rather, for Beckett, that we can and do trust adds to our incomprehension of the horrors the world has to offer. "If life and death did not present themselves to us," said Beckett, "there would be no inscrutability. If there were only darkness, all would be clear. It is because there is not only darkness but also light that our situation becomes inexplicable" (Perloff 1996: 133).

Beyond this strong area of similarity between Wittgenstein and Beckett, there are important differences. I will not dwell long on these because I am interested in how Wittgenstein and Beckett complement and illuminate one another's work and world view. Suffice, for now, to notice how Beckett's pessimism places him, albeit imperfectly, in the tradition of existentialist thinkers like Sartre and Camus who perceived the absurdity of the world and described it in terms of meaninglessness and exile. Wittgenstein, to the contrary, was more optimistic. If we were to start with Dostoyevsky's pronouncement, "if God is dead, anything is possible," and focus on the reading of this line offered by Beckett and Wittgenstein, we would see the former taking it as a prediction of future moral and political decline as inevitable as death itself; the latter would regard the "anything is possible" as a call to a version of self-creation we associate with Nietzsche and Foucault. Beckett employed humor most

159

often to expose the extent of the damage done by war and genocide and the consonance of this damage with ordinary experiences of corporeality and mortality; for Wittgenstein, the fact of language showed that at some level trust remains.

The main area of comparison for this chapter is in the rough ground of immanent theorizing; both Wittgenstein and Beckett offer tools and insights for theorizing politics that resists temptations to heroic transcendence in the form of the "epic" or synoptic stance, and the equally alluring desire to conceive of retrospection or timeliness as a privileged perceptual vantage. By contrast, both Wittgenstein and, more famously, Beckett, work from a street-level where no God's-eye point of view is possible, though we may find ourselves waiting for it. The difficulty in distinguishing the perceptual vantages of the philosopher and the playwright gives way to insight into the relation between cultural and political theory (Wolin 1997; Dean 2000; Chambers 2006; Robinson 2009). Travel between these language-games enriches and pluralizes our descriptions of political life by noticing its propinquity to popular culture. This mobile perspective gives "bare life" animation: a way of looking at, and acting upon, the world, a feature oddly lacking in the rendering offered by Agamben.

II. POLITICS AND *CATASTROPHE*

Politics at its dramatic origins was tied integrally to peace, or, more accurately, to a collective desire to replace vengeance and war as the predominate forms of conflict resolution with something nonviolent and reasonable. In the two great poetic and symbolic presentations of the emergence of politics as a mode of peace, *The Odyssey* and *The Oresteia*, peace is inaugurated as a divine intervention, which becomes a human enterprise with the re-definition of justice as a matter of due process, deliberation, and an acknowledgment that humans cannot see as the gods see. Following from the acknowledgment that human knowledge will always be provisional, verdicts must be open to appeal and re-investigation, and the discovery and administration of justice both serve to cultivate trust in the political community.

In contemporary political society, especially in the United States, there is a dual condition, both conceived and described conventionally as political. On one side is the politics of unity or order identified most closely with Hobbes and conceived originally by equating stability and safety with peace. Maintaining this equation has led to increasing bureaucratization,

160

even as the historical record shows bureaucracy's complicity in genocidal violence against portions of the population it was supposed to protect. In large part, this bureaucratization has occurred in response to advances in the destructive capacity of military technology and the military mindset. The existence of nuclear arsenals has been justified in terms of national defense, for example. Bureaucracy's justification lies, in part, in its promise to protect the arsenals by replacing the passion and vicissitudes of political forms of governance with steady, rigid formalism. On the other side is the politics of resistance or dissent, an activity conceivable in spatial terms, but the spaces are sporadic. That is, a space becomes political when it is the locus of a political event – a march, a demonstration, a strike, or a moment of street theatre. The space loses its political character when the event ends. These two sides to conventional political life do have points of overlap. Even a protest vote, for example, signals the continued legitimacy of the form of governance; and the politics of dissent can exhibit the same distrust, exhibited here in the form of cynicism, endemic to the politics of unity. However, as the politics of order becomes increasingly militarized, it sways so far from its historical tethers to peace that political theorists and those engaged in the politics of resistance do well to note the danger this shift in order entails and the corresponding distancing from those historical conventions that distinguished politics from other forms of collective life. The politics of unity today has surrendered peaceful ambition to become an instrument of suspicion, and this should be conceived as an antipolitical ploy and ambition.

The dangers have come into stark view in the politics of the United States since 9/11, an event often touted in terms of uniqueness – "the day the world changed" – but that functioned in actuality to unleash the violence that was already at the disposal of the military order. Violence is business as usual even as the state declares itself transformed from "normal" to a "state of emergency." For political theorists, however, I might argue that September 11th, 2001, really did involve historical disjunction. Prior to that day, arguments against transcendence and privileged political knowledge were couched largely in terms of ethics, epistemology, and religion. We could contend, like Levinas (1987) and Bauman (1989), that the perceptual distance celebrated in epic political theory as heroic and synoptic was the same dehumanizing distance built into the concentration camps. Or we might argue against the gnostic quality of claims to knowledge in the Platonic and Straussian traditions by turning to forms of linguistic philosophy and social constructionism that show attempts to escape the imprecision and prejudices of ordinary language or to fashion conceptions of unprejudiced truth are matters of self-delusion. Or, finally, we might argue against the existence of an Archimedean stance, past and future, as an onto-theological fantasy with totalitarian tendencies. But after the attacks on the World Trade Center and the Pentagon, transcendence could be argued against on political grounds. The governmental response of the United States was overwhelmingly military and unilateral. The politics of unity played its hand, renounced any thought of peaceful diplomacy, and made abundantly visible its antipolitical orientation by condemning domestic dissent and employing the history of military tactics, including torture, in the name of national security. If theorists wish to continue to talk about politics, therefore, the only form of political life that remains is in the form of resistance. Examining the military order and calling it governance has become an example of being trapped in a picture of politics that has become antiquated and a source of blindness. Theorists, like dissenters, must work surreptitiously, and "in the larger and less clearly demarcated, disciplined, and territorialized fields of thought and existence" that reward with perceptual vantages heretofore unnoticed and the promise of wider vision afforded by peripatetic liberty, as Brown (2004: 115) and Chambers (2006) have noted. The marginal field of this essay is that vantage composed of those who have suffered the injustice of exile, torture, and the loss of citizenship. "One misses a great deal by looking only at justice," wrote Shklar (1990). Political theorists, she continued, "can and should raise every possible question about injustice as a personal characteristic, as a relation between individuals, and as a political phenomenon" (15–50). Giving voice to victims is more than an expression of justice; it is an opening to a point of view on political life we all have the potential to explore involuntarily.[5] Samuel Beckett staged what bare life sees in a work titled, *Catastrophe*.

Beckett's *Catastrophe* is set during the rehearsal of a play's final scene. This larger dramatic context is not revealed; nor is it ascertainable from what follows. There are three figures present on an otherwise bare stage: The Director, "D"; his female assistant, "A"; and the Protagonist, "P," who is "midstage standing on a black block 18 inches high. Black wide-brimmed hat. Black dressing-gown to ankles. Barefoot. Head bowed. Hands in pockets" (Beckett 2006: 483–9). There is another character, a lighting technician named Luke, who is offstage throughout. The play opens with a prolonged silence as the Director studies the Protagonist. What happens to P is the product of premeditation.

The exchange that follows is marked by the authority of the Director who issues uncompromising assertions, the acquiescence of the Assistant, who regards her boss as a contagion, and the utter, shivering malleability of the Protagonist, so titled as an act of bitter irony or as a way of devising the ultimate antihero or as a foreshadowing device. The communication is solely between D and A, and is reminiscent of the primitive language-game presented by Wittgenstein (1958b) that includes the command, "Bring me a slab!" (secs. 117, 119–21). The orders, apparently comprehensible, are followed. "I make a note," says A repeatedly. Yet, there is incomprehension in the direction of A's utterances to D. When A observes P shivering with cold, for example, she expresses what might be taken for concern. There is no response from D, and, for A's part, she does nothing to comfort P. This momentary compassion, her tacit repulsion for D, and her ultimate complicity make her the most complicated character in the play. As the audience our eyes may settle upon the Protagonist at the center of the stage, but our attention is drawn to the cruelty of the Director, expressed in the coldness of his orders and the terse surety of his criticisms, which, in turn, makes what could be regarded as the cruelty and complicity of the Assistant seem warm, deep, and humane by comparison. We are listening to an exchange of two perpetrators, one ordering and the other obeying, in a context that recalls the experiments of Stanley Milgram and Philip Zimbardo.

What does happen to the Protagonist? The goal of the Director appears to be to reduce P to a corpse. This is achieved by baring P's head, stripping away his black gown to expose the ash-colored underclothes. Hands, head, feet, and ankles are whitened. Head remains bowed. The baring reaches completion with an offstage order to the lighting technician, Luke, to dim the light on the body while maintaining the light on the head.

D: Lovely.
[Pause.]
A: [timidly] What if he were to . . . were to . . . raise his head . . . an instant . . . show his face . . . just an instant.
D: For God's sake! What next? Raise his head? Where do you think we are? In Patagonia? Raise his head? For God's sake! [Pause.] Good. There's our catastrophe. In the bag. Once more and I'm off.

The scene's rehearsal is repeated. The light illuminating the stripped and whitened body of P fades, and the light on the bared and bleached head remains. D is pleased. "Terrific! He'll have them on their feet. I can hear it from here." With that a recorded "distant storm" of applause can be heard. As the sound rises, however, "*P raises his head, fixes the audience. The applause falters, dies.*" The audience, cast as bystanders, watched in silence as the Protagonist was humiliated, exposed, and dehuman-ized. Their passive complicity in letting this happen is captured by the recorded praise of the result. The actual audience does not applaud and this works to make their guilt of inaction obvious. They, in effect, join in the shamed silence of the recording engendered by the resistance and gaze of the Protagonist (Owens 2003: 74–81).

The moment is powerful. When we hear A ask, "What if he were to . . . raise his head?" initially, we take it as a dramatic suggestion that D refuses. After P does in fact raise his head, the audience reaction forces us to rethink A's suggestion. She is not asking for P to raise his head; rather, she fears he might do this. D, for his part, is not refusing a suggestion. He is responding mockingly to A's suspicion that his power over P is not as complete as he thinks.

Commentators have noted that *Catastrophe* stands as something of an oddity in Beckett's body of work because of its explicitly political themes of subjugation, authority, and resistance. It was a late work, written in 1982, and dedicated to Václav Havel. Beckett was invited to write a piece, along with Arthur Miller, André Benedetto, Victor Haim, and Elie Wiesel, by the International Association for the Defense of Artists. It was staged at the Avignon Festival as part of "A Night for Václav Havel" (Knowlson 1996: 595–6). As Beckett biographer Knowlson (1996) reports,

> While the play is no simple, straightforward political parable, its final political message is unambiguously presented in the image of the Protagonist's raising of his head. Beckett told me that in referring to what one might describe as the "grand finale," a reviewer had claimed that it was "ambiguous." "There's no ambiguity there at all," he said angrily. "He's saying: You bastards, you haven't finished me yet!" (597)

There is comedic force behind the moment of the Protagonist's defiance. Up to this point, all the conventions supporting the total power of the Director over P, and the authority of D over A, appear seamless. The pres-sure that builds through the drama reaches an apex with no expectation of release or corresponding exformation. But, then, this is precisely what occurs. Conventions supporting even apparent total power are shown to be, well, conventional.[6] P surprises and shames the audience and the recording into silence, perhaps because we, as the audience, may feel anguish for the cold and malleable P, but we focus and identify with A. To empathize with P would be to react differently to his heroic gesture. Instead of silence, there would be relief, or, stronger still, triumphant laughter. Deleuze observes this power in Beckett's work in a comparison with the grotesque art of Francis Bacon. "Bacon, no less than Beckett," writes Deleuze (2003),

> is one of those artists who, in the name of a very intense life, can call for an even more intense life. He is not a painter who "believes" in death. His is indeed a figurative *misérabilisme*, but one that serves an increasingly powerful Figure of life. The same homage should be paid to Bacon that can be paid to Beckett or Kafka. In the very act of "representing" horror, mutilation, prosthesis, fall, or failure, they have erected indomitable Figures, indomitable through both their insistence and their presence. They have given life a new and extremely direct power of laughter. (53)

But it is laughter reserved for those who see what lies before them, too familiar, perhaps, to be seen by most. Yes, P looking up is an act of defiance, but there is ambiguity, *pace* Beckett. More is being communicated than, "You haven't finished me yet!" The gaze that silenced the applauding audience is both a call to solidarity and an expression of betrayal: "You were supposed to oppose this!"

As an aside, there was a performance of *Catastrophe* at Colorado State University in September 2007. Both the playbill and the publicity posters featured the most iconic of the graphic photos depicting torture of prisoners by American soldiers at Abu Ghraib prison: A prisoner stands on a chair in a black gown, and a pointed head covering. His arms are stretched outward as if crucified, and in his hands are wires. There is ambiguity here too. Our silence in the face of the photograph signals a sense of complicity and shame. But this silence does not signal a unified "we." Some may consider torture as necessary in the war on terror; others experience their powerlessness to oppose torture as a policy effectively; and for still others, silence is relieved acceptance that a semblance of justice was restored by trials of a few of the enlisted guards and a single officer (Wittman 2007: 8–17).

III. POLITICS AND TRUST:
DESCRIBING THE BARE LIFE IN *CATASTROPHE*

In displaying what can be termed the spiritual torture of P, Beckett examines the antipolitical direction of the politics of order expressible in terms of betrayal and mistrust, and the only tactic available to the politics of resistance – the restoration of trust. Beckett was drawn to the plight of Václav Havel, because his fellow playwright was imprisoned for participating in resistance politics, and a condition of this imprisonment was that Havel was refused permission to write. A politics of order that seeks to crush intellectual and artistic liberty has subverted thoroughly its own political reason for being. Its new reason for being is necessitated by its own tactics that efface trust, and can be described in terms of bureaucratic rigidity, militaristic violence, and self-perpetuation ensured by the muted and fearful passivity of its "citizens." Beckett experienced this in Vichy France, and remained a committed resister well after the war. *Catastrophe* is a testament to this.[7]

There is no political or activist Wittgenstein. This is a common line of criticism for those examining the implications of Wittgenstein's work for political theory. Here his claims limiting philosophy's work to description are taken as calls to acquiescence and the renunciation of the philosophical heroism of Marx's Eleventh Thesis. I have responded to this argument in Chapter 3. In what follows, I want to respond to a corresponding claim, a more cogent criticism of Wittgenstein in my mind, that he does not address scenes of coercion and oppression present in any shared practice or language-game. What I have been laboring to show is the potential for such a Wittgensteinian investigation.

Agamben (1998) draws out the relation between bare life and the political life by turning to Aristotle, who conceived of the transformation of the former into the latter in linguistic terms and as therefore unique to humans in his *Politics*.

> Among living beings, only man has language. The voice is the sign of pain and pleasure, and this is why it belongs to other living beings (since their nature has developed to the point of having the sensations of pain and pleasure and of signifying the two). But language is for manifesting the fitting and the unfitting and the just and the unjust. To have the sensation of the good and bad and of the just and the unjust is what is proper to men as opposed to other living beings, and the community of these things makes dwelling and the city. (7–8)

Humans as political animals, actualize their potential for politics through their creation of the *polis*, which, in turn, is the ground for the most human pursuit of the good and just life. This transition from *zoe* to *bios*, animal to human, bare life to the life of a citizen, also involves, for Aristotle, a transition from "voice (expressive forms of communication shared with animals) and language (the rational communication needed to establish justice in the *polis*)" (Bull 2007: 2). Political life is suffused with bare life. The step from life to political life is presented by Aristotle as progress toward the good life of human fulfillment known to us as an enhancement of happiness. Stepping back from political life into bare life is, conversely, an expression of corruption and regression into unhappiness.

166

The proper role of the city in Aristotle's schema is fostering thought and action in the pursuit of the good life. For Agamben, following Foucault, this role has been subverted in the modern state that has moved bare life from the invisible margins of political life to the center. The politicization of bare life – literally the new interest the state takes in its citizens as embodied beings – marks the "decisive event of modernity" and is exemplified in the state's sovereign power to determine for itself the line delineating the normal state from the "state of exception," which turns the political community into a concentration camp (*Lager*). This transformation is a reversal of the Aristotelian order of things. The state of exception's integral ties to and power over bare life is what animates the state's totalitarian form. This integral tie, missed by Marxist and Anarchist critics of the state, is termed the "catastrophe" by Agamben. He (1998) writes, "the transformation of politics into the realm of bare life (that is, into a camp) legitimated and necessitated total domination" (120). What he accomplishes in his etymological investigation of *Homo sacer* goes beyond discerning the fragility of citizenship, politics, and rights posed by the state. Agamben exposes the threat the state in its current form poses for life itself. If Wittgenstein and Beckett could respond directly to this insight, it would be in agreement with the added claim that life's survival rested in trust (as opposed to the politics of decision, the simple "yes" or "no" posited by Žižek (2002: 101) and opposed by Agamben as a re-affirmation of state sovereignty over life or death.)

This same catastrophe can be gleaned *writ small* in Beckett's play, *Catastrophe*. The dramatic goal of the Director is to make visible what has, until the climactic moment, remained invisible. The success of his creation is tied to the baring and the shaping of life. It is achieved through reversal of Aristotle's version of language as originating in speech and becoming a kind of writing in the *polis*. In Beckett's conception so reminiscent of the torture apparatus in Kafka's *In the Penal Colony*, A encodes the verbal orders of D that lead to, and are etched into, the transformation of P: "*I make a note.*" A's spoken response is simultaneous with the application of pencil to a pad, and is less a promise to commit the order to the page and more a confirmation of the correctness of the downward direction they are moving in.

No utterance by either the Director or his Assistant could be construed as "hate speech" outside the context of the play. There are no beatings or electric shocks. Moreover, there is a profound lack of animus toward the Protagonist, and this fact heightens our notice of the insensitivity marking their regard for him. The Assistant observes: "He's shivering. [*Pause*]" To which the Director responds, perhaps in reference to the sacredness of life itself, perhaps as a tip-off to his own godly self-image, but without personal concern for the Protagonist: "Bless his heart." P is a clothed manikin waiting to be stripped, whitened, and lit.

Wittgenstein's account of language contains a verticality that ties the fact of language to the usually invisible and unquestioned forms human life takes. These forms entail both commonalities and differences. That is, forms of life include the physiological isomorphism that unites humans, while distinguishing them from other non-human species – "If a lion could talk, we could not understand him" (1958b: 223) – and the pluralistic character of the natural history of humans shaped by cultural differences (1958b: secs. 7, 19; 1958a: 134; O'Connor 2002: 71). In Wittgenstein's well-known metaphor of the "stream of language" the form of human life is the relatively stable riverbed. Flowing over the top is our ordinary language use, arbitrary and dynamic, and yet it also creates pools of stability that can appear natural and necessary. The riverbed is the depth grammar of language; and the flow is the surface grammar. Both are tied integrally to notions of trust, community, and communication. Neither level possesses regulative force or is able to determine meaning in any causal or linear sense. We might refer to grammar in retrospect in order to describe why a certain use did not engender the desired communication with another, but we do not refer to grammar first in order to say something (1958b: secs. 496, 497). Moreover, disagreements on the surface of a language might give the appearance of divisiveness, but are shaped by and conform to deeper agreements.[8]

In their emphasis on the trust that precedes political life and coincides, it seems, with life itself, Wittgenstein and Beckett depart from Agamben's (1999) use of bare life as an extreme situation that sheds light on the face of sovereignty in the state of exception by limiting perspective from the top down (48–50). The subjectification of bare life in Agamben implies a single perspective – that of sovereign power. By contrast, the philosophical and dramatic work of Wittgenstein and Beckett is more empathic than comparative, horizontal as opposed to vertical, and makes room for exploration of how trust can function to build or rebuild a political movement from a context of profound distrust and inhumanity. This perceptual direction, it bears repeating, gives life (the horizontal motion toward others) to bare life in the form of resistance that cannot be detected in Agamben's study.

Further, there is a need to distinguish between the bare life of the refugee, the artist imprisoned, and the person interned in a *Lager*, from the *Muselmänner* examined by Agamben in his study of the literature of witnesses to the depravity of Nazi concentration camps. The *Muselmänner* were the "walking dead" or the "drowned" of the camps. It is difficult both to contemplate the extent of suffering that led to the *Muselmänner*, and it is painful to make the following distinction: In blurring the line between life and death, these people had exposed a mode of existence, transient, perhaps unconscious, *beneath* bare life. As Agamben (1999) notes, a distinguishing feature of this *Muselmänner* phenomenon is that it is "unbearable to human eyes" (51). The continuity both Agamben and Aristotle posited between bare life and the political life is breakable, and this break is manifested in the walking death of the *Muselmänner*. In the personage of the *Muselmänner*, in other words, equally difficult to write, there is room for moral outrage and tears, but there is nothing of political interest to be gleaned except to say that the politics of unity and suspicion can achieve complete victory over trust and resistance, and this ends life just as surely as a high explosive.

Bare life as a perceptual vantage is, by contrast, something that can be contemplated and, indeed, lived. Through the treatment of the Protagonist in *Catastrophe*, and in Wittgenstein's description of the relation between surface and depth grammars, bare life becomes a conduit for the investigation of the conventions distinguishing political life from other language-games. What may be described aptly as the foundation of politics is a membrane of trust, or, as in the case of Beckett's play, a reminder of what was once a trusting relation. Trust is both contingent and ephemeral, and yet it is resilient and an adhesive within a relation that can, when damaged, repair itself. But, once again, not always. We are to understand, for example, that there is no turning back to normal trusting life for the *Muselmänner*.[9] The Protagonist, by dint of his resistance, has proven himself still alive, and still (potentially) *bios politikos*.

Trust is an underinvestigated aspect of Wittgenstein's philosophical travels, perhaps because it runs afoul of the skepticism that is so central to philosophical training. It is a dimension of language that is so familiar that it stands as invisible and unremarked before us even as it suffuses the contexts and language-games for communication.

> The aspects of things that are most important for us are hidden because of their simplicity and familiarity. (One is unable to notice something – because it is always before one's eyes.) The real foundations of his enquiry do not strike a man

169

[sic] at all. Unless *that* fact has at some time struck him. – And this means: we fail to be struck by what, once seen, is most striking and powerful. (1958b: sec. 129)

Contemplation of bare life and catastrophe both function as a breach of the ordinary orientation to life and this upheaval brings relations of trust into view.[10] The condition of homelessness, rightlessness, and victimization are symptoms of trust's effacement, and a portal opening into deep insight into transformations in the larger political order that, if not based in trust, must be becoming something else.

For Wittgenstein, the relation of trust to language, like the relation of thought to language, is entwined to the point of identity (1958a: 3; 1958b: sec. 334). They are distinguishable, but not separable. The braid of trust/language leads us into Wittgenstein's conceptions of what we are, and, as formulated by T. M. Scanlon, what we owe one another.

> What can I rely on?
> I really want to say that a language-game is only possible if one trusts something (I did not say "can trust something."). (1969: secs. 508, 509)

Note the closeness to the formulation of the following, as observed by Holt (1997: 150):

> My attitude towards him is an attitude towards a soul. I am not of the *opinion* that he has a soul. (1958b: xi)

This attitude is what is conspicuously absent in the regard of D and A for P. Moreover, it has been, at the very least, suspended in the relation of the audience to P. That the relation of trust is restorable or even recallable is the power of the silence following P's resistance to the catastrophe sought after and celebrated by D.

If trust is, as Wittgenstein claims, so closely related to the very fact of language, then how can it be effaced, betrayed, and broken in speech?[11] This is a central concern of Beckett's, and he labored to pare language down to, in effect, speak silence.[12] The project of giving voice to silence, which reached fruition in the alienated, deathly silence of P, was the unifying theme for Beckett's trilogy of novels: *Molloy, Malone Dies, The Unnamable,* and the later, *Company.* "Beckett's work," notes Thiher (1983), "gives full expression to the voice alienated from itself, the voice for which the first and third person pronoun are a matter of indifference. The speaker lives the 'I' as an 'it,' for the voice is present to itself only as otherness" (87).[13] Even in Beckett's poetic comedies, as illustrated by the postapocalyptic landscape of *Waiting for Godot,* this silence is authentic.

It is the best possible response to "the mess" of existence. But to turn back toward politics, as P can be said to do in *Catastrophe*, in the spirit of resistance, is to tap into the mess's energy and regain language, speech, by struggling, however counterintuitive this may sound, to restore trust. Trust is imaginable without language, and not vice versa.

"The writings and contortions endured by Beckett's narrators and characters are orchestrated around a relentless confrontation between a poetic demand for a right to silence, and a political demand for speech" (Boxall 2002: 160). Both demands can and should be conceived as forms of resistance. This strikes me as a perfect description of both the Protagonist of *Catastrophe*, and the response of bare life (as individual anatomy or as a population) to its biopowerful re-creator – the late eighteenth-century mode of power/knowledge wherein "the ancient right to *take* life or *let* live was replaced by a power to *foster* life or *disallow* it to the point of death" (Foucault 1978: 138). The site of this confrontation is between the surface grammar and depth grammar of the language-game of politics. That is, between the play of rules as signposts (indeterminate guides to communication, friendship, and conflict that permit intra-game creativity and comedy) and the deeper framework of agreements that give the game shape.[14] In this liminal space of political potential, where resisters hide and *Muselmänner* fall to their death, reside the victims of biopolitical injustice: the tortured, the exiled, and the fastest growing population on earth today, the refugee. They bear traces of their lost political and pain-free past in the form of scars and in their longing for home, friendship, and safety.[15]

IV. CONCLUSION: RE-TURNING WORDS

The therapeutic turn Wittgenstein offers fellow philosophers is in the direction away from ideal language and metaphysical speculation and toward a more intimate and trusting relation with ordinary language (1958b: secs. 107, 116). This turn is performed within the philosophical language-game, the province of his immediate audience, but promises an erosion of the boundary separating philosophy from other activities. Wittgenstein, in other words, follows his own admonitions regarding the possibility of stepping out of a language to justify or reform it, while creating conditions for greater freedom within. Similarly, silence, in Beckett's view, is both a tragic desire to step out of language and a comedic acknowledgment of this desire's impossibility. In this unvarnished look

171

at mortality is the promise of politics as a form of resistance to an order that has spurned its political roots in exchange for a fearful and violent lexicon of self-justification. P is therefore able to raise his head and avert the catastrophe.

When P looks out from his bare life and *"fixes the audience,"* what does he see? In the surface of the play, P sees an audience. They are perfect spectators, quiet and unmoving. Their hands are still, and yet there is applause. Below the play's surface the audience's silence matches P's. The potential to speak remains for both. Earlier, A had suggested, "[*timidly*] What about a little . . . a little . . . gag?" "For God's sake!" responded D. "This craze for explicitation! Every i dotted to death! Little gag! For God's sake!" "Sure he won't utter?" asked A. "Not a squeak." The play ends before the solidarity of P and the audience can be absorbed. The light on his head goes out, casting the scene into darkness.

Again, we might read A's suggestion about the gag as a thought about how to heighten the drama, only to realize that she fears what would happen if P were to speak. D has already miscalculated regarding P's ability to resist and raise his head. Could D be wrong here too? The play ends with us, the audience, awaiting a word from P. Herein lies the comedic aspect of the play, for in waiting for P to speak, we, the audience, are acknowledging the resilience of trust. The silence will not give way to death. Rather, the membrane of trust, frayed and dangerously effaced, can still support a turn to speech, then to politics, benefited along the way by the restorative power of humor. In this sense, the play *Catastrophe* is described best as a prelude to comedy.

It is Beckett's most Wittgensteinian drama in that it gestures toward trust as the ground of human life and language. It is also an unusual burst of optimism when compared with characters from his other dramatic works and novels. For the Beckett of *Endgame*, for example, Clov responds to Hamm's question, "What's happening, what's happening?" with "Something is taking its course." "What is happening," explains Josipovici (1999), "is that our bodies are slowly moving toward decay and dissolution. Trying to make sense of life, as of history, is not simply misguided, it is a way of avoiding this central truth" (231). Beckett's entire writing life was dedicated to opposing this inhuman thrust of literature and philosophy (not to mention theology) away from countenancing mortality by paring down language to bare death. This point is reached in the bowed and silent inaction of P. It is one step from the living death of the *Muselmänner*. What is exposed is not death (because P looks up),

172

but what Wittgenstein conceived as the bedrock of language: trust. "Must I not begin to trust somewhere? That is to say, somewhere I must begin with not-doubting . . ." (1969: sec. 150).

Herein lies the ground for a Wittgensteinian examination of politics that resembles that of Aristotle, with one important difference. Politics, we can surmise, resides not in the nature of humans: their potential political-ness that requires a *polis* for fulfillment. Rather, politics is grounded in the trust exposed in the baring of language (performed here by Beckett). This is not to say that language is political. It is to observe that language and politics have at least one common genealogical strand. As Wittgenstein observed, trust precedes both language and politics. It is irreducible in the sense that to go deeper is to cease living a human life as *Muselmänner* or corpse. Trust is conceivable as an underlying community of silence formed not by consent, concord, or contract, but it makes these eventual political attributes of community possible. To ask about the source of trust is to try to get beyond the irreducible. There is, simply, trust. The main task of politics, which distinguishes it from all other activities once it grows beyond the inchoate state of the resistance embodied by P, is to repair and cultivate this bed of trust from which it emerged. A politics of suspicion is, by implication, a renunciation of politics.

This is a promise held out by Wittgenstein's description of language and trust as entwined, Beckett's gesture of resistance and solidarity written into the character of P, and in Agamben's (2000) own conception of "form of life" (3–11): The political path that originates in the act of rebellion against the sacrifice of life by the state of exception need not retrace the historical path that led from peace to the violence imprinted on the exposed bodies of refugees and exiles. A new path can be forged that leads to a politics that is human in form and scale, vital in its opposition to bureaucratic formalism, and resistant to sovereign power and its corresponding distrust of and control over human life.

In the frame or larger agreement about the play, P is the imprisoned future President of his country, Václav Havel. The play itself is an expression of solidarity with him, from one artist to another. The distance a prison is designed to create to separate inmates from society is subverted. Beckett turns the jail into a raised stage where P is visible from head to toe. The audience is there to witness his stoicism in the face of torment as a form of resistance. For the moment, the artist is silenced and exposed. He raises his head illuminating the heretofore invisible empathy between the audience and himself. The trust expressed by the resister can be described as well placed. Will it be enough to restore the trust that has been damaged? Imagine P speaking. Follow the trajectory of Havel's political life and a range of possibilities are opened.

NOTES

1. I am not employing Agamben's (1998) concept of "bare life" with complete felicity. He is exploring the roots of modern sovereignty and its relation to legal-institutional power, in particular the power to define itself as an exception to, or outside, the law, and the biopower ("the original activity of sovereign power") it exercises to include bare life inside the law (8).This exception and power emanate from, and are connected to, bare life, the pre-political origin of sovereignty. My use emphasizes the abject features of bare life as constitutive of a perceptual vantage onto the conventions (relations of trust) of contemporary politics as a language-game. The relations of distrust exhibited by modern state sovereignty so alter the trusting origins of politics, I will argue, that the state ought not to be regarded as political. The question by one whose life has been bared – "Can I trust again?" – has two answers: One leads to death, and the other to a re-founding of politics.

2. Beckett (1961) would note on occasion his indebtedness to certain concepts and images drawn from philosophy, while distinguishing what he did from the work of philosophers. "When Heidegger and Sartre speak of a contrast between being and existence, they may be right, I don't know, but their language is too philosophical. I am not a philosopher. One can only speak of what is in front of him, and that now is simply the mess."

3. "Is there any reason why that terrible materiality of the word surface should not be capable of being dissolved?"(Beckett 1969: 173).

4. "A person who exists in a diaspora is also a person very much of a place, time, and culture – perhaps of multiple cultures. And insofar as we are rooted in common linguistic practices, it is to be expected that such practices might become disfigured with the result that we experience common modes of alienation from the 'we' that is also 'I.' This is Marx's subject and it is also Wittgenstein's" (Herwitz 1998: 15).

5. Žižek (2002), for example, reads Agamben as exposing the *Homo sacer* in us all (100–1). The idea of giving voice to the affected is akin to Connolly's (1999) notion of "critical responsiveness," which he conceived as an extension of liberal tolerance to emerging, inchoate political movements that have yet to find a place or constituency in the political landscape (148). See also White's (2000) explication of this idea in Connolly's work (122–7).

6. "By laughing at power," notes Critchley (2002), "we expose its contingency, we realize that what appeared to be fixed and oppressive is in fact the emperor's new clothes, and just the sort of thing that should be mocked and ridiculed" (11).

7. Acknowledging this political side and set of values in Beckett was achieved first in T. W. Adorno's (1991) reading of the play *Endgame*. Adorno observes in Beckett's drama the parody of philosophy, dead and canonical, the death of nature in the barren landscape, and the echo-like voices of Hamm and Clov reflecting that all is artifice, reified, and hopeless; all is "corpsed," in the wake of some unnamed catastrophe. Also see the essays in Sussman and Devenney (2001). More recently a political

Beckett based in biographical detail has emerged. See Knowlson (1996); and Eagleton (2006).

8. Our communal identity as "we," does not preclude differences of opinion on even the most critical of political issues (Cavell 1979: 19–20).

9. This is not to say that the restoration of trust once broken is easy or complete. "Every morning when I get up," wrote Holocaust survivor Amery (1980), "I can read the Auschwitz number on my forearm . . . Every day anew I lose my trust in the world . . . Declarations of human rights, democratic constitutions, the free world and the free press, nothing can lull me into the slumber of security from which I awoke in 1935" (94–5; Roth 2005: 31).

10. There is irony here in that relations of trust can be revealed by fostering a spirit of distrust, as in the famous breaching experiments of Garfinkel (1963).

11. Speaking of torture, Scarry (1985) notes, "intense pain is . . . language-destroying: as the content of one's world disintegrates, so the content of one's language disintegrates; as the self disintegrates, so that which would express and project the self is robbed of its source and subject" (35).

12. As Davenport (1987) noticed in a review of Beckett's novel, Company, "the only punctuation in the book is the period. Beckett gave up semicolons years ago, and the comma several books back" (148).

13. "It is not simply that Beckett's writing opens literary spaces of freedom from the socio-political world," notes Boxall (2002) perceptively, "but that he creates spaces which disrupt and exceed the limits of written space. Beckett's writing opens up something akin to a black hole, a rupture in the universe of writing through which the image or the narrative voice escapes and is lost, and which destroys the world of the work by the action of its own negativity" (163).

14. Stern (1995) discusses this play of surface and depth in Wittgenstein as a contest between the voices of essentialism and conventionalism. It is a tension, argues Stern, Wittgenstein never resolved. "To both these voices, Wittgenstein responds that the depth the essentialist sees is . . . due to our nature; we have a deep need to see things that way, and that is itself an important fact that deserves our attention" (116). In my reading, frames or depth grammars are neither determinative nor static (essential); rather, they usually escape reflection and are therefore more stable than the play of surface grammars and meanings. This stability does tell us something important about who we are, how we see ourselves, and the room we create to change.

15. See Agamben's (2004) protest against the "data registration" and fingerprinting of foreign travelers wishing to enter the United States, as a form of biopolitical imprint (168–9).

Conclusion: The Personal is the Theoretical

At first, Wittgenstein's work struck me as beautiful visually. Because my college philosophy teacher had warned me about the difficulty of his work, I expected the problem of reading Wittgenstein to be one of density in the prose akin to the problem of reading a late dialogue of Plato or one of Kant's critiques. The spare, even hygienic, quality of Wittgenstein's remarks was therefore something of a surprise. But I soon found accuracy in my teacher's admonishment. Reading Wittgenstein as an author with coherent narrative or immediately comprehensible messages or points was, for a novice, all but impossible. Still I managed to read through much of Part One of the *Philosophical Investigations* well enough to at least intuit the importance of the work.

This first exposure to Wittgenstein came in the second semester of graduate school in a course on Contemporary Sociological Theory where we read Garfinkel's *Studies in Ethnomethodology*. Garfinkel cited Wittgenstein's descriptions of language-games as a way of accounting for the variety of meanings a word or action could take as a person seeks to cope artfully with the challenges of everyday life. Wittgenstein's work was far less important to Garfinkel's project than that of Husserl or Alfred Schutz, but there was just enough talk of language-games to inspire my interest. What attracted me to Wittgenstein was the initial contrast I could draw between the irreducible but superficial plurality of language-games that called to mind a mosaic, and the unified, but deep, life-world of the phenomenologist. Later this contrast led to suspicion and then criticism of the unified or synoptic political visions of theorists in the epic tradition.

Study of Wittgenstein's philosophy proceeded following my usual method: collecting books and articles until the pile presented the requisite gravitas necessary to embarrass me into working. I read Norman Malcolm's little biography and remembrance of Wittgenstein. After this, Wittgenstein ceased being an abstraction and became, at least in the silence of my notebooks, "Ludwig." Despite the conversations I could have now with Wittgenstein, continued reading of the *Blue and Brown Books*, *On Certainty*, and *Culture and Value*, in addition to the *Investigations*, yielded no real insight or connection to my study of political theory. Yet, Wittgenstein was being revived through Richard Rorty's recently published *Philosophy and the Mirror of Nature*, and Stanley Cavell's *The Claim of Reason*, a book based on what was probably the most widely read doctoral dissertation in American philosophy. It was possible for me to learn a great deal about what can be made of Wittgenstein's philosophy from these and other secondary sources. Hanna Pitkin's *Wittgenstein and Justice* was always opened on my desk.

Pitkin's study of Wittgenstein suggested that his approach to philosophical problems could transform the way we theorize politics. But, in the end, this suggestion remained a potential. *Wittgenstein and Justice*, as I have noted throughout this work, took Wittgenstein to be an aid to our reading of works of concern to political theorists today. All of my initial reading led me to formulate the question that guided my doctoral dissertation. I asked why Wittgenstein was not more influential on the discourse of contemporary political theory. He had written two of the most significant works of philosophy in the twentieth century and inspired two very different approaches to philosophy. Political theory's historical and intellectual closeness to philosophy and its weakness for new trends instigated by philosophers was all clear enough. Why, then, wasn't Wittgenstein riding the same wave of popularity among theorists as Heidegger, Foucault, or Derrida?

Looking back, I see that I made an error in that dissertation that could be traced to Hanna Pitkin. I could sense Wittgenstein was doing something of profound importance that political theorists in the late twentieth century needed to grasp. I knew Pitkin's suggestion that Wittgenstein offered a new way of doing political theory was correct. But, like Pitkin, I was trapped in a picture of theory as a historical artifact that permitted only the narrow view onto Wittgenstein's "significance" for reading theory. That is, I looked at contemporary political theory for traces of his influences and obstacles that would explain the limits of that influence. What I did not look at or think through was the activity of theorizing politics and the difficulties a theorist engaging in this activity confronts that are unique to this age.

177

What I have contended in the preceding chapters is that Wittgenstein's *Philosophical Investigations* are themselves an intimate view onto the process of theorizing. This is a contentious point because of Wittgenstein's stated antipathy for theory, an antipathy that can be adduced as one explanation for his peripheral place in contemporary social, cultural, and political theory. But I have shown that Wittgenstein's criticism of theory is more accurately a criticism of metatheory, and, more importantly, that his remarks on seeing are re-presentations – slower, illuminating examinations – of the activity and experience of, and style of life behind, theorizing. These remarks, in turn, can also be adduced as a second explanation for Wittgenstein's tenuous relationship to political theory. Political theory's self-identity is a product of encounters with the thinkers whose works compose the "Great Tradition" of political thought. From Plato onward, these philosophical writers lived on the outer bounds of political life as a result of delusions of privileged knowledge, political defeat, exile, and ostracism. Their peripheral perspective was cast in heroic terms that are blatantly divine. The work that followed was a result of a putatively God's-eye point of view, clear, panoramic, and profound.

In Wittgenstein we find a de-divinized description of theorizing that befits the challenges of living and seeing in political society today. These challenges begin with the question of where to look when you seek to "see" politics or political phenomena. In the epic tradition, politics was conceived spatially as a place – "the city," "the *polis*," "the government," that locale where the theorist cannot go without being subjected to punishment by those in power. Theorists today continue to try to conceive politics in similarly spatial or ontologically stable terms, like "the political" or "the public." These terms do not conform at all to the way we experience politics today, but rather fit the epic model of political theory where the place of the theorist and politics is clearly delineated by a line that creates a safe zone for truth and contemplation on one side and a dangerous zone of corruption and action on the other. There is no such line in the lived-life of the contemporary political theorist, or, rather, there are many such lines that are thinner and less noticeable, but no less dangerous. The politics of today is a politics of resistance and dissent. The drama arises sporadically in the form of protest and imaginatively in the playfulness of street theatre. Perceiving these acts requires the intimacy that the epic tradition eschewed. To theorize today is to pursue what I have offered as Wittgenstein's path to politics.

Bibliography

Adorno, Theodor W. (1974), *Minima Moralia: Reflections from a Damaged Life*, New York: Verso.

Adorno, Theodor W. (1991), *Notes to Literature, vol. 1*, trans. Shierry Weber Nicholson, New York: Columbia University Press.

Agamben, Giorgio (1998), *Homo Sacer: Sovereign Power and Bare Life*, trans. Daniel Heller, Stanford: Stanford University Press.

Agamben, Giorgio (1999), *Remnants of Auschwitz: The Witness and the Archive*, trans. Daniel Heller-Roazen, New York: Zone Books.

Agamben, Giorgio (2000), *Means Without End: Notes on Politics*, trans. Vincenzo Binetti and Cesare Casarino, Minneapolis: University of Minnesota Press.

Agamben, Giorgio (2004), "Bodies Without Words: Against the Biopolitical Tatoo," *German Law Journal*, 5: 168–9.

Althusser, Louis and Balibar, Etienne (1970), *Reading "Capital"*, New York: Verso.

Amery, Jean (1980), *At the Mind's Limits: Contemplations by a Survivor on Auschwitz and its Realities*, trans. Sidney Rosenfeld and Stella P. Rosenfeld, New York: Schocken Books.

Arendt, Hannah (1958), *The Human Condition*, Chicago: University of Chicago Press.

Arendt, Hannah (1990), "Philosophy and Politics," *Social Research*, 57: 73–103.

Arendt, Hannah and Jaspers, Karl (1992), *Correspondence, 1926–1969*, New York: Harcourt Brace Jovanovich.

Arendt, Hannah (1994), "'What Remains? The Language Remains': A Conversation with Gunter Gaus," *Essays in Understanding 1930–1954*, ed. Jerome Kohn, New York: Harcourt Brace.

Ashcraft, Richard (1983), "One Step Backward, Two Steps Forward: Reflections upon Contemporary Political Theory," in John S. Nelson (ed.), *What Should Political Theory be Now?*, Albany: State University of New York Press, pp. 515–48.

Badiou, Alain (2005), "The Adventures of French Philosophy," *New Left Review*, 35.

Ball, Terence (1995), *Reappraising Political Theory: Revisionist Studies in the History of Political Thought*, Oxford: Clarendon Press.

Ball, Terence (1997), "Political Theory and Conceptual Change," in Andrew Vincent (ed.), *Political Theory: Tradition and Diversity*, Cambridge: Cambridge University Press, pp. 28–44.

Bartley, W. W. (1973), *Wittgenstein*, LaSalle: Open Court.

Bauman, Zygmunt (1989), *Modernity and the Holocaust*, Ithaca: Cornell University Press.

Bearn, Gordon C. F. (1997), *Waking to Wonder: Wittgenstein's Existential Investigations*, Albany: State University of New York Press.

Beckett, Samuel (1961), "Interview," *Columbia University Forum*, Summer: 21–5.

Beckett, Samuel (1969), "The German Letter," in Ruby Cohn (ed.), *Disjecta*, New York: Grove Press.

Beckett, Samuel (2006), *Samuel Beckett: The Grove Centenary Edition*, ed. Paul Auster, 4 vols, New York: Grove Press.

Bennington, Geoffrey (2001), "Derrida and Politics," in Tom Cohen (ed.), *Jacques Derrida and the Humanities: A Critical Reader*, Cambridge: Cambridge University Press, pp. 193–212.

Berlant, Lauren (2005), "The Epistemology of State Emotion," *Dissent in Dangerous Times*, ed. Austin Sarat, Ann Arbor: University of Michigan Press.

Berman, Marshall (1982), *All That Is Solid Melts into Air: The Experience of Modernity*, New York: Penguin.

Bérubé, Michael (1998), *Life As We Know It: A Father, A Family, and an Exceptional Child*, New York: Vintage.

Binkley, Timothy (1973), *Wittgenstein's Language*, The Hague: Nijhoff.

Blanchot, Maurice (1986), *The Writing of the Disaster*, trans. Ann Smock, Lincoln: University of Nebraska Press.

Borowski, Tadeusz (1976), *This Way For the Gas, Ladies and Gentlemen*, trans. Barbara Vedder, New York: Penguin.

Borradori, Giovanna (1991), *The American Philosopher: Conversations with Quine, Davidson, Putnam, Nozick, Danto, Rorty, Cavell, MacIntyre, and Kuh*, Chicago: University of Chicago Press.

Boxall, Peter (2002), "Samuel Beckett: Towards a Political Reading," *Irish Studies Review*, 10: 159–70.

Brenner, William (1999), *Wittgenstein's Philosophical Investigations*, Albany: State University of New York Press.

Brown, Wendy (1997), "The Time of the Political," *Theory and Event*, 1.1.

Brown, Wendy (2004), "At the Edge," in Stephen K. White and J. Donald Moon (eds), *What Is Political Theory?*, Thousand Oaks: Sage, pp. 103–23.

Bull, Malcolm (2007), "Vectors of the Biopolitical," *New Left Review*, 45: 1–13.

Cavarero, Adriana (2004), "Politicizing Theory," in Stephen K. White and J. Donald Moon (eds), *What Is Political Theory?*, Thousand Oaks: Sage.

Cavell, Stanley (1976), *Must We Mean What We Say?*, Cambridge: Cambridge University Press.

Cavell, Stanley (1979), *The Claim of Reason: Wittgenstein, Skepticism, Morality, and Tragedy*, Oxford: Oxford University Press.

Cavell, Stanley (1988), *In Quest of the Ordinary: Lines of Skepticism and Romanticism*, Chicago: University of Chicago Press.

Cavell, Stanley (1996), "On the Opening of the *Investigations*," in Hans Sluga and David G. Stern (eds), *The Cambridge Companion to Wittgenstein*, Cambridge: Cambridge University Press.

Cavell, Stanley (2005), *Philosophy the Day After Tomorrow*, Cambridge, MA: Harvard University Press.

Cerbone, David R. (2003), "The Limits of Conservatism: Wittgenstein on 'Our Life' and 'Our Concepts'," in Cressida J. Heyes (ed.), *The Grammar of Politics: Wittgenstein and Political Philosophy*, Ithaca: Cornell University Press, pp. 43–62.

Chambers, Samuel A. (2003), *Untimely Politics*, Edinburgh and New York: Edinburgh University Press and New York University Press.

Chambers, Samuel A. (2006), "Cultural Politics and the Practice of Fugitive Theory," *Contemporary Political Theory*, 5: 9–32.

Chandler, Ralph C. (1977), "Political Theory as History, Philosophy, and Science," in David Freeman (ed.), *Foundations of Political Science: Research, Methods, and Scope*, New York: The Free Press, pp. 123–53.

Conant, James (1990), "Throwing Away the Top of the Ladder," *The Yale Review*, 79.3: 328–64.

Connolly, William E. (1983), *The Terms of Political Discourse*, 2nd edn, Princeton: Princeton University Press.

Connolly, William E. (1995), "The Uncertain Conditions of the Critical Intellectual," *Political Theory*, 23: 653–57.

Connolly, William E. (1999), *Why I Am Not A Secularist*, Minneapolis: University of Minnesota Press.

Cornell, Drucilla (1993), *Transformations: Recollective Imagination and Sexual Difference*, New York: Routledge.

Cornish, Kimberly (1998), *The Jew of Linz: Wittgenstein, Hitler, and Their Secret Battle for the Mind*, Melbourne: Century Hutchinson.

Crary, Alice (2000), "Wittgenstein's Philosophy in Relation to Political Thought," in Alice Crary and Rupert Read (eds), *The New Wittgenstein*, New York: Routledge.

Critchley, Simon (2002), *On Humour*, New York: Routledge.

Dallmayr, Fred R. (1984), *Language and Politics: Why Does Language Matter to Political Philosophy?*, South Bend: University of Notre Dame.

Danford, John W. (1976), *Wittgenstein and Political Philosophy: A Reexamination of the Foundations of Social Science*, Chicago: University of Chicago Press.

181

Davenport, Guy (1987), *Every Force Evolves a Form*, San Francisco: North Point Press.

Davidson, Donald (1984), *Inquiries into Truth and Interpretation*, Oxford: Clarendon Press.

Davidson, Donald (2001), *Subjective, Intersubjective, Objective*, Oxford: Oxford University Press.

Dean, Jodi (ed.), (2000), *Cultural Studies and Political Theory*, Ithaca: Cornell University Press.

De Certeau, Michel (1984), *The Practice of Everyday Life*, trans. Stephen Rendall, Berkeley: University of California Press.

Deleuze, Gilles and Guattari, Félix (1991), *What Is Philosophy?*, trans. Hugh Tomlinson and Graham Burchell, New York: Columbia University Press.

Deleuze, Gilles (2003), *Francis Bacon: The Logic of Sensation*, trans. Daniel W. Smith, Minneapolis: University of Minnesota Press.

Diamond, Cora (1991), *The Realist Spirit: Wittgenstein, Philosophy, and the Mind*, Cambridge, MA: MIT Press.

Dienstag, Joshua Foa (1998), "Wittgenstein Among the Savages: Language, Action and Political Theory," *Polity*, 30: 579–605.

Dumm, Thomas L. (2000), "Political Theory for Losers," in Jason A. Frank and John Tambornino (eds), *Vocations of Political Theory*, Minneapolis: University of Minnesota Press, pp. 145–65.

Dumm, Thomas L. (2008), *Loneliness as a Way of Life*, Cambridge, MA: Harvard University Press.

Duran, Jane (2002), "Wittgenstein, Feminism and Theory," *Philosophy and Social Criticism*, 28.3: 321–36.

Eagleton, Terry (1982), "Wittgenstein's Friends," *New Left Review*, 135: 64–90.

Eagleton, Terry (2006), "Political Beckett?," *New Left Review*, 40: 67–74.

Eldridge, Richard (1997), *Leading a Human Life: Wittgenstein, Intentionality, and Romanticism*, Chicago: University of Chicago Press.

Embree, Lester E. (1972), "Toward a Phenomenology of Theoria," *Life-World and Consciousness: Essays for Aron Gurwitsch*, Evanston: Northwestern University Press.

Farr, James, Dryzek, John S. and Leonard, Stephen T. (eds), (1995), *Political Science in History: Research Programs and Political Traditions*, Cambridge: Cambridge University Press.

Farr, James and Seidelman, Raymond (eds), (1993), *Discipline and History: Political Science in the United States*, Ann Arbor: University of Michigan Press.

Ferguson, Kathy E. (1984), *The Feminist Case Against Bureaucracy*, Philadelphia: Temple University Press.

Feyerabend, Paul (1968), "Wittgenstein's *Philosophical Investigations*," in George Pitcher (ed.), *Wittgenstein: The Philosophical Investigations*, South Bend: University of Notre Dame Press, pp. 108–18.

Feyerabend, Paul (1995), *Killing Time*, Chicago: University of Chicago Press.

Fish, Stanley (1995), *Professional Correctness: Literary Studies and Political Change*, Oxford: Clarendon Press.

Fish, Stanley (1999), *The Trouble with Principle*, Cambridge, MA: Harvard University Press.

Fodor, Jerry (1998), *Concepts: Where Cognitive Science Went Wrong*, New York: Oxford University Press.

Foucault, Michel (1978), *The History of Sexuality, Volume 1: An Introduction*, trans. Robert Hurley, New York: Random House.

Foucault, Michel (1980), *Power/Knowledge: Selected Interviews and Other Writings*, ed. Colin Gordon, New York: Pantheon.

Foucault, Michael (1985), *The Use of Pleasure: The History of Sexuality*, New York: Pantheon.

Frank, Jason, A. and Tambornino, John (eds), (2000), *Vocations of Political Theory*, Minneapolis: University of Minnesota Press.

Freeman, Michael and Robertson, David (eds), (1980), *The Frontiers of Political Theory: Essays in a Revitalized Discipline*, New York: St. Martin's Press.

Gadamer, Hans-Georg (1975), *Truth and Method*, New York: Seabury Press.

Gadamer, Hans-Georg (1998), *Praise of Theory: Speeches and Essays*, trans. Chris Dawson, New Haven: Yale University Press.

Garfinkel, Harold (1963), "A Conception of, and Experiments with, 'Trust' as a Condition of Stable Concerted Actions," in O. J. Harvey (ed.), *Motivation and Social Action*, New York: Ronald Press, pp. 187–238.

Garfinkel, Harold (1967), *Studies in Ethnomethodology*, New Jersey: Prentice-Hall.

Geertz, Clifford (1973), *The Interpretation of Cultures: Selected Essays*, New York: Basic Books.

Gellner, Ernest (1959), *Words and Things: A Critical Account of Linguistic Philosophy and a Study in Ideology*, Boston: Beacon Press.

Gellner, Ernest (1998), *Language and Solitude: Wittgenstein, Malinowski and the Habsburg Dilemma*, New York: Cambridge University Press.

Genova, Judith (1995), *Wittgenstein: A Way of Seeing*, New York: Routledge.

Geuss, Raymond (2008), *Philosophy and Real Politics*, Princeton: Princeton University Press.

Gier, Nicholas F. (1981), *Wittgenstein and Phenomenology: A Comparative Study of the Later Wittgenstein, Husserl, Heidegger, and Merleau-Ponty*, Albany: State University of New York Press.

Glendinning, Simon (2002), *On Being with Others: Heidegger, Derrida, Wittgenstein*, New York: Routledge.

Glock, Hans-Johann (1996), *A Wittgenstein Dictionary*, Malden: Blackwell.

Gould, James A. and Thursby, Vincent V. (eds), (1969), *Contemporary Political Thought: Issues in Scope, Value, and Direction*, New York: Holt, Rinehart and Winston.

Graham, George and Carey, George W. (eds), (1972), *The Post-Behavioral Era: Perspectives on Political Science*, New York: David McKay.

Griswold v. Connecticut (1965), 381 U.S. 479.

Gunnell, John G. (1979), *Political Theory: Tradition and Interpretation*, Cambridge, MA: Winthrope.

Gunnell, John G. (1986), *Between Philosophy and Politics: The Alienation of Political Theory*, Amherst: University of Massachusetts Press.

Gunnell, John G. (1993), *The Descent of Political Theory: The Genealogy of an American Vocation*, Chicago: Chicago University Press.

Gunnell, John G. (1998), *The Orders of Discourse*, New York: Routledge.

Gunnell, John G. (2003), "Desperately Seeking Wittgenstein," *European Journal of Political Theory*, 3.1: 77–98.

Habermas, Jürgen (1990), *The Philosophical Discourse of Modernity: Twelve Lectures*, trans. Frederick G. Lawrence, Cambridge, MA: MIT Press.

Habermas, Jürgen (1992), *The Structural Transformation of the Public Sphere: An Inquiry into a Category of Bourgeois Society*, trans. Thomas Burger, Cambridge, MA: MIT Press.

Habermas, Jürgen (1996), *Between Facts and Norms: Contributions to a Discourse Theory of Law and Democracy*, trans. William Rehg, Cambridge, MA: MIT Press.

Hadot, Pierre (1995), *Philosophy as a Way of Life*, trans. Michael Chase, Oxford: Blackwell.

Hartsock, Nancy C. M. (1997), "How Feminist Scholarship Could Change Political Science," in Kristen Renwick Monroe (ed.), *Contemporary Empirical Political Theory*, Berkeley: University of California Press.

Hauptmann, Emily (2004), "A Local History of 'The Political'," *Political Theory*, 32: 34–60.

Hauptmann, Emily (2005), "Defining 'Theory' in Postwar Political Science," in George Steinmetz (ed.), *The Politics of Method in the Human Sciences: Positivism and Its Epistemological Others*, Durham, NC: Duke University Press, pp. 207–32.

Havercroft, Jonathan (2003), "On Seeing Liberty As," in Cressida J. Heyes (ed.), *The Grammar of Politics: Wittgenstein and Political Philosophy*, Ithaca: Cornell University Press, pp. 149–66.

Heidegger, Martin (1977a), *Basic Writings of Heidegger*, ed. David Krell, New York: Harper and Row.

Heidegger, Martin (1977b), "Science and Reflection," in *The Question Concerning Technology, and Other Essays*, trans. William Lovitt, New York: Harper and Row.

Herwitz, Daniel (1998), "On the Exile of Words," in Elazar Barkan and Marie Denise Shelton (eds), *Borders, Exiles, Diasporas*, Stanford: Stanford University Press, pp. 149–77.

Heyes, Cressida J. (2000), *Line Drawings: Defining Women Through Feminist Practice*, Ithaca: Cornell University Press.

Heyes, Cressida J. (ed.), (2003), *The Grammar of Politics: Wittgenstein and Political Philosophy*, New York: Cornell University Press.

Hintikka, Jaakko (1991), "An Impatient Man and His Papers," *Synthese*, 87: 183–201.

Hirst, Paul (1994), *Associative Democracy*, Cambridge: Polity.

Hodges, Andrew (1983), *Alan Turing: The Enigma*, New York: Simon and Schuster.

Hoffman, Donald, D. (1998), *Visual Intelligence: How We Create What We See*, New York: Norton.

Holt, Robin (1997), *Wittgenstein, Politics and Human Rights*, New York: Routledge.

Honig, Bonnie (1992), "Toward an Agonistic Feminism: Hannah Arendt and the Politics of Identity," in Judith Butler and Joan W. Scott (eds), *Feminists Theorize the Political*, New York: Routledge.

Honig, Bonnie (1993), *Political Theory and the Displacement of Politics*, New York: Cornell University Press.

Hymers, Michael (2000), "Wittgenstein, Pessimism and Politics," *The Dalhousie Review*, 80: 187–216.

Irwin, T. H. (1992), "Plato: The Intellectual Background," in Richard Kraut (ed.), *The Cambridge Companion to Plato*, Cambridge: Cambridge University Press, pp. 51–89.

Isaac, Jeffrey (1995), "The Strange Silence of Political Theory," *Political Theory*, 23.4: 636–88.

Janik, Allan (1989), "Nyíri on the Conservatism of Wittgenstein's Later Philosophy," in *Style, Politics and the Future of Philosophy*, Boston: Kluwer, pp. 40–58.

Janik, Allan (2001), *Wittgenstein's Vienna Revisited*, New Jersey: Transaction.

Janik, Allan (2003), "Notes on the Natural History of Politics," in Cressida J. Heyes (ed.), *The Grammar of Politics: Wittgenstein and Political Philosophy*, Ithaca: Cornell University Press, pp. 99–116.

Janik, Allan and Toulmin, Stephen (1973), *Wittgenstein's Vienna*, New York: Simon and Schuster.

John, Peter (1998), "Wittgenstein's 'Wonderful Life'," *Journal of the History of Ideas*, 49.3: 495–510.

Jones, K. (1986), "Is Wittgenstein a Conservative Philosopher?," *Philosophical Investigations*, 9: 274–87.

Jonsen, Albert R. and Toulmin, Stephen (1988), *The Abuse of Casuistry: A History of Moral Reasoning*, Berkeley: University of California Press.

Josipovici, Gabriel (1999), *On Trust: Art and the Temptation of Suspicion*, New Haven: Yale University Press.

Kateb, George (1977), "The Condition of Political Theory," *American Behavioral Scientist*, 21: 135–59.

Kateb, George (2004), "The Adequacy of the Western Canon," in Stephen K. White and J. Donald Moon (eds), *What is Political Theory?*, Thousand Oaks: Sage.

Kiss, Elizabeth (1995), "Response," *Political Theory*, 23: 664–9.

Knowlson, James (1996), *Damned to Fame: The Life of Samuel Beckett*, New York: Touchstone Books.

Kompridis, Nikolas (1994), "On World Disclosure: Heidegger, Habermas and Dewey," *Thesis Eleven*, 37: 29–45.

Kripke, Saul (1982), *Wittgenstein on Rules and Private Language*, Cambridge, MA: Harvard University Press.

Kuhn, Thomas (1962), *The Structure of Scientific Revolutions*, Chicago: University of Chicago Press.

Kymlicka, Will (1995), *Multicultural Citizenship*, Oxford: Clarendon Press.

Laclau, Ernesto (1988), "Politics and the Limits of Modernity," in Andrew Ross (ed.), *Universal Abandon: The Politics of Postmodernism*, Minneapolis: University of Minnesota Press, pp. 63–82.

Laclau, Ernesto and Mouffe, Chantal (1985), *Hegemony and Socialist Strategy: Toward a Radical Democratic Politics*, New York: Verso.

Lane, Ruth (2004), "Pitkin's Dilemma: The Wider Shores of Political Theory and Political Science," *Perspectives on Politics*, 2.3: 459–73.

Laurence, Stephen and Margolis, Eric (1999), "Concepts and Cognitive Science," in Eric Margolis and Stephen Laurence (eds), *Concepts: Core Readings*, Cambridge, MA: MIT Press, pp. 3–81.

Levi, Albert W. (1978–9), "The Biographical Sources of Wittgenstein's Ethics," *Telos*, 38: 62–76.

Levin, David Michael (1999), *The Philosopher's Gaze: Modernity in the Shadow of the Enlightenment*, Berkeley: University of California Press.

Levinas, Emmanuel (1987), *Collected Philosophical Papers*, trans. Alphonso Lingis, Pittsburgh: Duquesne University Press.

Lewis, David (1975), "Languages and Language," in Keith Gundersom (ed.), *Language, Mind and Knowledge*, Minneapolis: University of Minnesota Press.

Lugg, Andrew (1985), "Was Wittgenstein a Conservative Thinker?," *Southern Journal of Philosophy*, 23: 465–74.

Luntley, Michael (2003), *Wittgenstein: Meaning and Judgment*, Malden: Blackwell.

Lyas, Colin (1982), "Herbert Marcuse's Criticism of 'Linguistic Philosophy'," *Philosophical Investigations*, 5: 166–89.

Lyotard, Jean-François (1984), *The Postmodern Condition: A Report on Knowledge*, trans. Geoffrey Bennington and Brian Massumi, Minneapolis: University of Minnesota Press.

Lyotard, Jean-François (1988), *The Differend (Phrases in Dispute)*, trans. Georges Van Den Abbeele, Minneapolis: University of Minnesota Press.

Lyotard, Jean-François (1993), *Jean-François Lyotard: Political Writings*, ed. Bill Readings and Kevin Paul Geiman, Minneapolis: University of Minnesota Press.

Lyotard, Jean-François and Thébaud, Jean-Loup (1985), *Just Gaming*, trans. Wlad Godzich, Minneapolis: University of Minnesota Press.

McAfee, Noelle (2000), *Habermas, Kristeva, and Citizenship*, Ithaca: Cornell University Press.

McCarthy, Thomas (1990), "Private Irony and Public Decency: Richard Rorty's New Pragmatism," *Critical Inquiry*, 16: 355–70.

Marcuse, Herbert (1964), *One-Dimensional Man: Studies in the Ideologies of Advanced Industrial Society*, Boston: Beacon Press.

Marcuse, Herbert (1998), *Technology, War and Fascism, Collected Papers of Herbert Marcuse, Volume 1*, ed. Douglas Kellner, New York: Routledge.

Michael H. v. Gerald D. (1989), 491 U.S. 110.

Miller, David and Siedentop, Larry (eds), (1983), *The Nature of Political Theory*, Oxford: Oxford University Press.

Monk, Ray (1990), *Wittgenstein: The Duty of Genius*, New York: The Free Press.

Monk, Ray (2007), "Bourgeois, Bolshevist or Anarchist? The Reception of Wittgenstein's Philosophy of Mathematics," in Guy Kahane, Edward Kanterian and Oskari Kuusela (eds), *Wittgenstein and His Interpreters: Essays in Memory of Gordon Baker*, Oxford: Blackwell, pp. 269–94.

Moran, John (1972), "Wittgenstein and Russia," *New Left Review*, 73: 83–96.

Mouffe, Chantal (1993), *The Return of the Political*, New York: Verso.

Mouffe, Chantal (1999), *The Challenge of Carl Schmitt*, Verso.

Mouffe, Chantal (2000), *The Democratic Paradox*, New York: Verso.

Mouffe, Chantal (2005), *On the Political*, New York: Routledge.

Mulhall, Stephen (1990), *On Being in the World: Wittgenstein and Heidegger on Seeing Aspects*, New York: Routledge.

Mulhall, Stephen (2001), "Seeing Aspects," in Hans-Johann Glock (ed.), *Wittgenstein: A Critical Reader*, Malden: Blackwell.

Nafisi, Azar (2003), *Reading Lolita in Tehran: A Memoir in Books*, New York: Random House.

Nagel, Thomas (1986), *The View From Nowhere*, Oxford: Oxford University Press.

Nails, Debra (2002), *The People of Plato: A Prosopography of Plato and Other Socratics*, Indianapolis: Hackett.

Nelson, John S. (ed.), (1983), *What Should Political Theory Be Now?*, Albany: State University of New York Press.

Neumann, Franz (1957), *The Democratic and Authoritarian State*, ed. Herbert Marcuse, New York: The Free Press.

Nietzsche, Friedrich (1964), "On Truth and Falsity in an Extra-Moral Sense," in *Early Greek Philosophy and Other Essays*, trans. M. A. Mugge, New York: Russell and Russell.

Nietzsche, Friedrich (1967), *The Birth of Tragedy*, trans. Walter Kaufmann, New York: Vintage.

Nietzsche, Friedrich (1974), *The Gay Science*, trans. Walter Kaufmann, New York: Vintage.

Norton, Anne (2004), *95 Theses on Politics, Culture, and Method*, New Haven: Yale University Press.

Norval, Aletta J. (2006), "Democratic Identification: A Wittgensteinian Approach," *Political Theory*, 34.2: 229–55.

Nussbaum, Martha C. (2000), *Women and Human Development: The Capabilities Approach*, Cambridge: Cambridge University Press.

Nyíri, J. C. (1976), "Wittgenstein's New Traditionalism," in *Essays in Honour of G. H. von Wright*, *Acta Philosophica Fennica*, 28: 501–12.

Nyíri, J. C. (1981), "From Eotvos to Musil: Philosophy and its Negation in Austria and Hungary," in J. C. Nyíri (ed.), *Austrian Philosophy: Studies and Texts*, Munich: Philosophia Verlag, pp. 9–30.

Nyíri, J. C. (1982), "Wittgenstein's Later Work in Relation to Conservatism," in Brian McGuinness (ed.), *Wittgenstein and his Times*, Chicago: University of Chicago Press, pp. 44–68.

Nyíri, J. C. (1986), "Wittgenstein 1929–31: The Turning Back," in Stuart G. Shanker (ed.), *Ludwig Wittgenstein: Critical Assessments*, Canberra: Croom Helm, vol. 4, pp. 29–59.

Oakeshott, Michael (1975), *On Human Conduct*, Oxford: Clarendon Press.

O'Connor, Peg (2002), *Oppression and Responsibility: A Wittgensteinian Approach to Social Practices*, University Park: Penn State University Press.

Osborne, Andrew (2004), "'A Little Hard to See': Wittgenstein, Stevens, and the Uses of Unclarity," *Wallace Stevens Journal*, 28.1: 59–80.

O'Sullivan, Noel (ed.), (2000), *Political Theory in Transition*, New York: Routledge.

Owens, Craig N. (2003), "Applause and Hiss: Implicating the Audience in Samuel Beckett's *Rockaby* and *Catastrophe*," *Journal of the Midwest Modern Language Association*, 36: 74–81.

Patterson, Dennis M. (ed.), (1992), *Wittgenstein and Legal Theory*, Boulder: Westview Press.

Perloff, Marjorie (1996), *Wittgenstein's Ladder: Poetic Language and the Strangeness of the Ordinary*, Chicago: University of Chicago Press.

Peterman, James F. (1992), *Philosophy as Therapy: An Interpretation and Defense of Wittgenstein's Later Philosophical Project*, Albany: State University of New York Press.

Pitkin, Hanna Fenichel (1972), *Wittgenstein and Justice: On the Significance of Ludwig Wittgenstein for Social and Political Thought*, Berkeley: University of California Press.

Pleasants, Nigel (1999), *Wittgenstein and the Idea of a Critical Social Theory: A Critique of Giddens, Habermas and Baskar*, New York: Routledge.

Pohlhaus, Gaile and Wright, John R. (2002), "Using Wittgenstein Critically: A Political Approach to Philosophy," *Political Theory*, 30.6: 800–27.

Prigogine, Ilya and Stengers, Isabelle (1984), *Order Out of Chaos: Man's New Dialogue with Nature*, New York: Bantam.

Putnam, Hilary (1981), "Convention: A Theme in Philosophy," *New Literary History*, 13: 1–14.

Pylyshyn, Zenon W. (2003), *Seeing and Visualizing: It's Not What You Think*, Cambridge, MA: MIT Press.

Quigley, Austin W. (2004), *Theoretical Inquiry: Language, Linguistics, and Literature*, New Haven: Yale University Press.

Quinton, Anthony (1982), "Wittgenstein," *Social Research*, 49.1: 4–31.

Ragland, C. P. and Heidt, Sarah (eds), (2001), *What is Philosophy?*, New Haven: Yale University Press.

Rhees, Rush (ed.), (1981), *Recollections of Wittgenstein*, Oxford: Oxford University Press.

Ricci, David M. (1984), *The Tragedy of Political Science: Politics, Scholarship, and Democracy*, New Haven: Yale University Press.

Robinson, Christopher C. (2009), "Theorizing Politics after Camus," *Human Studies*, 32: 1–18.

Rochberg-Halton, Eugene (1986), *Meaning and Modernity: Social Theory in the Pragmatic Attitude*, Chicago: University of Chicago Press.

Roe v. Wade (1973), 410 U.S. 113.

Rorty, Richard (1982), *Consequences of Pragmatism (Essays: 1972–1980)*, Minneapolis: University of Minnesota Press.

Rorty, Richard (1985), "Habermas and Lyotard on Postmodernity," in Richard Bernstein (ed.), *Habermas and Modernity*, Cambridge, MA: MIT Press, pp. 161–75.

Rorty, Richard (1991), *Objectivity, Relativism and Truth: Philosophical Papers, Volume I*, Cambridge: Cambridge University Press.

Roth, John K. (2005), *Ethics During and After the Holocaust: In the Shadow of Birkenau*, New York, Palgrave Macmillan.

Roth v. United States (1957), 354 U.S. 476.

Said, Edward (1983), *The World, the Text, and the Critic*, Cambridge, MA: Harvard University Press.

Sandwell, Barry (2000), "The Agonistic Ethic and Spirit of Inquiry: On the Greek Origins of Theorizing," in Martin Kusch (ed.), *The Sociology of Philosophical Knowledge*, Dordrecht: Kluwer.

Sass, Louis (1994), *The Paradoxes of Delusion: Wittgenstein, Schreber, and the Schizophrenic Mind*, Ithaca: Cornell University Press.

Saward, Michael (2006), "Democracy and Citizenship: Expanding Domains," in John Dryzek, Bonnie Honig and Anne Phillips (eds), *The Oxford Handbook of Political Theory*, Oxford: Oxford University Press.

Scarry, Elaine (1985), *The Body in Pain: The Making and Unmaking of the World*, Oxford: Oxford University Press.

Scheman, Naomi (1996), "Forms of Life: Mapping the Rough Ground," in Hans Sluga and David G. Stern (eds), *The Cambridge Companion to Wittgenstein*, Cambridge: Cambridge University Press, pp. 383–410.

Schlozman, Kay Lehman (2002), "Citizen Participation in America: What Do We Know? What Do We Care?," in Ira Katznelson and Helen V. Milner (eds), *Political Science: State of the Discipline*, New York: Norton.

Schmitt, Carl (1996), *The Concept of the Political*, trans. George Schwab, Chicago: University of Chicago Press.

Schulte, Joachim (1986), "Wittgenstein and Conservatism," in Stuart G. Shanker (ed.), *Ludwig Wittgenstein: Critical Assessments*, Canberra: Croom Helm, vol. 4, pp. 60–9.

Shapiro, Michael J. (1981), *Language and Political Understanding: The Politics of Discursive Practices*, New Haven: Yale University Press.

Shklar, Judith N. (1990), *The Faces of Injustice*, New Haven: Yale University Press.

Shusterman, Richard (1986), "Convention: Variations on a Theme," *Philosophical Investigations*, 9: 36–55.

Shusterman, Richard (1997), *Practicing Philosophy: Pragmatism and the Philosophical Life*, New York: Routledge.

Skinner v. *Oklahoma* Ex. Rel. Williamson (1942), 316 U.S. 535.

Staten, Henry (1984), *Wittgenstein and Derrida*, Lincoln: University of Nebraska Press.

Stern, David G. (1995), *Wittgenstein on Mind and Language*, New York: Oxford University Press.

Sussman, Henry and Devenney, Christopher (eds), (2001), *Engagement and Indifference: Beckett and the Political*, Albany: State University of New York Press.

Szabados, Bela (1992), "Autobiography after Wittgenstein," *Journal of Aesthetics and Art Criticism*, 50.1: 1–12.

Taylor, Mark C. (1991), "The Politics of Theo-ry," *Journal of the Academy of Religion*, 59.1: 1–37.

Thiher, Allen (1983), "Wittgenstein, Heidegger, the Unnamable, and Some Thoughts on the Voice in Fiction," in Morris Beja, S. E. Gontarski and Pierre Astier (eds), *Samuel Beckett: Humanistic Perspectives*, Columbus: Ohio State University Press, pp. 80–90.

Thomas, Emyr Vaughn (1999), "From Detachment to Immersion: Wittgenstein and the Problem of Life," *Ratio*, 12: 195–209.

Tobias, Michael, Fitzgerald, J. Patrick and Rothenberg, David (eds), (2000), *A Parliament of Minds: Philosophy for a New Millennium*, Albany: State University of New York Press.

Toulmin, Stephen, Rieke, Richard and Janik, Allan (1979), *An Introduction to Reasoning*, New York: Macmillan.

Tully, James (1989), "Wittgenstein and Political Philosophy: Understanding Practices of Critical Reflection," *Political Theory*, 17.2: 172–204.

Upham, S. Phineas (ed.), (2002), *Philosophers in Conversation: Interviews From the Harvard Review of Philosophy*, New York: Routledge.

Van Inwagen, Peter (1992), "There Is No Such Thing As Addition," in Peter A. French, Theodore E. Uehling, Jr. and Howard K. Wettstein (eds), *Midwest Studies in Philosophy 17. The Wittgenstein Legacy*, 138–59.

Van Oenen, Gijs, Irena Rosenthal and Ruth Sonderegger (2008), "The State is a Limitation on Human Existence: An Interview with Simon Critchley," *Krisis*, 2: 40–4.

Vincent, Andrew (ed.), (1997), *Political Theory: Tradition and Diversity*, Cambridge: Cambridge University Press.

Vincent, Andrew (2004), *The Nature of Political Theory*, Oxford: Oxford University Press.

Waismann, Friedrich (1979), *Ludwig Wittgenstein and the Vienna Circle: Conversations Recorded by Friedrich Waismann*, trans. Joachim Schulte and Brian McGuinness, New York: Barnes and Noble.

Walzer, Michael (1983), "Democracy and Philosophy," in John S. Nelson (ed.), *What Should Political Theory be Now?*, Albany: State University of New York Press, pp. 75–99.

Walzer, Michael (1987), *Interpretation and Social Criticism*, Cambridge, MA: Harvard University Press.

Walzer, Michael (1988), *In the Company of Critics: Social Criticism and Political Commitments in the Twentieth Century*, New York: Basic Books.

Watson, James R. (1999), *Portraits of American Continental Philosophers*, Bloomington: Indiana University Press.

Weber, Max (1978), *Economy and Society, Volume 2*, ed. Guenther Roth and Claus Wittich, Berkeley: University of California Press.

Wertheimer, Alan (1976), "Is Ordinary Language Analysis Conservative?," *Political Theory*, 4: 405–22.

White, Stephen K. (2000), *Sustaining Affirmation: The Strength of Weak Ontology*, Princeton: Princeton University Press.

Winch, Peter (1977), "The Idea of a Social Science" and "Understanding a Primitive Society," in Fred R. Dallmayr and Thomas A. McCarthy (eds), *Understanding and Social Inquiry*, South Bend: University of Notre Dame Press, pp. 142–58, 159–88.

Wittgenstein, Ludwig (1922), *Tractatus Logico-Philosophicus*, trans. C. K. Ogden, London: Routledge and Kegan Paul.

Wittgenstein, Ludwig (1958a), *The Blue and Brown Books*, ed. Rush Rhees, New York: Harper.

Wittgenstein, Ludwig (1958b), *Philosophical Investigations*, trans. G. E. M. Anscombe, New York: Macmillan.

Wittgenstein, Ludwig (1967), *Zettel*, trans. G. E. Anscombe, ed. G. E. M. Anscombe and G. H. von Wright, Berkeley: University of California Press.

Wittgenstein, Ludwig (1969), *On Certainty*, ed. G. E. M. Anscombe and G. H. von Wright, New York: Harper.

Wittgenstein, Ludwig (1978), *Remarks on the Foundations of Mathematics*, ed.

191

G. H. von Wright, Rush Rhees and G. E. M. Anscombe, Cambridge, MA: MIT Press.

Wittgenstein, Ludwig (1980a), *Remarks on the Philosophy of Psychology, Volumes 1 and 2*, trans. G. E. M. Anscombe, ed. G. E. M. Anscombe and G. H. von Wright, Chicago: University of Chicago Press.

Wittgenstein, Ludwig (1980b), *Culture and Value*, trans. Peter Winch, Chicago: University of Chicago Press.

Wittgenstein, Ludwig (1993), *Philosophical Occasions, 1912–1951*, ed. James C. Klagge and Alfred Nordmann, Indianapolis: Hackett.

Wittgenstein, Ludwig (2003), *Private and Public Occasions*, ed. James C. Klagge and Alfred Nordmann, Lanham: Rowman and Littlefield.

Wittman, Rebecca (2007), "Torture on Trial: Prosecuting Sadists and the Obfuscation of Systemic Crime," *South Central Review*, 24: 8–17.

Wolcher, Louis E. (2006), "How Legal Language Works," *Harvard Journal of the Legal Left*, 2: 91–125.

Wolin, Sheldon S. (1970), *Hobbes and the Epic Tradition of Political Theory*, Los Angeles: William Andrews Clark Memorial Library, University of California.

Wolin, Sheldon S. (1982), "Revolutionary Action Today," *Democracy*, 2: 17–28.

Wolin, Sheldon S. (1985), "Postmodern Politics and the Absence of Myth," *Social Research*, 52: 217–35.

Wolin, Sheldon S. (1996), "Fugitive Democracy," in Seyla Benhabib (ed.), *Democracy and Difference: Contesting the Boundaries of the Political*, Princeton: Princeton University Press, pp. 31–45.

Wolin, Sheldon S. (1997), "What Time Is It?," *Theory and Event*, 1.1.

Wolin, Sheldon S. (2001), *Tocqueville between Two Worlds: The Making of a Political and Theoretical Life*, Princeton: Princeton University Press.

Wolin, Sheldon S. (2004), *Politics and Vision: Continuity and Innovation in Western Political Thought*, Expanded edn, Princeton: Princeton University Press.

Young, Iris Marion (1990), *Justice and the Politics of Difference*, Princeton: Princeton University Press.

Young, Iris Marion (2000), *Inclusion and Democracy*, Oxford: Oxford University Press.

Zerilli, Linda M. G. (2003), "Doing Without Knowing: Feminism's Politics of the Ordinary," in Cressida J. Heyes (ed.), *The Grammar of Politics: Wittgenstein and Political Philosophy*, Ithaca: Cornell University Press.

Zerilli, Linda M. G. (2005), *Feminism and the Abyss of Freedom*, Chicago: University of Chicago Press.

Žižek, Slavoj (2001), *On Belief*, New York: Routledge.

Žižek, Slavoj (2002), *Welcome to the Desert of the Real*, New York: Verso.

Index

Adorno, T. W., 66, 174–5
Agamben, Giorgio, 156–60, 166–9,
173–4
Arendt, Hannah, 89, 140–1
Aristotle, 9, 33, 39, 52, 56, 64n, 83,
91, 146n, 166–7, 169
aspect change, 83, 94, 116–17, 144
Augustine, 30–1, 35, 51, 60, 103,
126
Austin, J. L., 10–11

bare life (*homo sacer*), 20, 156,
159–60, 162, 166–73, 174n
Beckett, Samuel, 158–60, 162–75
behaviorism, 16, 64n, 65n
biopolitics, 171, 175n
Brennan, William, 124–5, 133n
Brown, Wendy, 31–2
bureaucracy, 24n, 154n, 61–3, 89–90,
105–8

Catastrophe (Beckett), 162–5, 167–9
Cavell, Stanley, 50, 64
Chambers, Samuel, 64
citizenship, 66–70, 73–4, 81–5
coercion, 55–7
comedy, 170–2
communitarianism, 6–7
community, 58–60

concepts, 42n, 67, 70–4, 84–5
Connolly, William E., 31–2
conservatism, 40, 61, 89, 98–102,
109–10
of science, 104–5
conventionalism, 62, 90–7, 111n,
175n
conventions, 93–6, 104–7, 110n,
174n
criteria, 11–13, 60, 94, 116, 129–30,
158
culture
high and low (Spengler), 114n

Davidson, Donald, 58–60, 65
deconstructionism, 62, 64n
Deleuze, Gilles, 70, 165
democracy, 4–6, 82–4
democratic citizenship, 6, 70, 84
depth grammar, 91–2, 110n, 157, 167,
171, 175n
or frame conditions, 92, 110n,
111n, 175n
description, 2, 67, 96–7, 128–9,
147–52
dichotomies, 38–41
disagreement, 74–5, 108, 150, 168
dissent (political), 67–9, 79–81,
145–51